The Symbolic Impetus

Charles T. Stewart

The Symbolic Impetus
How Creative Fantasy Motivates Development

FREE ASSOCIATION BOOKS / LONDON / NEW YORK

First published in Great Britain by
Free Association Books
57 Warren Street
London W1T 5NR

www.fa-b.com

ISBN 1 85343 535 X pbk; 1 85343 536 8 hbk

A CIP catalogue record for this book is available from the British Library

10 09 08 07 06 05 04 03 02 01
10   9   8   7   6   5   4   3   2   1

Designed, typeset and produced for Free Association Books Ltd by
Chase Publishing Services, Fortescue, Sidmouth, EX10 9QG
Printed in the European Union by TJ International, Padstow, England

Contents

Part III: Summing Up

List of Tables

To Matilda B. Stewart

Foreword

John Beebe
President of the C. G. Jung Institute of San Francisco

When I was a little boy, my father and mother were "stationed" in Nanking, China, where he was an Assistant Military Attaché for the United States government, in its failing diplomatic efforts to stabilize the Kuomintang regime. By 1948, not only the country of China, but my parents' marriage, was coming apart as a consequence of long civil war, and as an only child, many miles from anything I could regard as "home," I had to take care of myself as best I could. I recall spending an inordinate amount of time after school sitting in a little dark room reading the Oz books alongside the daughter of another discouraged diplomat. She was willing, like me, to spend long, hopeful hours with Dorothy, Glinda, Jack Pumpkinhead, Ozma, the Patchwork Girl, the Scarecrow, and the rest of the enthralling Oz characters. I realize now that the symbolic community of Oz celebrities probably saved my social attitude from early annihilation, and that this world of shared fantasy was actually the original circuitry for the tireless networking extroverted ego I have drawn upon to become an analyst viable in the international Jungian community.

I wouldn't have always given my early Oz book reading, at the expense of development in sports or skills, so uncritical an endorsement. For those doctors who were educated in psychiatry, as I was, in the years of the Vietnam war, a fantasy solution to a developmental crisis, however consoling or "interesting," was nevertheless a schizoid solution, something that our patients and ourselves would have to relinquish if we really wanted to grow and adapt. Even the Jungian training that I took up soon after taught me that indulging in archetypal fantasy (such as my play activity of endlessly drawing the mandala-map of the Land of Oz with my little girlfriend) was at best a temporary *temenos* for the soul. It was, that is, a meaningful shelter from the storms of development, a way of defending the self against the pressure of outer reality until it felt strong enough to take up realistic ego-adaptation again.

That is why I believe that Charles Stewart's *The Symbolic Impetus* is so important. It asks mental health clinicians who work with children, or the "child" in adults, to reconsider the role of fantasy in their patients' lives. Stewart demonstrates, with his elegant readings of the key clinical literature (from Piaget to Axline), that the symbol is far more than a refuge, far more than a way of "transcending" the conflicts that put ego development at risk. Rather, he shows us that the symbol, in tandem with the archetypal affects it supports, is the way the ego develops the attitudes it needs to grow.

To my knowledge, no previous psychologist has set out to do quite what Dr. Stewart succeeds so handsomely in doing here. He demonstrates that the symbol not only accompanies development but also guides it. To read his book is to become excited about what children have always found exciting about their own childhoods, the chance to live compelling fantasy in meaningful play. Anyone who troubles to read his text will find it impossible to read the literature of child development the same way after. Dr. Stewart has restored the element of interest to the professional duty to discover how children reinvent themselves through the use of symbols. His demonstration that this creativity is more than defensive – that it is not just magical thinking, and that it serves to motivate healthy adaptation – is entirely convincing.

This is not just a book about healing; it is a book that heals. It has the power to overcome our field's resistance to taking up Jung's practical suggestion that the symbol is the energy-source for individuation. *The Symbolic Impetus* can also lead us to recover moments in our own development when we gave ourselves over to the care of symbols, and learn that what most interested us was just what we needed to be able to go on.

Preface

A major turning point in my career as a child psychiatrist occurred when I decided to select the natural process of psychological development as my model for psychotherapy. From then on, I felt the need to construct an open-ended, integrated theory of development as a prism through which to focus the major trends in human psychological growth. I'd like to argue for the value of such an approach by applying it to the assessment of one of my own earliest memories.

When I was four years old, I lived in a house with a fish pond in the backyard. Next door lived a girl of the same age, whose mother was a seamstress. That lady worked at home and kept jars of buttons by her sewing machine. One day I told my friend that I had invented a game, and the little girl accepted my invitation to play it with me. We were to take a jar of her mother's buttons down to the pond. Once there, we would take turns dropping buttons into the water. Both of us watched with fascination as the iridescent buttons oscillated and sank slowly through the sunlit water to the murky green bottom below. I was so proud of the game I had invented that bursting with pride, I told my mother of my achievement. I was surprised and taken aback by her outraged response: "No!"

Now this was my memory, a nugget of early symbolic experience and ego-development in a particular peer and parental context. My interpretations of it are next, each a refraction through the prism of an integrated theory of the essential meaning that has long attached to that experience in my psychological life.

From the standpoint, first, of Piaget's theory of the "correlative development of cognitive operations and social co-operations," we might understand the memory as portraying the beginning of sociodramatic peer play, when play roles like initiator and follower begin to be differentiated and eventually become complementary. The first step in this development is taken, as I took it, at about three to four years, and consists in children being able to collaborate in their social play as long as they assume roles that are similar or identical.

Within the framework of the psychoanalyst Erik Erikson's view that individual psychological growth proceeds through a sequence of psychosocial crises, we might interpret the events I have recalled here as marking the creative completion of the stage Autonomy versus Shame and Doubt and the anxious beginning of the stage Initiative versus Guilt. In the former context, my friend's and my dropping of the buttons would signify our increased, even insouciant control over elimination functions. But from the standpoint of the next, more phallic stage lying in wait, my game provided an opportunity for the little girl and I to make "babies." In that regard my appropriation of her mother's buttons required my mother's aggressive intervention. We might speculate that my superego was being structured as my initiative in game invention came into conflict with guilt feelings induced by my mother's prohibition.

Interpreting this memory from the perspective of Kohut's psychoanalytic self psychology, however, we might infer that my mother's response was less guilt-inducing than shaming. Viewed through this lens, I had incurred a narcissistic trauma due to her failure as my chief mirroring selfobject in confirming and approving the grandiose self that had invented the game. At the same time, I still had my little girlfriend's approval, and so I had begun to establish an important relationship with an alter-ego.

If, from the optical box of theories, we next select as our refractive lens Winnicott's notion of potential space, then we might think that my playmate and I had also created between us a potential space, where additional symbolic play, as well as cultural activities, would be likely to occur.

Within the context of Jung's analytical psychology, several symbolic interpretations suggest themselves. The game might be viewed through an alchemical lens as a symbolic act, a ritual divination performed by me as an adept with a *soror mystica*, my friend, in a mercurial fountain. My playmate and I might be seen as an anima and animus coming together to express the mythological motif of a female–male *coniunctio*, which was followed by the birth of a series of divine "children." The numinous quality of the game, its "fascination" for us, indicates that a constellation of the unconscious had taken place. The game was thus a true symbol, produced by creative fantasy, and its meaning could not be fully known until a future stage in my/her psychological development, when that symbol had ripened into new consciousness.

Application of this approach of integrating perspectives from many theories over the past thirty years of practical psychotherapy with children and adolescents has taught me many lessons. The following two are probably the primary reasons for writing this book.

First, I have learned that, depending on the clinical context, any one of the interpretive lenses mentioned above may turn out to provide the optimal container for a particular treatment. When, however, the therapeutic task has been to support the patient's efforts to maintain, or to re-establish connection with his/her own healthy, developmental base, the Jungian refraction, with its emphasis on the symbol, has been consistently the most effective. In his *Collected Works* and other writings C. G. Jung has provided us with the richest and most complex under-standing of the "living" symbol as a necessary condition for psychological development. His own life makes clear that at the bottom of memory, every childhood is symbolic. As he did not say, but might have, the being of childhood lives the images of reality in total imagination.

Second, I have learned that there are gaps in our understanding of symbolic development itself. The prevailing view during the past thirty years certainly has been that the first year of life is presymbolic, and that the symbolic function only begins with the acquisition of language during the second year. This standpoint was controverted by Jung's thesis that the symbol was a necessary bridge, at all stages of the life cycle, between the developmental unconscious and the emerging ego-con-sciousness. Jungians had even suggested that mythological or symbolic apprehension was present at birth, but of course they could not easily document this claim, except through reconstructions. Studies of the various symbolic modes, that is, pretend, imaginary companion, daydream, etc., tended to be piecemeal and there was no conception of the growth of the symbolic process as a whole. I wanted to fill in the blanks in the theory I trusted.

All this led me to conduct a systematic study, both in normal devel-opmental and in clinical contexts, of the development of the symbolic process itself from Infancy through Early Adolescence and to investigate the importance of symbols during the same stages for psychological development and healing. The results of this study are presented here.

I should record that the theory-building described in this work has been helpful to me and to the parents of my patients, and I trust it will prove useful to the readers of this book.

Acknowledgments

My late brother was the Jungian analyst and author Louis H. Stewart, who died in 1998; for forty years we met regularly to discuss our clinical research interests. We borrowed so freely from one another that his ideas became mine, and mine his. Lou liked to say that I was becoming a Jungian "by osmosis." What is apparent throughout this book is my debt to his pioneering theory of the archetypal affect system. The preface of his major work on the influence of birth order and family atmosphere on social creativity, which he titled *Changemakers*, begins with a description of his reaction to my birth. Lou inscribed the copy he gave to me as follows: "For my brother Charles, without whom this book would never have been written." I imagine giving him a copy of *The Symbolic Impetus* similarly inscribed. Sibling bond and symbol are united in the archetype of the family.

The ideas of my sister-in-law, Joan Chodorow, also a Jungian analyst and author, with her own gift for finding affect in its home in the body, have also informed this work. That she has been unstinting in her enthusiastic support for my work has made it easier to bring it to fruition.

Discussions with Barbara Rosenkrantz, Emeritus Professor at Harvard University and my wife's second cousin, and her husband, Nat Marshall, encouraged me not to obscure my original ideas in an excess of quotes from other sources. Barbara referred me to my first professional editor, Kenny Lyman, of Cambridge, Massachusetts, who worked a minor miracle in two editorial consultations. In the first, she sent me back to my desk to rework the entire manuscript, with both her own critical comments and a copy of Orwell's essay, *Politics and the English Language*, to guide me. A year later, she felt able to declare that my revisions had made the first two chapters "light years better." Now, she said, I needed a clinically trained editor.

John Beebe, Jungian analyst and author, became that editor and he has worked a major miracle. He has shepherded me through two complete editings of the manuscript, during which my stilted, pedantic prose was given a refreshing infusion from his lively, imaginative style. Our editing was also an educational experience, for John helped me expand my understanding of the symbolic process through the archetypal lens of classical analytical psychology. But John did more. In his introduction to Iris Murdoch's *The Black Prince*, the "editor" of the book indicates what assistance the work's "author" required from him: "He needed someone to believe him and someone to believe in him. He found me, his *alter ego*, at the time needful." John might well have written this about me and what he brought to our relationship. This was symbolically confirmed when he agreed to write the foreword.

In David Stonestreet, psychology editor at Free Association Books, I found the ideal professional to guide me through my first preparation of a manuscript for publication. In response to my avalanche of e-mails, David made his extensive knowledge and experience available to me throughout the entire process of preparation and publication. It has been a pleasure to work with him.

Our New York attorney, Renee Schwartz, guided me through my first encounter with the legalisms specific to book contracts.

Margaret LaLiberte, Jennifer Giveen, Shirley Armintrout, and Moon Eng were colleagues who expressed interest in my views, applied them in their clinical activities, and provided me with critical feedback and moral support. The same, of course, can be said of the many trainees in child therapy whom I have instructed (and been instructed by) with my developmental perspective as a framework for their supervision. But the impetus for this book remains a series of remarkable youngsters, the child and adolescent patients, who simply by being themselves made the symbolic impetus evident to their therapists, to me, and I now hope, to the reader of this book.

In 1991, at the invitation of Alicia Lieberman, I presented my ideas to the developmental seminar of the San Francisco Infant–Parent Program, and in the same year, at the invitation of Rosa Chiu, I discussed them with the interns at the San Francisco C. G. Jung Clinic. These were milestones, as they were my first presentations of my views to the public.

My wife, Matilda, L. C. S. W., psychotherapist, and clinical supervisor, is the only person who has experienced all phases of my work: germination, realization, and publication. I discussed my ideas with her, she read the manuscript in all its forms, and she provided me with invaluable suggestions. This book would not have made its way to a larger community's perusal without her interest and encouragement.

But I cannot hide behind my helpers. I am solely responsible for the contents of this book.

The author and the publisher would like to thank the following for permission to quote from copyrighted material:

From *Dibs: In Search of Self* by Virginia Axline. Ballantine Books, 1964: New York; reprinted by permission of Lichter, Grossman, Nichols & Adler, Inc., Los Angeles, CA, for the Estate of Virginia Axline.

From 'The development of an adult's imaginary companion' by Helene Bass. *Psychoanalytic Review*, 70 (4), 519–33, 1983; reprinted by permission of The Psychoanalytic Review.

From C. G. Jung, *The Development of Personality, Collected Works*, Volume 17. Copyright © PUP; reprinted by permission of Princeton University Press.

From the *Fifty-Minute Hour* by Robert M. Lindner. The Other Press, 1999: New York; reprinted by permission of Harold Ober Associates Incorporated.

From *The Origins of Intelligence in Children* by Jean Piaget. International Universities Press, Inc., 1952: Madison, Conn.; reprinted by permission of International Universities Press, Inc.

From *The Origins of Intelligence in Children* by Jean Piaget. Routledge and Kegan Paul, 1952: London; reprinted by permission of Taylor & Francis Books Ltd.

From *Play, Dreams and Imitation in Childhood* by Jean Piaget. Routledge and Kegan Paul, 1962: London; Reprinted by permission of Taylor & Francis Books Ltd.

From *The Moral Judgment of the Child* by Jean Piaget. Translated by Marjorie Gabain. Reprinted with the permission of The Free Press, a Division of Simon & Schuster, Inc. Copyright © 1965 The Free Press.

From *The Moral Judgment of the Child* by Jean Piaget. Translated by Marjorie Gabain. London: Routledge, 1965; reprinted by permission of Taylor & Francis Books Ltd.

From Unpublished Manuscripts of Louis H. Stewart; Reprinted by permission of Joan Chodorow.

Cover illustration:
Classification: Painting
Full title: *The Infant Krishna Floating on the Cosmic Ocean*: episode from the "Bhagavata Purana"
Date of work: c. 1840
Culture: Indian
Place of creation: South Asia, India, Rajasthan, Mewar at Nathadwara
Credit line: Courtesy of the Arthur M. Sackler Museum, Harvard University Art Museums, Gift in gratitude to John Coolidge, Gift of Leslie Cheek, Jr., Anonymous Fund in memory of Henry Berg, Louise Haskell Daly, Alpheus Hyatt, Richard Norton Memorial Funds and through the generosity of Albert H. Gordon and Emily Rauh Pulitzer
Photo credit: Photographic Services
Image copyright: © President and Fellows of Harvard College, Harvard University.

Abbreviations

References to C. G. Jung are to the *Collected Works* (*CW*) and by volume, paragraph, and page (*CW* 17: 227,131), edited by H. Read, M. Fordham and G. Adler, translated by R. F. C. Hull, Routledge, London, and Princeton University Press, Princeton, New Jersey.

Introduction

Theory-building is the outcome of discussion among many.
——C. G. Jung, *Two Essays on Analytical Psychology*

The Symbolic Impetus did not emerge fully formed. Rather, the particular theoretical perspective that informs its view of the symbol's development and function arose from the confluence of four interrelated currents of observation and study, all grounded in the experience of the child: the symbolic life of the child; the child's emotional life; the natural processes of psychological development and healing in the child; and the child's construction of the ego-complex. A brief description of these currents, which have served the author, a child psychiatrist, as theoretical foundation for his practice of psychotherapy, will serve to introduce the reader to the perspectives which inform this work.

THE SYMBOLIC LIFE OF THE CHILD

Clinical work with children, however challenging, is imbued with a peculiar excitement, which arises out of the therapist's necessary immersion in the kaleidoscopic flow of symbolic images that inform the child's play, dreams, fantasies, drawings, modelings, paintings, singing, and dancing. Observing all this, one is very close to the matrix of creativity itself, for the average child patient sets up shop, so to speak, next to the Faustian realm of the Mothers.

> For regression, if left undisturbed, does not stop short at the "mother" but goes back beyond her to the prenatal realm of the "Eternal Feminine" to the immemorial world of archetypal possibilities, where "thronged round with images of all creation, slumbers the "divine child," patiently awaiting his conscious realization. This son is the germ of wholeness, and he is characterized as such by his specific symbols. (*CW* 5: 508,330)

For the child, however, this experience usually is not felt as a matter of regression, for in the early years life is lived near the world of "the

Mothers," and it is natural to return to them again and again for inspiration as new developmental challenges arise in the course of the maturation of the ego. The profusion of "images of all creation," which arises from the depths of the collective unconscious in the child's growing up, impels the child therapist to search for a way to classify these symbolic expressions.

The first distinction which offers itself is between "natural" and "cultural" symbols. Creative fantasy produces natural symbols by combining unconscious contents of the psyche with the appropriate conscious representations. As Jung notes, this activity of the creative imagination is also described in Goethe's *Faust*: "Formation, transformation, Eternal Mind's eternal recreation." Every parent has observed this natural symbolizing process in a developing child and Jean Piaget (1962) has organized many such observations of his own children.

Cultural symbols, on the other hand, "have gone through many transformations and even a process of conscious elaboration and in this way have become the collective representations of civilized societies" (*CW* 18: 579,253). C. G. Jung is the pre-eminent observer of these collective representations, which he understood as archetypal ideas constellated, through the medium of what his later follower Joseph Henderson has called the cultural unconscious, to become the dominant representations of a particular age.

The phantasmagoria of natural symbols presented by a developing child may also be classified according to the level of the unconscious from which they seem to be derived, that is, according to whether they are personal, cultural, or archetypal. Within the culture of childhood, moreover, the corresponding categories of cultural symbols, which mirror the intrapsychic personal, cultural, and archetypal, are easy to locate in children's games, the various materials of childlore, and the fairytales and myths which children read perennially.

The developmental significance of symbols arising from the collective unconscious is the impetus they provide for psychological growth. The archetypal or developmental unconscious can only be reached and expressed by symbols, and for this reason the child's process of development can never do without the symbol. In addition, archetypal symbols are truly whole structures, which ensure that the growth potential they transmit to the child's consciousness will be presented in its totality. Cultural symbols may also motivate a child's development if they are "living symbols," that is, if they are sufficiently charged with energy to constellate the developmental unconscious.

One aspect of the child's symbolic life which requires emphasis is its objectivity. Jung has gone so far as to argue that the unconscious is a natural process which, as such, never deceives. James Hillman also directs our attention to the phenomenology of the imaginal realm, which he says is characterized by its own precision:

Precision is an attribute of the psyche prior to all its manifestations ... In other words, the imaginal ego ... can have the Cartesian's ego clear and distinct virtues. The art of memory shows that the imaginal realm presents itself with exactitude and requires qualitative precision in its handling. (Hillman 1972: 209)

Or, as William Blake might say, autonomous imaginative development is the Mother of Minute Particulars, the irreducible source of individuality in every human being.

In his frequent descriptions of two contrasting and even opposed methods of interpretation, the retrospective/reductive/analytic/causal method versus the prospective/constructive/synthetic/final method, Jung has drawn attention to the importance of the psychotherapist's distinguishing those symbols originating in the personal unconscious from those formed from the contents of the collective unconscious.

Just as through *analysis* and *reduction* of individual events the *causal* method ultimately arrives at the universal principles of human psychology, so through the *synthesis* of individual trends the *constructive* method aims at universal goals. The psyche is the point of intersection, hence it must be defined under two aspects. On the one hand it gives a picture of the remnants and traces of all that has been, and, on the other, but expressed in the same picture, the outlines of what is to come, in so far as the psyche creates its own future. (*CW* 3: 404,184–5)

As the contents of the personal unconscious are acquired during the individual's lifetime, images arising from this level are referred to as *signs*, indicating that they point to something already known to the subject:

A symbol is an indefinite expression with many meanings, pointing to something not easily defined and therefore not fully known. But the sign always has a fixed meaning, because it is a conventional abbreviation for, or a commonly accepted indication of, something known. (*CW* 5: 180,124)

The "reductive" or retrospective method of psychoanalytic exploration is appropriate when the patient is engaged in symbolic healing of pathological family-complexes and other structures of the "personal" or what might be called the acquired unconscious, such as the deep reactions to trauma and loss. The "constructive" or prospective method of analytical psychology is appropriate when the child is engaged in actualizing or, as Jungians say, realizing symbols originating in the archetypal or developmental unconscious: "The symbol, in its prospective meaning, points the way to the further psychological development of the individual" (CW 4: 674,291). By making these distinctions between sign and symbol and the respective reductive and constructive methods of exploring the two types of images in understanding the child's play, the therapist is better positioned to facilitate both healing and development.

One fact which is of considerable help in making such discriminations is that the psyche itself guides the therapist. Archetypal symbols are characteristically *numinous* (Otto 1958; CW 18: 1273,541), inducing us to take them as "just so" and to respect (and sometimes revere) their natural arrangement of energy. The numinosity of a symbol, natural or cultural, is a measure of its dynamic, energic aspect, its life-promoting and motivational significance. When the child, regressing in psychotherapy, enters the "realm of the Mothers," archetypal symbols are constellated which transforms the consulting room into a vessel for the *numinosum*, which encompasses and suffuses patient and therapist alike. Although the numinosity of a symbol is an expression of its affective or emotional intensity, it also protects that intensity from a carelessly reductive approach to it.

THE EMOTIONAL LIFE OF THE CHILD

The second of the four currents which coalesced to generate *The Symbolic Impetus* concerned the emotional life of the child. Compared with adult psychotherapy, which is more challenging intellectually, treatment of children is, on the average, more lighthearted and joyful. One reason for this is that play, and only the most seriously disturbed child patient is unable to play, is, even at its most serious, intrinsically *fun*. In addition, when the vitality of the child's expressive world is analyzed, there is no doubt that an effervescent, upwelling of emotion is at the root of this aliveness. We learn from the Gnostic myth of Sophia's departure from the pleromatic realm of light and entry into relation with the darkness, that affects are cosmogonic:

> The sufferings that befell her took the form of various emotions – sadness, fear, bewilderment, confusion, longing: now she laughed, now she wept. From these affects ... arose the entire created world. (CW 13: 452,334–5)

The complexity one encounters in establishing a psychological perspective on the affects is highlighted by James Hillman's classic study *Emotion* (1962/1992), in which his analysis of the phenomenology of the extant theories of emotion required him to define eighteen classificatory groups just to categorize them.

For years, I studied emotion alongside my late brother Louis, a Jungian analyst, whose legacy is an archetypal theory of affect. In addition, three of Jung's perspectives on the affects have served as the foundation stones for my own thinking about the emotions. The first is that the affects are *the primary motivational system* in humans: "The essential basis of our personality is affectivity. Thought and action are, as it were, only symptoms of affectivity" (*CW* 3: 78,38). The second is that the basic emotions are *universal*:

Emotional manifestations are based on similar patterns, and are recognizably the same all over the earth. We understand them even in animals, and the animals themselves understand each other in this respect, even if they belong to different species. (*CW* 18: 540,234)

The third is that humans have an *innate capacity for the perception of emotions*:

We have a highly differentiated subjective system for recognizing and evaluating affective phenomena in others. There is present in each of us a direct instinct for registering this, which animals also possess in high degree, with respect not only to their own species but also to other animals and human beings. We can perceive the slightest emotional fluctuations in others and have a very fine feeling for the quality and quantity of affects in our fellow-men. (*CW* 8: 25,14)

This innate capacity is referred to by Ernst Cassirer (1957, chapter 2) as the "perception of expression," and by Heinz Werner (1957) as "physiognomic" perception. Jung assigns it to the archetypes, which are thus organs of perception just as much as they are innately structured internal objects. In fact, one can speak of them just as easily as internal subjects conditioning our affectivity with their own.

Detailed studies of the emotions by the founder of contemporary affect theory, Silvan Tomkins (1962, 1963), have amply demonstrated that the affects are the primary motivational system in humans. Cross-cultural study of emotions by P. Ekman and W. Friesen (1971) confirmed the universality of the innate emotions. And recent studies of infants' perception of emotion, both in normal developmental (Field and Fox 1985) and experimental (Tronick 1989) contexts, indicate that this capacity is present from the beginning of postnatal life.

Tomkins made another advance in our understanding of the affects when he identified seven affects as the hereditary or innate elements of emotional life. In the study my brother and I made of the relation between play, games, and the affects, we summarized his contribution as follows:

Tomkins presents his theory as a necessary correction of Freud's psychoanalytic theory (Tomkins 1962, 1963). For Freud the prime motivators are the drives and the libido which derives from them. Tomkins' view is that the affects are the primary motivational system and that the drives represent a secondary system dependent upon the affects for amplification in order to function effectively. His justification of this view is based on an analysis of the evolution of the affects as a more flexible system than the drives allowing for choices necessary to complex organisms which can no longer survive on programmed instincts or drives linking need and object. He concludes that the affects have evolved in response to three types of stimuli, novelty, people, and threats to survival. Moreover, he identifies a specific set of affects which he characterizes in terms of phenomenology, facial expression, and characteristic response patterns. He specifies three categories: 1) positive affects, Interest–Excitement and Enjoyment–Joy; 2) negative affects, Distress–Anguish, Fear–Terror, Shame–Humiliation, Contempt–Disgust, and Anger–Rage; and 3) the resetting affect, Surprise–Startle. His view is that Interest evolved in relationship to novelty, Joy in relation to people, and the negative and the resetting affects in relation to survival needs. (L. H. Stewart and C. T. Stewart 1981: 44)

Each of the innate affects has a distinctive pattern of physiological reaction, a characteristic phenomenology of feelings and images, an identifiable facial expression, and a particular postural stance.

Hillman concludes his book on emotion with his own theory, based on Aristotle's four types of cause, which enable us to see the main foci of the different theories of emotion currently at hand: for Hillman, the material cause of emotion is *energy*, the efficient cause is the *symbol*, the formal cause is the *soul*, and the final cause is *transformation*. In his view these "causes" are not to be understood in a temporal way as motives producing effects in time, but as four *simultaneous* aspects participating in the manifestation of an emotion where before there was none.

In his elegant theory of the archetypal affect system, my brother, L. H. Stewart (1985, 1986, 1987a, 1987b) specified the efficient cause of each of the innate affects as a symbol composed of a Life Stimulus and a Primordial Image, the conscious and unconscious components of the symbol respectively (see Table 1).

I hope these illustrations point out how inextricably interrelated are the symbolic and emotional life of the child. During psychotherapy with children, the therapist can fill in with clinical material the particular Stimuli, Images, and Affects presented in Table 1. Doing so systematically can assist the therapist in maintaining therapeutic rapport with the child patient, for this chart can provide a sensitive compass to guide the therapist's affective attunement. But there is a second reason, which is even more important. *The emotional components of those archetypal symbols that motivate the natural process of psychological development are these selfsame innate affects.* The right kind of attention to them gives the symbolic impetus its chance to move psychological development and healing along.

Table 1: Symbolic Evocation of the Innate Affects

Life Stimulus	Symbol Primal Image	Innate Affect (Range of Intensity)
1 The Novel →	2 Focused Insight →	3 INTEREST–EXCITEMENT
2 The Familiar →	Diffuse Illumination →	JOY–ECSTASY
7 The Unexpected →	Darkness →	SURPRISE–STARTLE
3 The Unknown →	the Abyss →	FEAR–TERROR
4 Loss →	the Void →	SADNESS–ANGUISH
7 Restriction of Autonomy →	Chaos →	ANGER–RAGE
6 Rejection →	Alienation →	CONTEMPT/SHAME– DISGUST/HUMILIATION

THE NATURAL PROCESSES OF PSYCHOLOGICAL DEVELOPMENT AND HEALING IN THE CHILD

A third current began its flow when I settled on the natural processes of psychological development and healing as my model for child psychotherapy. Such a model, developed from one's own observations and the close reading of the observations of others, cannot tell one how to do psychotherapy, but it does provides a firm anchor for the clinician when participating with the patient in the creative aspects of treatment. I was interested to learn, long after I had started to use this developmental approach to the psychological resilience and creativity of humans, that Jung had chosen a similar model for analysis of adult patients during the "second half" of life (for him, after age thirty-six):

The transcendent function does not proceed without aim and purpose, but leads to the revelation of the essential man. It is in the first place a purely natural process, which may in some cases pursue its course without the knowledge or assistance of the individual, and can sometimes forcibly accomplish itself in the face of opposition. The meaning and purpose of the process is the realization, in all its aspects, of the personality originally hidden away in the embryonic germ-plasm; the production and unfolding of the original, potential wholeness ... For these reasons I have termed this the *individuation* process. This natural process of individuation served me both as a model and guiding principle for my method of treatment. (*CW* 7: 186–7,110)

This raises the question of whether there is individuation in childhood. During his pre-analytic years as a kindergarten teacher, my brother realized that the children under his tutelage were passing through stages of an autonomous process of creative development that found expression in their painting, dancing, singing, dramatics, and play. When he became a Jungian analyst, this experience was not forgotten:

> Thus, when years later I had become immersed in Jung's analytical psychology, and had experienced his ideas embodied in my own analysis, and then in my analytic work with others, it seemed self-evident to me that what he described as the individuation process which led to "wholeness," and which, moreover, was facilitated, I should say rested upon, active imagination, was precisely what I had observed in the kindergarten children, only in that context we called it "development." (L. H. Stewart 1985: 89–90)

The Jungian child analyst and theoretician, Michael Fordham (1994), came to a very similar conclusion. In my own case, although I had chosen the symbol-led, natural process of psychological development as a model specifically for my work with children as a child psychiatrist, it was now evident that it would serve as a model for the entire life cycle. I saw that the development of the personality throughout the life cycle can be viewed as the realization of its hereditary potential, an unfolding of the original wholeness, which is conditioned not only by interpersonal relationships, participation in cultural activities, mythic experience, and interactions with the animal, plant, and physical worlds, but also by the developmental symbols that appear in the midst of these extensions of selfhood.

My choice of the affective-symbolic model for child therapy faced me, however, with the fact that even with the enormous advantages offered by Jungian concepts, there was still no theory which, in my judgment, captured the complexity of the early psychological growth that symbols facilitate. This realization led me to begin the task of formulating an integrated, comprehensive theory of psychological development with the maturation of capacity to symbolize at its center, for only in this way could I provide myself with a sufficiently specific framework for monitoring the progressive development of my patients through their creative play.

I began by integrating Jean Piaget's (1967, 1969) cognitive stages of ego-development, Erik Erikson's (1950/1963, 1959) psychosocial description of the "life cycle," and Erich Neumann's (1954, 1990) archetypal exegesis of the development of ego-consciousness (see Table 2). These theories lend themselves to integration because (a) the chronology of their stages correspond and (b) their contents – cognitive, psychosocial, and archetypal – are distinct but complementary domains.

Table 2: An Integrated Theory of Development

Stage (Age in Years)	Cognitive Stages (Piaget)	Psychosocial Stages (Erikson)	Archetypal Stages (Neumann)
1	2	3	4
Infancy (Birth to 1½)	Sensorimotor	Trust vs Mistrust	Phallic-Chthonian
2 Early Childhood (1½ to 3–4)	Intuitive Thought	Autonomy vs Shame/Doubt	Magic-Phallic
3 Preschool Period (3–4 to 6–7)	Articulated Intuitive Thought	Initiative vs Guilt	Magic-Warlike
4 Middle Childhood (6–7 to 12–13)	Logico-Mathematical Thought	Industry vs Inferiority	Solar-Warlike
5 Early Adolescence (12–13 to 15–16)	Hypothetico-Deductive Thought	Identity vs Identity Diffusion	Solar-Rational

The reader will find references to these various stages of development throughout this work, as well as elements drawn into my integration of these theories from the views of other well-known child therapists and developmental psychologists such as Winnicott, Bowlby and Ainsworth, Fraiberg, Sander, Malatesta, Stern, and Emde.

One of the values of any developmental perspective is the objectivity it confers (Piaget 1970: 35–6). Thinking developmentally does this in several ways. First, a complex acquired structure is only truly comprehensible through an understanding of its formation; that is, developmental understanding is explanatory. Second, it is extremely difficult to mold a body of objective developmental observations to fit a narrowly subjective theory, that is, a structure that exists only in the mind of the investigator. Third, it is possible to study and verify the effects of a newly constructed structure on the individual's pattern of behavior and thought.

A psychopathology grounded in the natural process of psychological development will explain psychological disturbances as compromises between the normal, healthy functions of the psyche and pathogenic influences. Jung states that neurosis is, at one and the same time, a failed attempt at adaptation and an effort at self-cure, and goes on to say that "hidden in the neurosis is a bit of still undeveloped personality, a precious fragment of the psyche ..." (CW 10: 355,167). Thus, at the center of those psychic structures (or "complexes") which result from blocks to development are healthy developmental nuclei, which require therapeutic nurturance to foster their realization and their capacity to release healing energy. Winnicott writes: "But we do need to try to get at a theory of normal growth so as to be able to understand illness and the various immaturities, since we are no longer contented unless we can cure and prevent" (Winnicott 1965: 67). Both Jung and Erikson consider analysis as a process of quickened maturation, an accelerator of developmental processes. As a corollary of this view, the psyche is to be understood as a self-regulating system, which has its capacity for self-healing just as the body does.

In the context of pointing to the self-regulating nature of the psyche, Jung speaks of the *compensatory* function of unconscious processes, which coincides with his view that the "unconscious does not consist only of morally incompatible wishes but is largely composed of hitherto undeveloped, unconscious portions of the personality which strive for integration in the wholeness of the individual" (CW 18: 1156,482). Jung found that this compensatory function (so easily demonstrable in dreams and play) has not only day to day but also long term effects. The former is a momentary adjustment of one-sidedness in some conscious attitude or an equalization of disturbed balance, as when the psyche has dwelled on something too long and the unconscious responds by trivializing the conflict. These compensations viewed over time, however, like so many beads on a string, can appear as successive steps in an orderly pattern of development, the individuation process itself, as sort of a necklace of the soul. Thus, self-regulation leads to development, and development to individuation, and these three phases of growth are seamlessly interrelated. Both Winnicott (1971) and Piaget (1962) have given us vivid examples of the self-healing function of play, Winnicott in clinical and Piaget in normal developmental contexts. Jung also emphasized play, defining it as the dynamic principle of fantasy and demonstrated the healing power of improvised creativity in processes like active imagination and the drawing of pictures from the unconscious, which are basically like play therapy for adults. As he puts it:

The best way of dealing with the unconscious is the creative way. Create for instance a fantasy. Work it out with all the means at your disposal. Work it out as if you were it or in it, as you would work out a real situation in life which you cannot escape. All the difficulties you overcome in such a fantasy are symbolic expressions of psychological difficulties in yourself, and inasmuch as you overcome them in your imagination you also overcome them in your psyche. (Jung 1973b: 109)

My brother has compared the Jungian technique of active imagination with the symbolic play of childhood: "For the child, then, it would appear that symbolic play is a direct analogue to adult active imagination, and, as a spontaneous activity of the psyche, serves the purposes of 'individuation' in childhood" (L. H. Stewart 1981a: 27). In this book, the term *individuation* will be used to refer to the spontaneous process of psychological development, whereas the *process of individuation* can be taken to refer to that psychological development as stimulated by analysis.

Analysis is, of course, not confined to interpretation. It is also, as Winnicott has shown, a "holding" of the patient that makes growth safe. By providing non-interpretive support for the child patient's expressive activities, the therapist protects against a deleterious engagement with the unconscious and facilitates a healthy trust that the energy for development welling up from the Self can somehow be safely contained:

A real, systematic dream-analysis is hardly possible, because with children the unconscious should not be stressed unnecessarily: one can easily arouse an unwholesome curiosity, or induce an abnormal precociousness and self-consciousness, by going into psychological details which are of interest only to the adult. When you handle difficult children, it is better to keep your knowledge of psychology to yourself, as simplicity and common sense are what they need most. (CW 17: 211,120)

In his later writings, Winnicott increasingly sounds a note of caution about interpretation, expressing his fear that external definitions will steal the patient's creativity and inflate the developing potential space with the analyst's own creative imagination: "It does not really matter, of course, how much the therapist knows provided he can hide this knowledge or refrain from advertising what he knows" (Winnicott 1971: 57).

Finally, it is necessary for a comprehensive theory of development to take into account those cultural forms which mirror and reflect the construction of the ego-complex. Brian Sutton-Smith (1972), folklorist and developmental psychologist, has taken this approach with his notion of the *expressive profile*. He defines expressive forms as "ways of presenting or representing human experience, sufficiently consistent across individuals to permit functional and formal analyses" (Sutton-Smith

1972: 522). Some of the folk forms included in these, and other of his studies, are games, riddles, rhymes, jokes, pranks, superstitions, magical practices, wit, lyrics, guile, epithets, nicknames, torments, parody, oral legislation, seasonal customs, tortures, obscenities, codes, and ganglore. (Fairytales need to be added to this list.) Sutton-Smith's goal is to identify the normative expressive profile for each developmental age group, as well as the unique profile of the individual.

When Sutton-Smith's numerous studies of childlore are combined with the three encyclopedic studies by the Opies, *The Oxford Dictionary of Nursery Rhymes*, *The Language and Lore of School Children*, and *Children's Games in Street and Playground*, we have in hand the basic data for constructing expressive profiles for each stage of development from Infancy through Early Adolescence. On two previous occasions, I have presented a developmental hierarchy of games, as a partial rendering of the expressive profile, and a model for stages of ego-development (C. T. Stewart 1981a, 1981b). The present work builds on this evidence that there are specific stages in the growth of the symbolic capacity and that each stage has its own characteristic style of symbolization.

THE CHILD'S CONSTRUCTION OF THE EGO-COMPLEX

When L. H. Stewart extended his theory of the archetypal affect system to show how the innate affects provide both the dynamic forces and the building blocks for the construction of the ego-complex, he provided a model for an entirely new current of developmental and clinical research (Table 3).

With the notion of affects as archetypal in mind, the child therapist, as developmental psychologist, is able to monitor both the *patterning* of the affective forces which drive the developmental process itself and the child's *construction* of the personality in the form of the Jungian feeling-toned complexes and ego-functions, and what the Jungian analyst Joseph Henderson (1984) has called cultural attitudes. (In a previous study, my brother and I demonstrated the construction of an Aesthetic cultural attitude during the stage of Infancy (L. H. Stewart and C. T. Stewart 1981).)

Both the positive affects (Columns 2 and 3, Row 3) and the existential affects (Columns 5–8, Row 3) are motivators of the developmental process.

The Positive Affects

Two positive affects, Interest and Joy, and their respective dynamisms, curiosity/exploration and play/fantasy (Columns 2 and 3, Rows 3, 6, 9), function as the dynamisms of the life instinct, making it certain that newborn mammals, and particularly humans, will enter the world with *joie de vivre* and divine curiosity. This assures an active engagement with the world through which the fundamentals for survival are acquired.

Interest and Joy are the twin affects of the life instinct, and they develop a dialectical relation with each other which is the driving force of the entire developmental process. The dynamic interrelation between the Interest and Joy is based on their respective Life Stimuli (Columns 2 and 3, Row 2). Reproductive and generalizing acts of exploration lead the individual to "recognition" of the cognitive structures under construction. As the Familiar is the Stimulus to Joy, there is a reciprocal activation of this affect and its dynamism, play/fantasy. Play is not only integrative, but also creative, and deeply enjoyable, so that play produces novel expressive structures in the affective psyche. As Novelty is the Stimulus to Interest, activation of this positive affect and its dynamism, curiosity/exploration, results, and a dialectical movement is inaugurated. As the form of the communication between Joy and Interest, which is always symbolic, follows a spiral course, the subsequent progression in the cognitive realm begins at a higher level.

Within the dialectical process, the two affects retain their autonomy: beginning in Infancy, Interest–curiosity/exploration is the force which drives equilibration of the symbolic structures which underlie conceptual or noetic consciousness; Joy–play/fantasy, on the other hand, drives the formation of the symbolic structures which underlie expressive consciousness. Interest–curiosity/exploration is the general principle of discrimination, which in the Jungian literature is often referred to as Logos.

> For example, the Logos element, being a principle of discrimination, not only allows one but forces one to give equal dignity to any object of thinking or observation. It enables a man to devote himself with almost religious concentration to the classification of lice, or to the different qualities of faeces, to put it quite drastically, as well as to counting the stars ... (Jung 1984: 700)

On the other hand, Joy–play/fantasy is the general principle of relatedness, which in the Jungian literature is also referred to as Eros: "Eros brings things together, establishes dynamic relations between things ..." (ibid.: 700).

> There can be little doubt but that to play is to be related, to oneself and to others – a state of "being oneself." Curiosity, on the other hand, inevitably leads to discrimination and discovery – a state of "becoming aware of the 'other,' and new potentials." The dialectic between play and curiosity – relatedness and discrimination – continually interweaves these two opposites into the fabric of our life, creating the

Table 3: The Archetypal Affect System

THE PRIMORDIAL SELF

1	2	3	4	5	6	7	8
1 PRIMAL INNATE IMAGES OR IMPRINTS:	FOCUSED INSIGHT	DIFFUSE ILLUMINATION	DARKNESS	THE ABYSS	THE VOID	CHAOS	ALIENATION
2 EXISTENTIAL LIFE SITUATION:	THE NOVEL	THE FAMILIAR	THE UNEXPECTED	THE UNKNOWN	LOSS	RESTRICTION OF AUTONOMY	REJECTION
3 THE INNATE AFFECTS:	INTEREST	JOY	STARTLE	FEAR	GRIEF	ANGER	CONTEMPT AND SHAME develop out of the primal affective reflex DISGUST
4 RANGE OF INTENSITY FROM MILD TO EXTREME:	INTEREST, EXCITEMENT	ENJOYMENT, JOY, ECSTASY	SURPRISE, ASTONISHMENT, STARTLE	APPREHENSION ANXIETY FEAR, TERROR, PANIC	DISTRESS, SADNESS, GRIEF ANGUISH	IRRITATION, ANNOYANCE, FRUSTRATION, ANGER, RAGE	DISDAIN, DISLIKE, CONTEMPT, DISGUST (REJECTION TOWARD OTHER) SHYNESS, EMBARRASSMENT, SHAME (REJECTION TOWARD SELF)

5 THE COMPLEX FAMILY EMOTIONS:	The complex family emotions (Stewart 1988, 1992) are mixtures, modulations and transmutations of the innate affects. They develop in the family. The innate affects have clear prototypical expressive patterns. By contrast, the expressive behavior of a complex emotion tends to be subtle, indistinct, idiosyncratic. The complex family emotions include jealousy envy, revenge, hatred, suspicion, deceit, slyness, guilt, despair, helplessness, and of course, love, affection, tenderness, devotion, deference, consideration, generosity, satisfaction, awe, trust, admiration, respect, reverence, compassion, mercy and many others.					
6 EXPRESSIVE DYNAMISMS:	CURIOSITY	PLAY	REFLECTION	RITUAL	RHYTHM	REASON	RELATIONSHIP
7 SYMBOLIC CULTURAL ATTITUDES:	ANIMUS	ANIMA	SELF REFLECTIVE PSYCHOLOGICAL ATTITUDE	RELIGIOUS	AESTHETIC	PHILOSOPHIC	SOCIAL
8 APPERCEPTION:	BECOMING	BEING	ORIENTATION	INTANGIBLE	TANGIBLE	QUANTITATIVE ORDER	QUALITATIVE ORDER
9 EGO FUNCTIONS:	EXPLORATION	FANTASY (DAYDREAM)	EGO CONSCIOUSNESS	INTUITION	SENSATION	THINKING	FEELING
10 EVOLVED IMAGES:	SOL	LUNA	MANDALA	HOLY MOUNTAIN	ABUNDANCE AND BEAUTY OF NATURE	ORDERED COSMOS	UTOPIAN COMMUNITY
11 HIGHEST VALUE:	LOGOS	EROS	WHOLENESS "KNOW THYSELF"	THE SACRED	THE BEAUTIFUL	THE TRUE	THE GOOD

THE REALIZED SELF

Source: Reproduction from L. H. Stewart (1996) (a similar chart appears in L. H. Stewart 1987b).

intricate web of consciousness of ourselves and of the world. (L. H. Stewart 1992a)

Through this dialectical process new stages of consciousness and self-consciousness are constructed.

During the natural process of psychological development, these two principles also "inform" each other.

> I may add here that the ideal Logos can only be when it *contains* the Eros; otherwise the Logos is not dynamic at all. A man with only Logos may have a very sharp intellect, but it nothing but dry rationalism. And Eros without Logos inside never understands, there is nothing but blind relatedness. (Jung 1984: 701)

In the body of this work, we will show that the principle of individuation guides both social and individual developmental pathways. Here, we follow Jung, who has pointed out the dual nature of the individuation process, which is as much a social maturation as an individual one:

> Although the conscious achievement of individuality is consistent with man's natural destiny, it is nevertheless not his whole aim. It cannot possibly be the object of human education to create an anarchic conglomeration of individual existences. That would be too much like the unavowed ideal of extreme individualism, which is essentially no more than a morbid reaction against an equally futile collectivism. In contrast to all this, the natural process of individuation brings to birth a consciousness of human community precisely because it makes us aware of the unconscious, which unites and is common to all mankind. Individuation is an at-one-ment with oneself and at the same time with humanity, since oneself is a part of humanity. (CW 16: 227,108)

Not surprisingly, Jung's prerequisite for individuation is a dialectical relation to the unconscious, which involves a dialogue with a human partner (on whom so much of the past, present, and future of the psyche gets projected). During child treatment, the therapist has to become one of the patient's human partners if out of their dialogue new symbols are going to emerge to guide development.

As basic developmental forces, the positive affects and their dynamisms confer a broader perspective in two basic ways. First, the flexible nature of the affects, as compared with the drives, means that they can be invested in any and every aspect of the world, including, as Jung noted above, the classification of lice, faeces, or the stars. There seems to be nothing which humans cannot be interested in or enjoy. Second, this same flexibility makes possible the investment of these vitality affects in all the functions of the psyche.

> Perhaps for the time being we could leave it with the statement that the functions are vehicles for the forces, or influences, or activities, which emanate from those two principles, those two gods, Logos and Eros. And perhaps you can also understand that if there were not principles outside of the functions, one could never hope to detach anything from the unconscious. There must be something which helps one to detach a function, some principle outside which allows one to tear it away from the original lump of the unconscious. (Jung 1984, p. 701)

The original lumps of the unconscious, from which the dialectic extracts psychic functions from "outside" are the existential affects.

The Existential or Crisis Affects

Fear–Terror, Sadness–Anguish, Anger–Rage and the bipolar affect of Shame/Contempt–Disgust/Humiliation (Row 3, Columns 5–8) are oriented to (and arise out of) the existential spiritual crises of life in the world as it is.

> In each case the pain and suffering they cause us are proportionate to the need we have for them to make us aware of an aspect of life that is of critical importance to our human existence. In this sense these affects could as well be called the existential affects. They are in the last analysis the source of our ability to exist in an alien universe, they are the source of our human values. (L. H. Stewart 1984: 4)

The seventh primal affect of the self, Surprise–Startle (Column 4), is the affect of centering and reorientation. Its function is to prevent the occurrence of an inappropriate response before the stimulus evoking it has been evaluated.

L. H. Stewart has described the relation between these affects and the Jungian ego-functions and cultural attitudes (Table 3, Rows 3, 7, 9).

> The process by which both the ego functions [e.g. sensation, thinking, etc.] and the cultural attitudes [e.g. the aesthetic, social, religious, philosophical] are structured is, as I have suggested, the interaction of the twin dynamisms of the libido, joy/play and interest/curiosity, with the world and the self. I should further like to suggest that the seeds of these differentiated functions of the psyche are to be found in the unique 'behaviour patterns' of the archetypal affects of the primal self, (terror, anguish, rage and disgust/humiliation), each of which

embodies both an expressive and a noetic factor. We surmise that the expressive factors are the seeds of the cultural attitudes, the noetic factors the seeds of the ego functions (L. H. Stewart 1987a: 44)

This standpoint makes it possible to view even Winnicott's "primitive agonies" as potential spurs to development (see Table 4). I have placed Primal Image and Primitive Agony in Columns 2 and 3 to facilitate comparison.

Table 4: Crisis and Reorienting Affects and Primitive Agonies

Life Stimulus 1	Primal Image 2	Primitive Agony 3	Crisis Affect 4
1 Restriction	Chaos	Going to pieces	Anger–Rage
2 The Unknown	The Abyss	Falling forever	Fear–Terror
3 Loss	The Void	Having no relation to the body	Sadness–Anguish
4 Alienation	Rejection	Complete isolation	Contempt/ Shame–Disgust/ Humiliation
5 The Unexpected	Disorientation	Having no orientation	Surprise–Startle

Winnicott (1962, 1989) has identified five "primitive agonies" or "unthinkable anxieties" (Column 3) which result in the annihilation of being. I have compared these emotions with the crisis and reorienting affects (Column 4), and more particularly the primal images (Column 2). This correlation suggests that whether or not the "agonies" lead to development of the ego-complex or to its disruption depends both on the intensity of activation and on the adaptive and modulating capacities of parents and child.

Feeling-Toned Complexes

"*Every affective event becomes a complex*" (CW 3: 140,67) is the basic principle which determines the formation of feeling-toned complexes. The nuclear element of a such a complex consists of a factor determined by experience and causally related to the environment and an individual, innate factor. Parents induce affects in their children through contagion and by affect-specific stimuli (Table 3, Row 2). The individual factor is determined by the constitutional or temperamental character of the innate affects in the child.

Taking the stage of Infancy as a paradigm, we can predict that the development of feeling-toned complexes will be conditioned first of all by the quality of the affective life of the parents, which may be measured by their level of curiosity and playfulness. The emotional structure of these complexes will also be conditioned by the frequency and intensity of the parents' expression of crisis affects, their activation of these emotions in the infant, and the capacity of both parents and infant for affect modulation.

The people who Winnicott calls "good enough" parents are those who are able to ensure that the emotional structure of the parent-complexes will be composed of a balance of positive and existential affects, so that the crisis emotions will enter relatively smoothly into the developmental process. The array of crisis affects in the parent-complexes being constructed by the infant also determines the typological characteristics of the developing ego-complex, for the existential affects are the raw materials for the construction of the lasting ego-functions and cultural attitudes for all of us.

Ego Functions and Cultural Attitudes

When we speak, following Jung, of "ego-functions" in this work, we are referring specifically to the *Jungian* ego-functions, Sensation, Intuition, Feeling, and Thinking. When we speak of cultural attitudes, on the other hand, we are referring to the Jungian analyst Joseph Henderson's (1984) classification of Aesthetic, Religious, Social, and Philosophic attitudes, which should not be reduced to the functions or confused with them.

The dialectic between the positive affects, Interest and Joy, provides the driving force for the construction both of the ego-functions and the cultural attitudes that Jungian psychology has discovered. The existential or crisis affects provide the raw materials, the building blocks, for their construction.

Our hypothesis is that the prototypical behavior patterns of Fear, Sadness, Anger, and Contempt/Shame may be characterized in their *expressive* aspects, as: "ritual," "rhythmic harmony," "reason," and "relationship." These are the irreducible elements, respectively, of Religion, Art, Philosophy and Society. And, as we have said, these are the Categories of the Imagination, and appear as Henderson's Cultural Attitudes, the Religious, the Aesthetic, the Philosophic and the Social. On the other hand, the prototypical behavior patterns of these same archetypal affects may be characterized in their *noetic* aspects, as an apperceptive focus on fundamental domains of the world: the intangible, the tangible, quantitative ordering and organic ordering. These are the irreducible elements of our experience of the World and Kant's Categories of Understanding (Intellect): time and causality, objects in space, quantitative-logical order, and qualitative-organic order. As psychological functions these are represented in Jung's Ego

Functions: Intuition, Sensation, Thinking, and Feeling. (L. H. Stewart 1987b: 138–9)

These relations appear in Table 3, Columns 5–8, Rows 6–9. As I have said above, with this formulation in mind the child therapist is able to monitor the patient's ongoing construction, and reparative reconstruction of the ego-complex.

We have now reached the point of confluence of what I initially described as four currents of experience, observation, and study, a coalescence which gave rise to this work.

THE SYMBOLIC IMPETUS

As I have already suggested, the confluence of the four currents, children's symbols, emotions, natural psychological development and healing, and construction of the ego-complex brought into startling focus a deficit in the integrated theory I was formulating. This concerned the development of the symbolic process. For it was at this juncture that I realized there were no studies which had determined exactly how symbolic development itself proceeded. We simply did not know if it occurred in an invariant, stage-specific sequence, i.e. in a pattern similar to Erikson's psychosocial, Neumann's archetypal, and Piaget's cognitive stages of ego-development. In his systematic, empirical, but very incomplete study of the early development of the symbolic function, Piaget (1962, chapter VII) had explained its maturational patterning in a circular way, as determined by the immaturity of the thought of the child. In her study of the symbolic play of children from Early Childhood through Adolescence, Linn Jones, on the other hand, had demonstrated a more precise correlation between cognitive and expressive stages.

When the children in this study created their worlds in the sand, they revealed a cross-section of structural process ordered in the same chronological stages and by the same principles of development as those discovered by Piaget to govern the structuring of adaptive intelligence and thereby suggested an expressive reality which is the equivalent of the external world whose reality we all so readily accepts. (Jones 1982: 183)

These results caught my attention, because they clearly argued in favor of a stage-specific progression in the emergence of the symbolic process.

L. H. Stewart (1984) had also argued in favor of this notion when he formulated the following sequential pattern in the development of the imagination: Vision (Infancy); Pretend (Early Childhood); Imaginary Companion (Preschool Period); and Daydream (Middle Childhood), and suggested that the mechanism of this emergence was interiorization; i.e. Pretend results from the interiorization of Vision, the

Imaginary Companion results from the interiorization of Pretend, etc. This suggests that prior to interiorization the contents in question appear in projected form.

George Hogenson has explained Jung's view of the primacy of projection (over repression) as referring to the fact that "recognition of the world itself rests on a primordial investiture of the world [through the projection of unconscious symbolic contents] with psychic energy, libido" (Hogenson 1994: 124). As these primal images are integrated into consciousness, they provide a symbolic impetus for progressive development. David Elkind has pointed to the part that projection plays at each step in cognitive development: "*Once a concept is constructed, it is immediately externalized so that it appears to the subject as a perceptually given property of the object and independent of the subject's own mental activity*" (Elkind 1967: xii). Hans Furth (1969) has shown that Piaget viewed cognitive development as dependent upon interiorization of these projected structures. By interiorization, Furth means dissociation of form and content, and not internalization of external actions. Furth points out that the latter is substituted for the former by those translators of Piaget who do not fully understand his distinction between these two terms and the processes to which they refer. In our view, the mechanism of interiorization is the lifelong dialectical process between Interest–curiosity/exploration and Joy–play/fantasy: "Meditation or critical introspection [fantasy] and objective investigation of the object [exploration] are needed in order to establish the existence of projections" (*CW* 14: 710,499).

At this juncture, in an attempt to understand psychological development in terms of what was happening to the imaginative life of the child, I decided to use L. H. Stewart's notion of specific stages in symbolic development, along with Piaget's detailed empirical observations of the symbolic life of children, to carry out a study of the emergence of the symbolic process to determine if there was, indeed, an invariant sequence of specific stages. What I found was that each stage of development from Infancy through Early Adolescence is characterized both by a mode of the symbolic process and by a new symbolic instrumentality specific to that stage for the assimilation of the world (see Table 5).

Table 5: Stages of Symbolic Development

Stage	Symbolic Mode	Symbolic Instrument
Infancy	Waking Dream	Symbolic Act
Early Childhood	Pretend/Make-Believe	Symbolic Scheme
Preschool Period	Imaginary Companion	Symbolic Narrative
Middle Childhood	Social Realm	Symbolic Community
Early Adolescence	Cultural Attitude	Symbolic Form

Each of these stages is nothing less than a apperceptive revolution, for at each emergence the child sees the world in an entirely novel way. This transformation may be compared with Jung's characterization of the Zen Buddhist's *satori* or enlightenment: "*It is not that something different is seen, but that one sees differently*" (*CW* 11: 891,546). A new, wider horizon has opened up.

A comment on the notion of a stage may be useful at this time, since this is the sort of conception that can seem too "pat" on the one hand and too limiting on the other. But if one uses stage in the metaphoric sense of a dramatic performance space for the enactment of symbolic experience as well as in the sense of a way station along the road of development, the concept opens up considerably. Like a theater stage, I consider a developmental stage to have a preformed, fixed aspect and an open, variable aspect. I refer to the predetermined character of a stage by the term *mode*: Waking Dream, Pretend, Imaginary Companion, etc. are symbolic modes. They can be likened to ways of using the theater stage as a potent medium for dramatic expression. In this view, we are following the great theorist of symbolic forms, Ernst Cassirer, who distinguishes between *quality* of a symbolic expression, e.g. space, time, and causality, and its *modality*, for instance, whether it follows the style of scientific cognition or that of mythical thinking. The mode changes the form or quality:

> ... the general form of *causality* appears in a totally different light accordingly as we consider it on the plane of scientific or mythical thinking. Myth also knows the concept of causality, which it employs both in the general theogonies and cosmogonies and in its interpretations of all sorts of particular phenomena which it "explains" mythically on the basis of this concept. But the ultimate motive of this "explanation" is entirely different from that which governs the study of causality by theoretical, scientific concepts. The *problem* of the origin as such is common to science and myth; but the type and character, the modality of the origin changes as soon as we move from the one province to the other – as soon as we use the origin and learn to understand it as a scientific *principle*, rather than a mythical *potency*. (Cassirer 1955: 96–7)

A mode, in other words, depends essentially on the *structural* principle which is operative and dominant in the expression of a symbolic quality, and this form cannot be reduced to any other principle.

We can therefore understand the possibilities inherent in a "stage" of development in the following way. Pretend is a symbolic mode which provides the frame for a particular stage in which development occurs. The realization of this virtual developmental potential into symbolic schemes is locally, temporally, interpersonally, and individually conditioned, as in a theater which is dependent on cast, director, playwright, audience, and publicity. This explains the fact that the actualization (Piaget would say "equilibration") by the individual of a stage of symbolic development is infinitely variable. This state of affairs may also be compared to the state of quantum superposition, known since the advent of modern physics. Quantum theory holds that until it is observed, a particle remains suspended in a state of pure potential consisting of all the possible positions it would conceivably occupy. Under the influence of different kinds of environments, this quantum-like ambiguity is quickly resolved and the particle assumes a particular position. Analogously, before its actualization, Pretend is a state of symbolic superposition, which is then resolved into actual symbolic schemes through the effect of environmental influences and the activity of the individual. The field possibilities out of which a particular realization emerges is determined by the infinite variability of the individuals and psychological fields conditioning this constructive process. Yet the field that "stages" these qualities has its own distinct mode of being what it is.

It remains to clarify three ways that the stages of symbolic development are related to each other. First, they are linked by an innate or hereditary factor, although one that is poorly understood. Piaget conceives of an endogenic factor in nervous maturation as accounting for the invariant sequence of stages in his cognitive theory. Erikson postulates the virtual existence of his psychosocial stages in an innate ground plan before their actualization in the epigenetic developmental process. Neumann refers to a series of developmentally articulated hereditary archetypes as the preformed structures underlying the stages in his theory. This view provides us with the deepest insight into the innate aspect of the symbolic process, for archetypes are expressed as symbols, characterized by primordial images, numinous innate affects, and specific patterns of behavior. Second, as we have just shown, interiorization or actualization of the symbolic mode of one stage prepares for the emergence of the symbolic mode of the succeeding stage. Third, once a symbolic mode is constructed it persists throughout the life cycle and remains available as a "superposition" to be utilized by the ego as life circumstances and developmental needs dictate. Fourth, the relation between earlier and later symbolic modes is one of what a systems linguist would call hierarchical integration, which means that, once assimilated, no mode can be reduced to an earlier form, nor can it be entirely subsumed by a subsequent mode. In other words, all modes continue to function throughout the life cycle.

In Table 6, an elaborated Table 1 and Table 5 are combined.

The purpose of this book is to describe the emergence of the complex symbolic process at each stage of its maturation from Infancy through Early Adolescence. In so presenting the results of my study of this neglected line of development, I hope to demonstrate the significance of

Table 6: Symbolic, Cognitive, Psychosocial, and Archetypal Stages

Stage (Age in Years)	1 Symbolic Stages (Symbolic Instrument)	2 Cognitive Stages (Cognitive Instrument) (Piaget)	3 Psychosocial Stages (Erikson)	4 Archetypal Stages (Neumann)
1 Infancy (Birth to 1½)	Waking Dream (Symbolic Act)	Sensorimotor (Action Scheme)	Trust vs Mistrust	Phallic-Chthonian
2 Early Childhood (1½ to 3–4)	Pretend/ Make-Believe (Symbolic Scheme)	Intuitive Thought (Representative Scheme)	Autonomy vs Shame/Doubt	Magic-Phallic
3 Early Childhood 2 (3–4 to 6–7)	Imaginary Companion (Symbolic Narrative)	Articulated Intuitive Thought (Configurative Scheme)	Initiative vs Guilt	Magic-Warlike
4 Middle Childhood (6–7 to 12–13)	Mythical Realm (Symbolic Community)	Logico-Mathematical Thought (Concrete Operations)	Industry vs Inferiority	Solar-Warlike
5 Early Adolescence (12–13 to 15–16)	Cultural Attitude (Symbolic Form)	Hypothetico-Deductive Thought (Formal Operations)	Identity vs Identity Diffusion	Solar-Rational

the symbol-producing function, creative fantasy, as the motor of development itself. An ancillary goal is to show how particular symbols can facilitate the healing of blocks to maturation that may arise in each stage of psychological development from Infancy through Early Adolescence.

Each chapter in Part I will describe a new phase of the symbolic process as it emerges in typical fantasies that accompany a stage of normal development. Chapter 1 analyzes the importance of symbols in parent-infant bonding. Chapters 2–7 proceed successively from Infancy through Early Adolescence, tracing the role of stage-specific symbols in fostering the child's construction of the ego-complex.

In Part II, each chapter of the book will be devoted to the exposition of the particular *healing* role played by symbols at different stages of development. The clinical material is drawn from psychotherapy with infants, children, adolescents, and adults. Although I hope all the above is richly filling, I do not expect it fully to convince the reader or satisfy the appetite for the point of looking at things this way. In Part III, Chapter 13 is intended to serve as the proof of the pudding. It summarizes and illustrates the themes and aims of the book by presenting a symbolic analysis of Virginia Axline's classic case of child psychotherapy, *Dibs*. I believe this clinical masterpiece can be appreciated best when the notion of the symbolic impetus is applied to it.

Part I

Symbolic Fantasies that Foster Normal Development

It is exceedingly difficult to write anything definite or descriptive about the progression of psychological states. It always seemed to me as if the milestones were certain symbolic events characterized by a strong emotional tone.
——C. G. Jung, *Letters* 1

1

Parent–Infant "Chemistry": The Double Bond

> For everybody the birth of a child is quite the most important event there can possibly be.
> —— C. G. Jung, *Collected Works* 17

It seems hard to believe that the notion of "bonding" is so new, but the idea of this particular, crucial moment in the mother–infant relationship was introduced into child psychology only thirty years ago by the pediatricians Klaus and Kennell. The notion of 'imprinting' from ethology was of course earlier, but their definition of the specifically human interactional event they were addressing was based on the view that "a bond is a unique relationship between two people that is specific and endures through time." The necessary condition in the case of mother–infant bonding was not just a hard-wired readiness to "receive the mother" on the part of the infant brain, but "early and extended contact" between the mother and her newborn engaging the full psychologies of both in a creative encounter. Since its introduction the concept has been the subject of controversy, and by 1984 three independent reviews of the mother–infant bonding literature had reached different conclusions. Kennell and Klaus themselves concluded: "At present there are no definitive studies to either confirm or refute the presence of a sensitive period or to assess the length of time required in the first few hours and days after birth to produce an effect" (Kennell and Klaus 1984: 277); Myers drew quite a different conclusion: "The research both favoring and not favoring the bonding hypothesis is critically reviewed, with the evidence generally not supporting the notion that early and extended contact is crucial to the mother–infant bonding" (Myers 1984: 240); and Goldberg, agreeing with Kennell and Klaus that the hypothesis had not been tested, added:

One of the striking features of the reviewed literature is that, although much effort has been directed toward establishing that early contact affects subsequent maternal behavior, there has been little conceptualization of causal mechanisms underlying such effects and little hypothesis testing of alternative explanations (Goldberg 1984: 44–5)

Obviously, another key to the process we think of intuitively as "bonding" is needed to unlock the subject to meaningful developmental research. The approach of this chapter will be to present a phenomenological view of the natural process of parent–infant bonding that emphasizes the fantasies involved, particularly those of the parents. It is the present author's view that such an approach will be more fruitful than simple behavioral description.

THE DOUBLE BOND

"Chemistry" is a word used to define a branch of science and to point, more poetically, to the mutual attraction, sympathy, or rapport between persons. A chemical "double bond" is defined scientifically as "a type of linkage between atoms in which two pair of electrons are shared equally." But a bond can also be a way of referring to the uniting force or ties in any affiliation between people, e.g. *the bonds of friendship, the familial bond*; so we use the term *double bond* here in this psychological, relational sense to refer to a paradox, that the parent–infant relationship consists of two contexts.

First, right from birth, parents have a conscious, personal relationship with their infant, which becomes the context for all their intentional acts of adaptation to the infant. The "object" of this bond is the real, human infant. There is, however, a second context to the relationship. Even before physical birth occurs, parents start to develop an unconscious, symbolic relatedness with their infant, and this becomes the context for many of their instinctual acts of adaptation to the infant's natural need for them. This symbolic context fully manifests itself only when, at the completion of Pregnancy and the beginning of Infancy, an "infant" symbol is constellated in the parent who is able to project it onto the infant as Divine Child. Because the conscious personal context and the unconsciously determined symbolic context exist side by side throughout the stage of Infancy, it sometimes seems as if there are actually two infants undergoing development, a personal human one and a much mythologized archetypal one. As we shall see, these two infant-objects affect each other, through a process of reciprocal assimilation of their qualities and features.

Nevertheless, each of the parent–child relationships that arise in this double context has its own characteristic phenomenology. The phenomenology of the conscious relationship includes (1) individual "images" of the person that the infant is, (2) a variety of complex emotions, and (3) a busy set of intentional actions. The phenomenology of the parent's symbolic relatedness to the infant as archetype includes (1) supraordinate "divine child" images, (2) innate affects, and (3) instinctual patterns of parent–child behavior.

The complexity that emerges out of this dual phenomenology precludes any simplistic account of early parental behavior as merely the activation of a maternal instinct in the caretaking parent and a reciprocal readiness to receive the mother in the infant. Nor is the symbolic component of this complexity easy to recognize right away. In the following example, the context of the mother–infant relationship seems, for the first thirty-six hours, to be conscious, personal, and no more complex than that.

> Several years ago a woman who had extensive experience with normal newborn infants told us about the birth of her first baby in a hospital where mothers and their infants stay together throughout the hospital course. She checked her newborn over carefully following the birth and found the baby to be healthy, normal, pink, and breathing easily. She proceeded to feed and care for her baby but did not sense any special reaction to the neonate. (Klaus and Kennell 1982: 53)

Nevertheless, thirty-six hours after birth, this mother found that she had been transfixed by an arrow from the bow of golden-winged Eros – her infant was now transfigured in her fantasy, as was she herself:

> ... she described *a remarkable warm glow* that *came over her*. At that point she suddenly realized that she had *the most beautiful, gorgeous, most responsive baby in the world*. And she had *strong feelings of love for her infant*. (ibid.: 53; italics added)

In some versions of his myth, Eros, interestingly, has two mothers: as the son of Aphrodite, Goddess of Love, his darts excite *sexual passion*, whereas as the son of Eileithyia, Goddess of Childbirth, the same darts evoke *mother–love*.

The observation of mother and infant above records the psychological moment when an "infant" symbol is constellated in the "everyday" mind of the mother. This symbol is of course readily projected upon her infant; in fact, it is discovered in projection, which is what the word "constellated" implies. The first indication that a new supraordinate gestalt – the archetypal stardom of the infant – will be governing the interaction is the "*remarkable warm glow*" that comes over the mother. This glow is shed by the awe-inspiring, luminous affects evoked by the "infant" symbol. The mother's further statement that the warm glow "*came over her*" expresses the autonomous and numinous nature of the emotional process that was set in motion by the archetype. The very next indication of the appearance of the archetype is the articulation of the symbolic "image" of the divine child which appeared in the mother's realization that she had "*the most beautiful, gorgeous, most responsive baby in the world.*" The superlatives used to qualify this symbolic expression, which was composed of conscious representations of the infant organized around the innate "image" of the ideal baby, express the supraordinate nature of the emergent "infant" symbol, in other words, its archetypal status. The last indication that an archetype has, indeed been constellated, was the evoked affect, the mother's "*strong feelings of love for her infant.*" These confirm that the active projection of the divine infant symbol onto the infant has occurred. Through this healthy mechanism of projection, the positive affects comprising the infant symbol become a loving mother–infant bond, which then will serve as the foundation for mother–infant relatedness throughout this baby's infancy.

In the rest of this chapter, we will examine the characteristics of the process described as "constellation," in both mothers and fathers, alongside the developmental significance of idealized "infant" symbols.

CONSTELLATION OF "INFANT" SYMBOLS

According to classical Jungian theory, during the natural course of psychological development, whenever environmental or developmental demands require the construction of a new attitude, a process of *introversion* and *regression* of libido may occur. It is as if the libido, faced with the challenge of crossing a developmental threshold, first steps back to take a better leap. When the introverted libido regresses to the level of the developmental ground plan, it stimulates the creative activity of the psyche to form a *developmental symbol*. This symbol then converts regression into progression, and conscious *realization* of the contents of the symbol results in the attainment of a new attitude. In a discussion of the dynamics of regression and progression, Henderson used the wave design in Greek ornamental art to correct "several errors commonly encountered when evaluating this pair of contrasts": "Progression leads the whole cycle forward and upward; regression returns to redefine the center of the whole cycle, as if the movement were a self-concealing, self-restorative creative act" (Henderson 1990: 51).

In the case of the symbol of the divine child, because it is a developmental symbol, the new attitude that is conveyed is an orientation to progressive unfolding and developing. The dynamism associated with the divine child is richly elaborated in creation myths, which tell of the creative activities of cosmogonic gods and goddesses, who, through introversion, are fertilized, inspired, regenerated, and reborn. One example of this group of deities is the Indian creator-god Prajapati, "Lord of Creation."

As Hiranyagarbha (the Golden Germ), Prajapati is the self-begotten egg, the cosmic egg from which he hatches himself ... He creeps into himself [introversion], becomes his own womb [regression], makes himself pregnant with himself [symbol formation] in order to hatch forth the world of multiplicity [realization]. (*CW* 5: 589, 380)

Given the pluripotentiality of the child in this cosmogonic myth, it is not surprising that the constellation of a developmental "divine infant" symbol has the power to transform the parents' relation to their infant, to themselves, and to the world, giving each of these aspects of their involvement with parenting a new energy.

In a society that attends to its symbolic life, this process of introversion, regression, symbol formation, and realization is guided and regulated by cultural practices. These safeguard the stability of the personality (and the community) during the transition from one psychological attitude to another. Van Gennep's (1960) analysis of the rites of passage invoked at birth, puberty, marriage, and death has demonstrated that these different ceremonies have in common three phases of purpose: (1) separation, (2) transition, and (3) incorporation. We can find these stages in the natural process of a mother's becoming initiated into the parental role with her infant. *Separation* would correspond to severance of the libido-attachments of everyday life during "confinement," a time of *introversion*. *Transition* suggests the period of relative isolation just after the child is born, when there is often regression and symbol formation. *Incorporation* belongs to the return to everyday life, in which can be observed progression to a growing confidence in being a mother and realization of the meaning of the divine child. Many traditions assure that mothers will go through these stages with full cultural sanction and support. When these traditional cultural forms are no longer effective, the individual faces the hazards of the developmental unconscious in unmediated form. Psychological treatment may be needed to offer support to the individual struggling to persevere through the process of symbolic developmental transformation.

As psychotherapists who have accompanied their long-term patients through many such transformations know, each stage of the life cycle is a stimulus for the same sequence of events. We will now show that at the completion of Pregnancy and the beginning of their child's Infancy new parents experience a process of introversion, regression, and symbol formation in preparation for parenthood.

Introversion

Introversion, the *turning inward* of psychic energy or libido, is well-documented in studies of prospective mothers during their pregnancies, although different terms have been used to refer to this process, for instance *aloneness* (Shereshefsky and Yarrow 1973), *self-preoccupation* (Leifer 1980), and *centering* (Gloger-Tippelt 1983).

In his account of Primary Maternal Preoccupation, that state of heightened sensitivity in the mother that begins towards the end of pregnancy and lasts a few weeks after birth, Winnicott has presented a graphic description of the process of introversion.

> Experience shows, however, that a change gradually takes place in the feeling as well as in the body of the girl who has conceived. She'll always say her interest gradually narrows down. *Perhaps it is better to say that the direction of her interest turns from outwards to inwards. She slowly but surely comes to believe that the center of the world is in her own body.* (Winnicott 1964: 19; italics added)

In this way, the prospective mother can be said to creep into herself. So does the prospective father.

May has described prospective fathers passing through a *focusing* phase, which begins around the twenty-fifth to thirtieth weeks of pregnancy and extends until the onset of labor.

> The expectant father's attitudes and feelings about the pregnancy change. The man *focuses on his own experience of pregnancy*, and, in so doing, he feels more in tune with his wife. He begins to redefine himself as a father and the world around him in terms of his future fatherhood. (May 1982: 341; italics added)

I would add that many men feel maternal at this stage, as if in possession of a psychological womb that is his inner preoccupation with the coming infant. Once the process of establishing the "infant" symbol is underway, this introversion of libido is followed, both in mothers and in fathers, by its regression.

Regression

Regression, the *turning backward* of libido to earlier objects or modes of adaptation, can occur in two basic forms: (1) regression to the personal unconscious, which means regression to less conscious ways of coping in the service of adaptation of the ego-personality; and (2) regression to the developmental ground plan, which means an activation of the deeper Self in the service of the growth of the whole personality. As regression from control of the ego to reliance upon the Self involves a returning to the foundation of the total personality, we can anticipate that it will be accompanied by profound effects.

Winnicott's description of the alteration of the mother's state during Primary Maternal Preoccupation gives witness, I believe, to regression to the developmental ground plan.

> This organized state (that would be an illness were it not for the fact of the pregnancy) could be compared with a withdrawn state, or a dissociated state, or a fugue, or even with a disturbance at a deeper level such as a schizoid episode in which some aspect of the personality temporarily takes over. (Winnicott 1956: 302)

Winnicott points out, on the other hand, that this profound regression prepares the mother for the initial phase of mother–infant bonding.

> I do not believe it is possible to understand the *functioning of the mother at the very beginning of the infant's life* without seeing that she must be able to reach this state of heightened sensitivity, almost an illness, and to recover from it. (ibid.; italics added)

Twenty-three years after Winnicott's observations, and without reference to them, Brazelton and Als interviewed prospective mothers and encountered similar psychic turmoil.

> We found in our research at Putnam Children's Center that the prenatal interviews with normal primiparas [first-time mothers], in a psychoanalytic interview setting, uncovered anxiety which seemed at first to be of almost pathological proportions. The unconscious material was so loaded and distorted, so near the surface, that before delivery the interviewer felt inclined to make an ominous prediction about each woman's capacity to adjust to the role of mothering. (Brazelton and Als 1979: 350)

They also discovered that the regressive turmoil experienced by the mothers was an integral part of a progressive developmental process.

> Yet, when we saw each in action as a mother, this very anxiety and the distorted unconscious material seemed to become a force for reorganization, for readjustment to an important new role. We began to feel that much of the prenatal anxiety and distortion of fantasy was a healthy mechanism for bringing a woman out of the old homeostasis which she had achieved to be ready for a new level of adjustment. (ibid.: 350)

In this way, the prospective mother becomes her own womb and broods upon herself.

So does the prospective father. For, during the above study of first-time mothers, Brazelton (1973) interviewed their husbands and found that during the third trimester they experienced psychic upheavals similar to those of their wives.

In the natural course of the development of infant symbols, introversion and regression are followed, both in mothers and in fathers, by constellation and projection of infant symbols.

FORMATION AND PROJECTION OF INFANT SYMBOLS

When the introversion and regression of psychic energy reaches the level of the developmental ground plan, it stimulates creative fantasy, that is the symbol-forming activity of the psyche. It is this creative activity that produces any developmental symbol: in this instance the infant symbol arises composed of both conscious and unconscious contents and corresponding in its nuances to the adaptive needs of the moment. This infant symbol becomes manifest in the dreams and fantasies of parents, gets projected upon the infant, and is realized by the parents through their progressive development and adaptation to parenthood.

The phenomenology of infant symbols appearing in the dreams and fantasies of prospective and newly-minted parents includes supraordinate images, innate emotions, and instinctual patterns of behavior. The cultural analogues to the natural infant symbols most parents take for granted are stories of the *primordial child* as formed in myths, legends, and fairytales (Jung and Kerenyi 1963). In the dreams and fantasies of parents we do not find such fully-formed mythological figures, but nevertheless the structural elements of myth are in place and can be readily identified in the actual utterances of parents. Jungians refer to such mythological utterances as mythologems or mythical motifs.

These facts make it possible to compare the attributes of infant symbols appearing in the dreams and fantasies of parents with those of the primordial child, thus giving us a way to identify the supraordinate nature of the imagery.

PHENOMENOLOGY OF "INFANT" SYMBOLS: MOTHERS

Image

One attribute shared by symbolic "infant" and primordial child is *precocity*. Thus, both Deutsch (1945) and Van de Castle (1994) recorded dreams of prospective mothers in which they gave birth to "infants" who were far advanced in development, *walking and talking at birth*. The only explanation another mother could find for her breasts feeling rather empty in the morning was that her three month old daughter was "so 'cunning' that ... the baby jumped from her crib to the adjacent parental bed to sneak a feeding while the mother was asleep and then jumped back to her crib" (Lieberman 1999). In a foundational myth of Western

Civilization, the Homeric *Hymn to Hermes* (1970), the primordial child, Hermes, spent the late afternoon of his day of birth in thieving.

> Born in the morning,
> he played the lyre
> by afternoon, and
> by evening had stolen the cattle
> of the Archer Apollo (Homeric Hymns: 19)

Similarly, on the day of his birth, the Finnish child hero, Kullervo, was swaddled and laid in his cradle, while his mother sat rocking it, but after three days of rocking, "the boy kicked out with his feet before and behind, tore off the swaddling-clothes, crawled out, and broke the lime-wood cradle to pieces" (Jung and Kerenyi 1963: 34).

Another correspondence between symbolic "infant" and the primordial child in parent's dreams is their astonishing *birth weights*. Mothers report dreams in which they give birth to "infants" with very large or very small birth weights: "Once born, the baby usually possesses unusual physical characteristics such as weighing 5 *ounces* or else tipping the scales at *35 pounds* ..." (Van de Castle 1994: 392). In myth, legend, and fairytale, certain child gods are born as "thumblings," others as "giants," and some as both: "The footprints of an Indian child god are always the footprints of a giant even though the child is a mere midget" (Jung and Kerenyi 1963: 57). At birth, the Finnish wonder-child, Samsa, was as big as a man's thumb. When he was challenged to perform heroic deeds, on the other hand, he grew into his giant form.

> Scarcely had he spoken these words when, before his eyes, the little man was transformed into a giant. He stamped with his feet on the earth and his head reached up to the clouds; his beard flowed to his knees and his hair to his heels. His eyes were fathoms wide and his legs fathoms long; his knees were one and a half fathoms and his girth and his hips two fathoms. (ibid.: 1963: 42)

Giving birth to a symbolic "heroine," however, has its frustrations. One mother dreams "I gave birth to a large girl in a very few minutes of labor. She was the size of a ten-year-old child! I was upset because I had no baby to hold!" (Sherwen 1981: 400).

A less frequent form of advanced development, in symbolic "infant" and primordial child alike, is *precocious smiling*. Just before the birth of her first child, while in a state of expectant introversion, "The baby has been on my mind almost constantly," a prospective mother had the following dream. She said it was the first time she really had a "picture of what he looked like."

I didn't see any of the labor ... we were in a church and I was singing in the choir. All of a sudden the baby was there and I got to see him. All I could see was his face, but he looked like a boy with a real round face and red hair like my husband. I looked down at him and said, "Oh, you're just beautiful." And he gave me a big smile. Just born, and my child smiling! (Leifer 1980: 193)

The initial situation is thus charged with numinosity: the dreamer is in a house of worship and, along with others, raises her voice in a hymn of devotion. The miraculous "sudden" appearance of the "baby", without the necessity of labor, marks the initial manifestation of a constellated "infant" symbol. When the mother likens the "red hair" to that of her husband, she is viewing the dream "infant" in a personal context. But viewed in a symbolic context, the "red hair" takes on special significance – it becomes a fiery corona, the classical attribute of a sun-hero or sun-god, e.g. Helios: "You will see a god, young, comely, with glowing locks, in a white tunic and a scarlet cloak, with a fiery crown" (CW 5: 155,103). The angelic beauty and beatific smile of the "baby" suggest it is a member of a celestial choir. The mother's reaction to the "big smile" concludes the dream. A bright-eyed social smile occurring on the day of birth is indeed precocious.

It is said that on the day of his birth, Apollo smiled when first nursed by his mother Leto: "So saying, she display'd her sacred breast, which, with his lips, the smiling infant prest, and sucked ambrosial juice ..." (Callimachus 1901: 401). Beroe, daughter of Aphrodite by Adonis, is said to have smiled on the day of her birth. The wonder-child in Virgil's IV Eclogue was encouraged to do so.

> Then begin, little boy, to greet
> your mother with a smile. The ten
> long months of her pregnancy
> have been hard on her. Begin,
> little boy. (Virgil 1980)

In *Infant Joy*, Blake's (1977) divine child *smiles* and *speaks* on the second day of life.

I have no name
I am but two days old. –
What shall I call thee?
I happy am
Joy is my name, –
Sweet joy befall thee!
Pretty joy!
Sweet joy but two days old.

Sweet joy I call thee:
Thou dost smile. I sing the while
Sweet joy befall thee.

Another attribute shared by "infant" symbol and primordial child is *monstrosity*. Mothers are understandably troubled by dreams in which their "infants" appear as monsters:

The dreams are not always so optimistic: the fear of giving birth to a monster is intensified in the last weeks of pregnancy, and cripples, idiots, monsters appear in the pregnant woman's dreams just as in her daytime anxieties. (Deutsch 1945: 214)

One mother had the following dream: "I dreamed that there was confusion over whether the baby is a boy or girl, like it was a *hermaph-rodite*" (Sered and Abramovitch 1992: 1407; italics added). Our culture has grown familiar with the monstrous primordial child born from the union of Aphrodite and Hermes, Hermaphroditos. In addition, many cosmogonic, creator gods are hermaphroditic, as is Eros in his manifestation as Protogonos.

The Eros of Athenian poetry and painting is unquestionably male, but the Protogonos of esoteric doctrine is not male or female but bisexed, resuming in mystic fashion Eros and Aphrodite. He is an impossible, unthinkable cosmic potency. (Harrison 1922: 647)

The realization of a cosmic potency corresponds to the pluripotential for the development, in the dreamer, of a new level of consciousness, in this case a loving symbolic relatedness with her god-like "infant."

The monstrous images in the following two dreams also point out the necessity of viewing such images from a symbolic perspective. When one mother dreams of giving birth to a "baby" with a "pig's head" and another dreams of giving birth to a "baby" with a "cat's face" (Schroer 1984), we need to recall that Demeter and Persephone had these very animal attributes, even though they were anthropomorphic deities most of the time. Pig and cat are among the most ancient symbols of fertility and the feminine. Like Jung, Schroer assumes that these dreams originate in "a deep collective level of the psyche," which, in my view, is the locus of the developmental ground plan.

The infant symbol may also appear *entirely* in theriomorphic form, as a prospective mother's waking fantasy shows.

In this fluid, she thought, the child swims like a fish in water; it feeds on the water and, like a fish, dies when it does not receive enough of its life element. She also referred facetiously to the fetus as "my little goldfish." (Deutsch 1945: 241)

Viewed as an unconscious product originating in the personal unconscious, the goldfish signifies the unborn child. Viewed more broadly as an unconscious product originating in the developmental unconscious, the goldfish is still an infant symbol, but with the elements of "gold" and "fish" pointing to a deeper archetypal meaning to the symbol of developing value, that is the typical meaning of a prized new child. Let us amplify this meaning by turning again to the storehouse of myth.

The Primordial Child, Vishnu, sleeping in the world-ocean, is fish, embryo, and womb at once. The fish is also one form of Greek child gods. The dolphin, sacred to Apollo, appears in Greek mythology as the changeling shape of a child god. And the boyish figure of Eros is portrayed being carried on the back of a dolphin. When the setting sun, Helios, sinks into the sea, it becomes primordial child and fish, thus literally a "goldfish." Further, in psychological terms, the "fluid," i.e. primal water, upon which the "goldfish" feeds, symbolizes the nourishing function of the instinctual unconscious for the "infant" symbol. Note that this is not just the sustenance provided by the mother's breast, or by the baby bottle offered by the mothering figure. It is the full amniotic surround of earliest unconscious life. Thus, the "goldfish," swimming or floating in the cradle of the mother's womb, implies a virtual or potential state of being that awaits realization.

We turn now to the emotions accompanying such a constellation.

Emotion

In the dreams just analyzed, we can identify emotional expressions of joy, consternation, dismay, puzzlement, and apprehension. As common experience tells us and the following examples show, however, the most frequent affects accompanying the initial manifestation of an infant symbol are a set of innate positive emotions that L. H. Stewart (1986) has described as Joy–Ecstasy and Interest–Excitement. These in turn are linked to, and help us in developing a way of approaching the complex emotion Love that has always been the most important of all affects to those who raise children.

In the introduction to this chapter, we observed a mother develop "strong feelings of love" for her infant thirty-six hours after childbirth. When 132 women were asked if they had any unusual (for them) experiences during childbirth, forty-three (32.6 percent) said that they felt an "unusually deep happiness." When the same group of women were asked the same question two to four days after birth, fifty-two (39.4 percent) said that, while daydreaming, they felt an "unusually deep happiness." (The authors do not tell us whether or not there was overlap between these two groups of respondents. If not, the number of women being pierced by a dart from the bow of Eros would be ninety-five, or nearly three-quarters of the mothers interviewed.) "Unusually deep happiness" is described as follows:

(It arises) uncontrollably, spontaneously, and frequently "in waves". It does not tend to be motivated, or to be conditioned by family background, of course of childbirth or future expectations. It is fairly often compatible with polar feelings (like grief). To sum up, subjects regard it as profoundly different from ordinary happiness. (Spivak et al. 1993: 240–1)

Deep happiness corresponds, I believe, to an innate affective component of the infant symbol itself, Joy–Ecstasy, which being archetypal is both autonomous and numinous with respect to the ordinary experience of the subject. The uncontrollable nature of the affect is an expression of its *autonomy*, whereas the difference of this deep happiness from ordinary happiness is a measure of its *numinosity*. (It would be interesting to know what images appeared in the dreams and fantasies of these women at childbirth and two to four days after.) It is reasonable to conclude that the authors are witness to the manifestation of the positive affective components of an evoking infant archetype. Additional support for this interpretation appears in the reports by forty-eight (36 percent) of the women at childbirth and (45 percent) two to four days after, that they were in an "unusual state of mind," characterized by an "overwhelming preoccupation with childbirth/childcare issues and a profound alteration of interior life."

One question that Tronick and co-workers (1997) asked was whether, during the postpartum period, the mothers in their study group were denying depression and distress. Their findings did not support this premise, but they did discover that these mothers were experiencing a highly positive postpartum state which the authors labeled "postpartum exuberance." The similarity of circumstance in which "usually deep happiness" and "postpartum exuberance" emerge and of their quality suggest that they are different names for the same phenomenon.

In the next example, we are witness to a mother falling under the spell of this archetypal Eros on the fourth day after childbirth.

When I held the baby for the first time I don't think I experienced any rush of maternal feeling. That came in gradually, and then on about the fourth day after, it really hit me. It was like falling in love for the first time. (Kitzinger 1972: 219)

We recall that this is the very same pattern that we saw in the example in the introduction – a matter-of-fact first few days of motherhood followed by a numinous moment, when the archetype is constellated, an experience which is likened to "falling in love for the first time." It is at this moment that an "infant" symbol has been constellated, has been projected onto the baby, and the initial phase of a loving mother–infant bond has been established.

An arrow from the bow of Eros transfixes yet another mother when she nurses her infant for the first time.

> When the nurse took my first child and put him to my breast his tiny mouth opened and reached for me as if he had known forever what to do. He began to suck with such force *it took my breath away* ... I began to *laugh*. I couldn't help myself. It seemed incredible that such a tiny creature could have such force and determination ... *Tears of joy* ran shamelessly down my cheeks while he sucked. I thought back to my past conviction that only when I had a baby would I *know* whatever it was I had to know. Now I *did* know. It is the only important thing I have ever learned, and so ridiculously simple: love exists ... *There in the midst of all that clinical green and white, I had discovered what love was all about. It was a meeting of two beings.* (Stevens 1990: 78–9; italics added)

The autonomy of the constellation of the affect-evoking infant symbol is expressed in the mother's exclamation, "I couldn't help myself" and in the spontaneous nature of the joyful laughter and tears. The intensity of the activated Joy is sufficient to take her breath away. The blissful "meeting of two beings" marks the projection of the "infant" symbol, which is accompanied by the numinous, ecstatic beginning of mother–infant bonding.

On occasion, the dart from the bow of Eros strikes in the middle of the night.

> Later that night, when I was too happy to sleep, I took the baby from his cot and held him, against my shoulder for the rest of the night. I seemed to breathe his very essence and he I believe mine too ... Every part of me seemed to fill with what I can only describe as "a loving ecstasy." (Kitzinger 1979: 57)

The initial manifestation of constellation is that the mother is "too happy to sleep." Then, the beginning of bonding with her infant, i.e. projection of the "infant" symbol, is marked by the numinous exchange of breaths, an intermingling of souls. (In the questionnaire study just mentioned, twelve mothers during birth and eleven mothers at two to four days after birth described experiencing an "unusual" form of "an almost telepathic contact" with their infants.) The rapturous culmination in the current example is a "loving ecstasy," which suffuses the mother's whole being. The experience of a developmental symbol is always an experience of wholeness, which we can explain psychologically (if we follow Jung) by recognizing that such a symbol is composed both of elements from consciousness and of contents from the deepest levels of the unconscious.

In the next hospital observation, a mother is inspired not by Eros but by the equally primordial cosmogonic Logos, the universal principle of revelation, thought, and word.

> I had an *uncontrollable curiosity* to find out about him – watch his funny little movements, take off his clothes and *examine* his fingers and toes. I think this *process of getting to know* your baby in the physical sense is underestimated at the very beginning – that women do in fact need long periods of privacy when they can be allowed just *to watch their baby and to explore* his or her body. I remember the feeling of never wanting to let him go from my bed. I wanted him to be with me, and I felt a terrible deprivation when he was taken away to the nursery ... I longed to get home to *total involvement* with my baby. (ibid.: 55–6; italics added)

The mythic Logos is to be understood in psychological terms as grounded in the innate archetypal affect Interest–Excitement, with its particular dynamism curiosity/exploration. The autonomy and intensity of the mother's experience can be discerned in the "uncontrollable" nature of her curiosity, her wish for "total" relatedness with her baby, and the "terrible deprivation" when this relatedness is interrupted. The numinous quality of her experience breathes through each of the mother's utterances. Her longing for "total involvement" anticipates the projection of the "infant" symbol and the initiation of mother–infant bonding.

We turn now to the patterns of behavior accompanying constellation.

Patterns of Behavior

An extensive list of patterns of behavior accompanying mother–infant bonding has been compiled by Klaus and Kennell (1982). These correspond, I believe, to the "intuitive" or "primary" parenting behaviors reported by Papousek and Papousek (1983). From our perspective, these patterns of behavior represent the instinctual components of "infant" symbols.

(Just after completing this analysis of mothers' images and emotions at childbirth, I discovered the recently published book *Dream Child*, by Abt, Bosch, and Mackrell (2000), which has as its subtitle: "Creation and New Life in Dreams of Pregnant Women.")

PHENOMENOLOGY OF "INFANT" SYMBOLS: FATHERS

Our understanding of the phenomenology of "infant" symbols in fathers is limited by the fact that there are, surprisingly, no studies of the dreams and fantasies of prospective fathers during the period of gestation. Both culture-lore and clinical observation are replete with descriptions of fathers' states of mind following the actual birth of their children, however. Greenberg and Morris have introduced the concept of engrossment to characterize the "enthusiastic response and intense involvement of fathers in their newborn infants."

> In our attempt to describe this involvement of the father with his newborn, we will employ the term *engrossment*, by which we refer to a sense of absorption, pre-occupation, and interest in the infant. The potential for engrossment in one's newborn is considered an innate potential, and it is hypothesized that it is the early contact with the infant which releases this potential for involvement. (Greenberg and Morris 1974: 521)

My analysis, based on the descriptions provided by Greenberg and Morris, will show that the correspondence between the phenomenology of paternal engrossment and "infant" symbols makes it possible to use descriptions of the former to illustrate the latter.

Image

Fathers in the grip of the numinous state of engrossment have perceptions of their infants which require supraordinate terms for their expression: "so beautiful," "a little gem," "larger than life," and the epitome of "perfection." The "jewel," one of the traditional images of the primordial child, the superlative "beauty" and "perfection," and the expansive, "larger than life" quality in these reports, indicate we are witnessing the manifestation of supraordinate "images," which mark the constellation in fathers of "infant" symbols.

Emotion

Fathers describe the "high" they experience at birth and over the next few days as feeling "stunned, stoned, drunk, dazed, off-the-ground, full of energy, feeling ten feet tall, feeling different, abnormal, taken away, taken out of yourself." These spontaneous moods of elevation and exaltation, of being moved out of the ego to a higher plane, are as characteristic as those we have seen in the case of mothers, and I think they too must be counted among the archetypal affects which accompany the constellation of an infant symbol. The immediate, powerful evocative effect of encountering the symbol of the divine child in projection onto one's baby is evident in the next observation, of a father:

I just sit and stare at it and talk to the wife and comfort her a bit. But the main thing is the baby. I just want to hold the baby ... And then I go look at the kid and then I pick her up and then I put her down and then I say, "Hi! is everything all right?" And then I go back to the kid, I keep going back to the kind. It's like a magnet. That's what I can't get over, the fact that I feel like that. (ibid.: 524)

The magical, magnetic attraction exerted by the infant is to be understood as a manifestation of the energic intensity of the image projected onto the child, which literally pulls the father into parent–infant bonding. In men such an attraction is often grounded in the affect Interest–Excitement. This of course does not preclude a father feeling "maternal" and experiencing many states of mind identical to the mother's, nor does his excitement and interest keep him from participating vicariously and taking pleasure in her enjoyment at being a mother.

Patterns of Behavior

Greenberg and Morris (1974), Klaus and Kennell (1982), and Parke (1981), among others, have described paternal instinctual patterns of behavior at birth and during the first months of life. That there is a sufficient degree of parallelism between the instinctual patterns of behavior in mothers and fathers points to a common factor in the evocation of both parents' fantasy and behavior, which can be found, we believe, in the constellated infant symbol.

It is not hard to conclude that such strong, archetypal affects are of major importance in fostering development. But we must now consider just what that significance might be for the developing child.

DEVELOPMENTAL SIGNIFICANCE OF "INFANT" SYMBOLS

Up to now, our focus has been on the profound effects on parents of the constellation of infant symbols as they affect parents. Once the infant symbol has been projected by them onto their offspring, however, it also begins to have profound effects upon the actual infant.

Initially, the infant is immersed in and suffused by the positive libido – Joy and Interest – streaming from the unconscious of the parents to the unconscious of the infant. These affects flow across the bridge thrown up by the constellated and projected symbol of the divine child. In order to capture the likely nature of this experience for the infant, we must turn to myths which speak of "floating" in the primal or cosmic "vessel," "womb," "ocean," "round," and "pond," or "shelteredness" in the "original home," "paradise," and even the Gnostic "pleroma." In our own day, the symbolic medium of relatedness is referred to in the quasi-scientific language of contemporary psychology as a holding environment, a container, or a primal envelope.

Soon the libido streaming out of the unconscious of the parents begins to activate both the developmental ground plan and the symbol-forming activity in the instinctual unconscious of the infant. The full developmental significance of these effects of the projected "infant" symbol will be discussed in Chapter 2, where the rise of consciousness in the infant during the first few weeks and months of life will be described and analyzed in detail.

But for now it is important to note that the developmental significance of the infant symbol is not exhausted by, or limited to the child's development in the earliest phases of its existence. In fact, the potentiating effect of the infant symbol endures throughout the stage of Infancy (see Chapter 3). In order to demonstrate this fact, we analyze studies of securely and insecurely attached infants. Our focus in these analyses will be on the emotional components of "infant" symbols. In the case of securely attached infants and their mothers, our focus will be on the positive affects Interest and Joy; in the case of insecurely attached infants and their mothers, our focus must be on the more painful existential or "crisis" affects – Fear, Sadness, Anger, Shame/Contempt.

Positive Affects and Secure Attachment

Mary Ainsworth and her co-workers have described four bipolar patterns of maternal behavior which condition infant-maternal attachment in its positive and negative aspects: "Sensitivity–insensitivity, acceptance–rejection, co-operation–interference, and accessibility–ignoring" (Ainsworth et al. 1974: 106). The sensitivity–insensitivity continuum is supraordinate to the other dimensions, inasmuch as sensitive responsiveness is incompatible with the predominance of rejection, interference, and ignoring, which block development. The sensitive mother is able to see things from her baby's point of view, whereas the insensitive mother gears her interventions almost exclusively in terms of her own needs. Sensitive mothers can be identified in the first three months of the infant's life.

Our premise here is that sensitivity in mothers is largely conditioned by the constellation and projection of the divine infant symbol, which ensures optimal activation of the positive affects Interest and Joy in the mothers, along with their respective dynamisms curiosity/exploration and play/fantasy, which consequently are strongly activated in the infant as well.

Blehar and co-workers demonstrated that there are two poles in the behavior of sensitive mothers.

One pole of Factor 1 is defined by routine maternal manner during face-to-face interaction [social exploration], and also substantially loaded in this direction is silent, unsmiling maternal initiation of interaction [social exploration]. Associated with these maternal behaviors is the infant response of merely looking at [curiously exploring] the mother ... (Blehar et al. 1977: 189)

These results show that a sensitive mother initiates social exploration with her infant and that a responsive infant reacts with curiosity of its own. The emotional component of the infant symbol which is motivating both the mother's and the infant's interpersonal curiosity and exploration is the affect Interest–Excitement: "I had an uncontrollable curiosity to find out about him ..."

The opposite pole of Factor 1 is defined by maternal *playfulness*, with maternal contingent pacing loaded moderately in the same direction. The positive infant behaviors – *vocalizing, smiling, and bouncing* – are associated with these maternal behaviors and, likewise, the dyadic measure of ensuing interaction ... (ibid.; italics added)

These results show that the sensitive mother is always looking for the opportunity to play with her infant: "How many days has my baby to play? ... My baby wants to play every day." The emotional component of "infant" symbols which motivates social play is the affect Joy–Ecstasy. The joyful response of the infant to its mother's playfulness establishes a mutual context for social play and games.

By the end of the first year, the effect of the sensitive mother's curiosity and playfulness on her infant are apparent. Securely attached one year olds, in contrast to insecurely attached toddlers, are more "cooperative and *playful* during Bayley testing, are more verbal during free play, *approach a playmate more fully, play a social ball game more actively*, and *explore a puzzle box with greater curiosity and interest*" (Main 1983; italics added). Thus, securely attached one-year-olds of sensitive mothers exhibit the same poles in their behavior – they explore and play more, both in social and in individual contexts, than their insecure age-mates. Thus, curious and playful mothers are a necessary condition for the creation of curious and playful infants.

This analysis leads to the following conclusion: beginning in earliest Infancy and continuing throughout this stage, sensitive mothers are best defined by their capacity for social exploration and social play with their infants, and this capacity, in turn, is based on the original, optimal constellation in the mothers of unambiguously divine infant symbols.

Further support for this view appears in the studies of C. Malatesta and her co-workers (1986). They found that in their interactions with their infants at two and a half, five, and seven and a half months, mothers instinctively made every effort to maximize their expressions of Joy, Interest, and Surprise. (They also minimized their expressions of the crisis affects, Fear, Anger, and Sadness.) The rates of total maternal expressions of Joy and Interest, both verbal and nonverbal, predicted increases in infant expressions of these positive affects. Finally, it appeared that mothers correctly understood the expression of Surprise by the infant as an index of maturing intelligence. The mothers often mimicked the child's expressions of Surprise and escalated the games and occasions for Surprise as a means of enhancing the child's cognitive growth. When asked to express negative feelings in such interactions, mothers found it almost impossible to do so.

Crisis Affects and Insecure Attachment

Turning our attention to more insecurely attached one-year-old infants, we find that they are classified into three groups, based on their behaviors in reunion episodes with their mothers: A (avoidant), C (ambivalent) and D (fearful), and subgroups, A1 A2 C1 C2. Mothers of A1 infants are the most rejecting, mothers of A1 and C1 infants are the most interfering, mothers of A2 and C2 infants are the most ignoring and inaccessible, and mothers of D infants are the most indecipherable.

These maternal behaviors may be compared with the Life Stimuli which contribute to the activation of the crisis affects (Table 7).

Table 7: Maternal Behavior and Crisis Affects

Maternal Behavior	Life Stimulus	Affect
Ignoring	Loss	Sadness
Interfering	Restriction of Autonomy	Anger
Rejecting	Rejection	Shame/Contempt
Indecipherable	The Unknown	Fear

These considerations led me to conduct an analysis to determine if there was, in fact, a correspondence between a maternal behavior viewed as a Life Stimulus and the crisis affect expressed by their insecurely attached infants. The results are as follows.

1. There is a correlation between *ignoring* maternal behaviors, interpreted as the life stimulus *Loss*, and the more frequent expression by their infants of the crisis affect *Sadness*, i.e. crying.
2. There is a correlation between *interfering* maternal behavior, interpreted as the life stimulus *Restriction of Autonomy*, and the predominant expression by their infants of the crisis affect *Anger*.
3. There is a correlation between *rejecting* maternal behaviors, interpreted as the life stimulus *Rejection*, and the predominant expression by their infants of the crisis affect *Shame/Contempt*.

4. There is a correlation between *indecipherable* maternal behaviors, interpreted as the life stimulus of *the Unknown*, and the predominant expression, by certain of the Group D infants, of the crisis affect *Fear*.

Just after completing the above analyses, I discovered the study by Malatesta and Wilson (1988) which correlates parental antecedents, emotion traits, and attachment categories. They found that C1 infants who were angry during reunion episodes, had parents who were chronically frustrating, and that C2 infants, who were sad during separation episodes, had parents who presented their infants with experiences of major or minor loss. For these two attachment categories, my conclusions are in agreement with those of Malatesta and Wilson. Our conclusions differ, on the other hand, with regard to the innate affect Fear. Malatesta and Wilson assign Fear to the A2 infants with overly stimulating parents; I assign Fear to the D infants, those whose parents present them with indecipherable behaviors. Since either overstimulation or confusion might in common experience seem to be a basis for a frightened response, further research can be expected to clarify this difference in our findings and emphases.

At this point, however, these analyses have led me to the conviction that it is reasonable to assume that one of the factors which conditions the behavior of mother's of insecurely attached infants is a less than optimal constellation of an infant symbol. Failure of this divine child archetype to prevail decreases the normal predominance of the positive affects and increases the tendency toward unmodulated activation of the crisis affects. The heightened activity of the innate affects Fear, Anger, Sadness, and Shame/Contempt motivate the negative maternal behaviors which result in the insecure attachments of their one-year-old infants. The predominance of a particular crisis affect in a particular mother is of course based on her individual life experience.

In Chapter 2 we continue our examination of the parent–infant bond, but shift our attention to the developmental changes in the infant, as the *infant–parent* bond is activated.

2

The Waking Dream of Infancy

> One has never seen the world well if he has not dreamed what he was seeing.
> ——G. Bachelard, *The Poetics of Reverie*

The stage of development that we analyze in this chapter extends from birth to one to two years and is referred to by Jean Piaget as the Sensorimotor period, when action schemata, the initial cognitive structures, are constructed. By developmental psychologists, however, it is known as the stage of Infancy, in which a number of psychic issues already exist. The psychoanalyst Erik Erikson found that it is marked by the crisis of Trust versus Mistrust and this formulation has had wide acceptance. The Jungian analyst Erich Neumann has challenged Freud's assumption that orality predominates at this age by calling it the Phallic-Chthonian stage, chthonian referring to the strong ground of instinct in general so prevalent in the psychological life of the infant at this stage, and phallic suggesting that primitive initiatives already can be observed as the infant seeks the world. The *symbolic* function which emerges at the beginning of this stage of Infancy is, however, the *waking dream* or *vision*, which gives meaning to both instinct and environment or "world." The new instrument used by the infant for the assimilation of these rich inner and outer experiences is the *symbolic act*.

The emergence of the symbolic process during the first weeks and months of Infancy occurs within a sequential, stepwise differentiation of consciousness that I believe is invariant once it is set in motion. Using a term Jung originally introduced, this rather complex sequence of ego-development can be referred to as the *primal experience*.

> By "primal experience" is meant that first human differentiation between subject and object, that first conscious objectivation which is psychologically inconceivable without an inner division of the human against himself – the very means by which he separated himself from the oneness of nature. (CW 5: 500n32,325)

The primal experience, then, begins with differentiation between subject and object; only later is it followed by differentiation between ego and self. Eventually the extraordinary consequences of these two differentiations lead to the creation of a new world view. Once established through this three-step process, the primal experience serves as a foundation for all the psychological development that ensues in the stage of Infancy. Moreover, throughout this book we will repeatedly discover this same three-step process as the sequence through which the assimilation of experience into symbolic psychological life takes place. This sequence (first differentiating subject from object, then ego from self, and finally creating a new world view) is the order invariably encountered as each new stage of the symbolizing capacity becomes established.

In the rest of this chapter, I will first discuss the theoretical and evidential basis for my view that the *waking dream* is the imaginal mode that characterizes symbolic development in the stage of Infancy. I will then describe in some detail the stepwise differentiation of consciousness that constructs the "primal experience" at this stage.

WAKING DREAM/VISION

In equating "vision" and "waking dream," I am again adopting the Jungian view of these phenomena.

> Visions are like dreams, only they occur in the waking state. They enter consciousness along with conscious perceptions and are nothing other than the momentary irruption of an unconscious content. (*CW* 8: 581,307)

During the process of psychological development an infant utilizes *dreaming* the world, as well as cognizing it, as a way of assimilating experience.

> Imagination occurs as a spontaneous visionary phenomenon; it causes the quality of an experience which is both "real" and "unbidden" but which does not replace external reality, appearing instead "alongside" the experience of the everyday world. (L. H. Stewart 1984: 17)

My own view, that the waking dream or vision is the imaginal mode at this stage of symbolic development, can be explicated along two lines of reasoning.

The first, which might be called a "regressive analysis" of these affairs, begins with the status of the dream as we find it at the beginning of Early Childhood. This is the stage immediately following Infancy. We know that at the beginning of Early Childhood, the child believes (1) that he or she dreams with his or her eyes, (2) that the dream comes from outside,

(3) that it takes place within the room, and (4), upon awakening, that it is true and objective (Piaget 1960). When we try to imagine what might be the dream's status at the beginning of Infancy, we are apt to conjecture that the waking dream is experienced simply as one event among all the others that constitute experience at that early stage.

> At the lowest and most primitive level we find a sort of generalized or cosmic consciousness, with complete unconsciousness of the subject. On this level there are only events, but no acting persons. (*CW* 10: 281,136–7)

This is consistent with Jung's view that at the beginning the infant does not think, that is, produce thoughts, but rather *perceives his or her mind functioning*.

Another line of reasoning, which we might refer to as progressive, begins with the observation that at least 50 percent of the newborn infant's sleep consists of active REM or dreaming sleep. (The corresponding figure in the adult is 20 percent.) Even the figure of 50 percent underestimates the amount of time the infant spends dreaming. When Emde and his co-workers studied endogenous smiling in the neonatal period, they made an unexpected discovery.

> A surprising finding was that endogenous smiling occurs not only during REM sleep when the eyes are closed, but also at times when there are behavioral activity patterns and polygraphic patterns of REM-sleep with eyes open. We decided to call this state, which appeared to be a behavioral form of drowsiness, "drowsy REM." The discovery of what some might consider to be a "nonsleep" REM state was soon enlarged to include other behavioral states. (Emde et al. 1976: 72–3)

These observations have led me, along with others, to believe that the "nonsleep" REM state is a waking dream state. Certainly, a similar if not identical state has been observed by other researchers.

> In newborns ... a unique state change was also observed when they responded as usual to a previously conditioned stimuli only to find their behavior was no longer reinforced; there was a sudden and dramatic shift from Waking State IV (agitation, distress) to Waking State I (eyes open, no movements or vocalization). It appeared that the difficult adaptation process in this case overextended the capabilities of these very young subjects, leading to a sudden inhibition or withdrawal during which the newborn stared motionlessly, breathing deeply as if *sleeping with its eyes open*. (Papousek et al. 1986: 97; italics added)

My own interpretation is as follows: faced with an obstruction in exploring the world, and experiencing "crisis affects" in response to this blockage, the infant resorts to *dreaming* the world. At this point in its development, the infant in search of adaptation requires a symbolic fantasy that will serve as a guide to overcoming the restriction in his or her sensorimotor repertoire.

Piaget also speculates that the thinking of the infant at this "sensorimotor stage" is analogous to deep dreaming. Here is how he describes the development of thought at this stage:

> First, the assimilation of the world to the self; second, the formation of emotional schemas charged with images; third, the special orientation of thought by emotional association and not by logical systematization. (Piaget 1927: 202)

The whole of the infant's mental activity, Piaget even says is "a sort of long waking dream" (ibid.: 205) in which emotion predominates. When the infant is happy or sad, "he colors his whole universe with his joy or grief" (ibid.: 200). I would say in the light of present day affect theory that the infant's first experience of the innate affects is a stimulus to dream the world, in such a way as to give image to those affects. But the images dreamed are also encountered qualities of the world itself.

Ernst Cassirer in his classic four-volume work, *The Philosophy of Symbolic Forms*, holds the view that the origin of all mythical consciousness is to be found in the perception of affective expression in the world that surrounds us:

> Where the "meaning" of the world is still taken as that of pure expression, every phenomenon discloses a definite "character," which is not merely deduced or inferred from it but which belongs to it immediately. It is in itself gloomy or joyful, agitating or soothing, pacifying or terrifying. These determinations are expressive values and factors adhering to the phenomena themselves; they are not merely derived from them indirectly by way of the subjects which we regard as standing behind the phenomenon. (Cassirer 1957: 72)

It is not hard to apply this view to the psychology of an infant, so tuned to the mothering figure's face. Cassirer's perspective is further differentiated in Heinz Werner's notion of physiognomic perception, i.e. the infant's reading of the expressions in the faces of those around him or her, including the "face" of whatever non-human environment is present to him or her in the form of flowers, trees, sun, moon, water, and animals.

> Physiognomic perception must be considered as the primary phenomenon, and personification as a more advanced and specific

form of childlike interpretation. It may be that the child apprehends persons physiognomically more readily than other objects in his surrounding world. This fact might give rise to the erroneous impression that the child first discovers physiognomic characteristics in human individuals and then transfers them to non-human objects. The more direct assumption, however, and one which is in greater accordance with the facts, is that the child, grasping the world as he does through his motor-affective activity, will understand the world in terms of physiognomics before personifying. (Werner 1957: 75–6)

Winnicott, moreover, has observed that in play the child invests external phenomena with the dramatic feeling and meaning of a dream: "Without hallucinating the child puts out a sample of dream potential and lives with this sample in a chosen setting of fragments from external reality" (Winnicott 1971: 51). All this, as I have been arguing, takes the form of a waking dream: "At the theoretical start," Winnicott wrote, "the baby lives in a dream world while awake. What is there when he or she is awake becomes material for dreams" (Davis and Wallbridge 1981: 171).

THE PHASE OF NON-RECOGNITION

I will now go back in developmental time to discuss the presymbolic period of development which extends from birth to the emergence of the primal experience. This period of development, when the newborn's apprehensions of the world and self are essentially unconscious, will be referred to as *the phase of non-recognition.*

This brief period of earliest postnatal development is of considerable importance because the infant's experiences during it are the main determinants of the quality of the primal experience, which is in turn the beginning of all later symbolic development. Although the primal experience is grounded in a virtual pattern already contained in the Self, and the genetic, constitutional, and physical health of the infant condition its realization, it is the quality of emotional and physical nurturance provided by the parents that is the primary influence on its maturation. We draw on Neumann's term, *personal evocation*, to refer to the vital role parents play as this stage in making archetypes come to life for their infant. As Neumann points out, it sometimes seems as if the constellating power of the archetype has called the good-enough parent into being, rather than vice versa. Certainly, however, parents serve to make the archetype real.

For the true evocation of an archetype, a concurrence between the tendency to form a psychic image of a certain kind and a factor in the world outside is indispensable in every case. But the factor in the world outside is not only a carrier of the image in the sense that the archetypal image is projected upon it; it has also to be seen as the mundane component of the archetype itself. (Neumann 1966: 82)

An essential condition during the period of non-recognition for "good enough" personal evocation of the symbolic archetype needed to guide the child's forward development of both ego and self is the constellation in parents, following the birth of their baby, of the symbol of the divine child. This is only effective of course, if it is projected upon the developing infant (Chapter 1), although this, as we have seen, is what normally happens.

During this same period, when the parents are projecting the Divine Child, they are also beginning to construct a conscious, personal, and particular relationship with their infant. Studies have shown, for instance, that soon after childbirth parents begin to recognize their own infants by visual, olfactory, auditory, and tactile cues (Kaitz et al. 1993).

Neumann, using the alchemical image of a snake swallowing its own tail, the uroboros, refers to this period in the infant's life as the postnatal *uroboric* phase, which he regards as an extension of intrauterine existence.

> The term uroboric has been selected for the initial pre-ego state, because the symbol of the uroboros, the circular snake, touching its tail with its mouth and so "eating" it, is characteristic of the oppositionless unity of this psychic reality. Thus the uroboros as the Great Round, in whose womb center the ego-germ lies sheltered, is the characteristic symbol of the uterine situation in which there is not yet a clearly delimited child personality confronting a human and extra-human environment. This undelimited state characteristic of the uterine embryonic situation is largely, though not fully, preserved after birth. (Neumann 1990: 10)

During this admittedly mythological phase, the infant's relation to the world and the Self is one of what Jung called unconscious identity: the world is revealed to the infant and the infant dreams the world. Yet, on the day of birth, at the center of the quiescent uroboric oneness, we can already discern innate developmental motivations of primary significance.

Activation of the innate affect Interest occurs during the birth process (Lagercrantz and Slotkin 1986). On the first day of life, after an initial period of high arousal, an endogenous sleep–wake cycle occurs.

> Following birth, all infants had an initial wakeful period, fell asleep, awoke, and then fell asleep a second time. Fifteen infants awoke again and fell asleep a third time during the ten-hour observation period.

Thus, all infants had wakefulness between sleep periods without an associated feeding. (Emde et al. 1975: 782)

These subjects' sleep cycles exhibited both NREM and REM periods, the latter predominating. The infants' REM periods of somnolence were accompanied by endogenous *smiling*. These research findings indicate that, on the first day of life, there is activation of a cycle relating the innate affect Interest, manifest in high arousal and wakeful periods, to the affect Joy, manifest in REM somnolence and endogenous smiling.

It has also been shown that parental behaviors influence these patterns from the outset. The initial differentiation of the sleep–wake cycle, which occurs during the first weeks of the phase of non-recognition, is conditioned by the quality and continuity of the caretaking environment (Sander 1977, 1983). During this period when their child is not able to recapture who they are, sensitive parents approach every caretaking encounter as an opportunity for social interaction, and they engage their baby in gentle social play *before* the infant is capable of initiating this activity on its own (Escalona 1968).

As a result of the unconscious identity between infant and parent (and the normally contagious nature of all emotions), the infant at the beginning of extrauterine life is suffused with affects originating in the parents' unconscious.

All affects, with the exception of startle, are specific activators of themselves – the principle of *contagion*. This is true whether the affect is initially a response of the self, or the response of another. By this we mean that the experience of fear is frightening, the experience of distress is distressing, the experience of anger is angering, the experience of shame is shaming, the experience of disgust is disgusting, the experience of joy is joying, the experience of excitement is exciting. These are the innate relationships. (Tomkins 1962: 296)

Under normal circumstances, the affects directed at the infant arising in the unconscious of the parent are primarily the positive emotions, Interest and Joy. As these numinous emotions play a crucial role in the personal evocation of the infant's own primal experience, the ways they are expressed and modulated are of considerable importance.

One expressive form which is closest of all to capturing the essence and totality of what parents evoke for the child during the period of non-recognition is the nursery rhyme.

The nursery rhyme, which by tacit and universal consent may be either said or sung, is resorted to by the mother for the soothing and amusement of her child without thought of its origin, except in that usually she remembers it from her own childhood. (Opie and Opie 1973: 3)

In fact, it is usually the infant's first introduction to the archetypal world of images that evoke affects and thus the magical possibilities of symbolic experience. The aesthetic quality of nursery rhymes and play songs makes them fitting symbols for introducing the infant to the numinous elements of the human voice.

> "The best of the older ones", says Robert Graves [writing of nursery rhymes], "are nearer to poetry than the greater part of *The Oxford Book of English Verse.*" "They have", says Walter de la Mare, "their own complete little beauty if looked at closely." "The nursery rhyme", says Professor Cammaerts, "is essentially poetical because essentially musical." They do not fail to satisfy the ear. "G. K. Chesterton", writes Ivor Brown, "observed that so simple a line from the nursery as 'Over the hills and far away' is one of the most beautiful in all English poetry", and, as if in confirmation, Gay, Swift, Burns, Tennyson, Stevenson, and Henley thought well enough of the line to make it their own. (ibid.: 2)

Lively rhymes and songs may be said or sung to evoke Interest and capture attention. Happy songs may be sung to evoke Joy and facilitate communion. Rhymes with unexpected twists and turns may be sung or said to evoke Surprise; they accustom the infant to conscious reorientation in the grip of a symbol. Lullabies are sung to soothe the infant and prepare for sleep.

> Little has been said about the lullaby, though it is a most natural form of song and has been declared to be the genesis of all song. As Sir Edmund Chambers has said: "It must be remembered that the dance was not the only primitive activity, the rhythm of which evoked the song. The rocking of the cradle was another." (ibid.: 18)

When circumstances dictate, there are dark lullabies and gruesome rhymes available to metabolize the "primitive agonies" of both parent and infant alike (Warner 1999).

THE PRIMAL EXPERIENCE

The completion of this "uroboric" phase of non-recognition of the fact of self and other is marked by the emergence of the symbolic mode of Infancy, the *primal experience.*

The primal experience is a differentiation of consciousness which occurs during the first four to twelve weeks of life. It emerges, invariably, through a sequential, stepwise process of development. The first event composing the primal experience is the ego's "recognition" of the other. This is really a new level of consciousness, which is marked by the infant's first bright-eyed, social smile. The next event is the ego's "recognition" of the self, also a new level of consciousness, which is marked by the infant's first individual laugh. The last event in the construction of the primal experience is the creation of a new world view. This last occurs when the infant begins to use the intellectual instrument forged during ego-self "recognition" to assimilate the world.

As always in the development of the ego's capacity to symbolize, the first step is a necessary condition for the second, and the second is a necessary condition for the emergence of the third. For the infant, the primal experience marks both the completion of the passive stage of Pregnancy and the beginning of the active stage of Infancy.

The Ego's "Recognition" of the Other

The first event in the primal experience is a *rise of consciousness* resulting from the beginning of differentiation of subject (infant) and outer object (parent). This is a landmark achievement that marks the beginning of the innate ego-nucleus as a differentiated entity. The emergence of the new level of consciousness that we refer to as the ego's "recognition" of the other, is marked by the infant's first, bright-eyed, social *smile*, nearly always a numinous moment for parent and infant alike.

At 0;1(0), just five days before his first social smile, one of Piaget's observations of his son Laurent catches the baby intently exploring the human face.

> When one leans over him, as when dressing him, he explores the face section by section: hair, eyes, nose, mouth, everything is food for his visual curiosity. (Piaget 1952: 68)

After five days of such almost continuous exploration, that face becomes *familiar*, and Laurent smiles.

> Laurent *smiled* for the first time at 0;1(15) at 6 o'clock, 10 o'clock and 11:30 while looking at his nurse who is wagging her head and singing. (ibid.: 72; italics added)

According to L. H. Stewart (Table 1), the Familiar is the life stimulus for the innate affect Joy, and that affect, I think, is the motivation for Laurent's smile here. Often accompanying an infant's first bright-eyed smiles are the baby's earliest vocal expressions directed to the other, primarily melodious "cooing."

This obviously joyful initial differentiation of ego-consciousness is accompanied by a significant increase in the infant's capacity for *social exploration* and *social play* generally. This is almost always impressive to the parents: "Now he [my baby] can see me! Now he [my baby] is fun to play with!" (Wolff 1961: 122). There is a nursery rhyme that asks, "How many days has my baby to play?", and answers itself, "My baby wants to play everyday."

We have seen that at the beginning of Infancy, an "infant" symbol is constellated in parents and projected onto the infant to form one of the ties in the parent–infant double bond (Chapter 1). In response to archetypal parent behavior, such as mirroring of the infant's progress during the phase of non-recognition, a "parent" symbol is now constellated in the infant and projected onto the parents, reinforcing their parent behavior. In other words, just as an "infant" symbol, the Divine Child, is evoked in the parents by the baby, so a complementary "parent" symbol, the Divine Mother, is evoked in the infant's psyche by the parents. Jungian psychology recognizing the supraordinate relationship-shaping power of these intrapsychic structures once evoked, speaks of them as "constellated." The implication is that the archetype, like a planet in the heavens as conceived by traditional astrology, has its coercive "field" of influence.

> The mother constellates the archetypal field and evokes the archetypal image of the mother in the child psyche, where it rests, ready to be evoked and to function. This archetypal image evoked in the psyche then sets in motion a complex interplay of psychic functions in the child, which is the starting point for essential psychic developments between the ego and the unconscious. (Neumann 1990: 24)

The evocation of the mother archetype in turn permits its projection upon the human mother, and that accomplishment is the central event of the first step in the primal experience.

> But within one to three months the infant has a startling revelation. It discriminates, out of the void of unconsciousness, the sound of the mother's voice and the sight of her face, and responds with its first clear-eyed smile of recognition. We may imagine that, for the infant, this is a vision of great beauty and wonder, a revelation of the visual-auditory archetypal image of the mother, the Great Goddess, a vision our dreams ever seek to recover. This revelation signals the approaching end of the earliest uroboric state, and leads on to the ensuing stages of development. (L. H. Stewart 1990: 2)

The symbolism adds a new value to the object – the personal mother – without any prejudice as to her own immediate value: the mother becomes numinous while remaining just as she is. The activations of the innate affects and their dynamisms, particularly Interest–curiosity/ exploration and Joy–play/fantasy, are manifestations of the constellation of the Great Mother–Divine Child pair, which forms the basis for the symbolic double "bond" which is the foundation for *infant–parent* "chemistry."

Once constellation of these reciprocal archetypes has occurred in parent and infant, a strong archetypal field is established which contains the intersubjective relationship of parent and infant. This is spoken of by Neumann as the *primal relationship*.

> The primal relationship has as its field a system of relatedness with mother and child as its poles; but in the pre-ego phase of child development this field is also a reality independent of the poles. The primal relationship, as a specifically archetypal constellation, embraces both individuals in its transparent reality, each pole – mother and child – appearing to the other and acting upon it as an archetype. This basic archetypal situation guarantees the formative functioning of the primal relationship with all its vital consequences for child development. (Neumann 1990: 22)

The symbolic field is actually characterized by *two* reciprocal bonds, one personal and one archetypal, guaranteeing that both parent and infant will engage in social exploration and social play. This symbolic field of their interaction is the social motor of development, which takes every opportunity given by the archetypal potential of the child to undergo social development. The bright-eyed social smile that Laurent flashed at his nurse suggested that this development in him was in full flower, fostered by the reciprocal interest in it shown by the parent figures.

The Ego's "Recognition" of the Self

The ego's "recognition" of the other is a necessary precondition for the ego's "recognition" of the self because, in order to be conscious of oneself, one must be able to distinguish that self from the selves of others. However, the ego has its own interest in itself, apart from the interest it takes in others interest in itself.

The second numinous event in the primal experience, which occurs some weeks after the first, is the ego's "recognition" of the self. This is a new level of consciousness expressed in the infant's first individual *laughs*, which occur during exuberant, joyful *self-motion*.

Piaget's daughter Lucienne's first social smile had occurred on 0;1(24) and four weeks later her parent observes her in her crib.

At 0;2(13), for example, she smiles at her hood. She looks attentively at a particular place, then smiles while *wriggling all over*, then returns to this place, etc. (Piaget 1952: 73; italics added)

For six more days, Lucienne explores "wriggling all over." Then she laughs in "recognition" of her capacity for self-motion.

At 0;2(19) the ribbon which always hangs from the hood arouses her hilarity; she looks at it, *laughs while twisting herself about*, looks at it again, etc. (ibid.: 73–4; italics added)

This is the beginning of that primal joy at *being oneself* which will hopefully accompany one throughout the life cycle. Piaget refers to the joy we take in being ourselves as *functional pleasure*.

Reading on in Piaget's classic descriptions, we are also treated to Laurent's first laughs. Four weeks after his first social smile, while engaged in enthusiastic wriggling all over and babbling, Laurent, like Lucienne, laughs in "recognition" of his capacity for self-motion.

At 0;2(18) he smiles five times in succession while looking at the mosquito net ... The same day he *laughs and babbles* with great excitement while watching the toy. As soon as he is naked he *laughs loudly, gesticulating* and looking at the objects surrounding him including the brown wall of the balcony. (ibid.: 73; italics added)

After three more days of such joyful "gesticulating," Laurent discovers that he can look at the world upside down.

At 0;2(21), in the morning, Laurent spontaneously bends his head backward and surveys the end of his bassinet from this position. Then he smiles [ego–other "recognition"], returns to his normal position and then begins again. I observed this several times. As soon as Laurent awakens after the short naps to which he is accustomed, he resumes this activity. At four o'clock in the afternoon after a long sleep he has barely awakened before he bends his head backward and bursts out laughing [ego–self "recognition"]. (ibid.: 70)

This observation shows Laurent's beginning differentiation of his capacity for self-motion.

Lucienne and Laurent demonstrate that the ego's "recognition" of the self is accompanied by a significant increase, easily identified by parents, in the infant's capacity for *individual exploration* and *individual play*. Such spontaneous self-aware playfulness and exploration is the motor of individual development.

The observations of the first laughs of Lucienne and Laurent were made by a loving father, but the laughs themselves were not shared with him. Rather, as we have indicated, these laughs mark vital moments of *self*-discovery. These facts have led me to conclude that ego–self "recognition" represents the first occurrence of what Winnicott refers to as the capacity to be alone.

> It is only when alone (that is to say, in the presence of someone) that the infant can discover his own personal life. The pathological alternative is a false life built on reactions to external stimuli. When alone in the sense that I am using the term, and only when alone, the infant is able to do the equivalent of what in an adult would be called relaxing ... The stage is set for an id [self] experience. In the course of time there arrives a sensation or an impulse [self-motion]. In this setting the sensation or impulse will feel real and be truly a personal experience. (Winnicott 1958: 34)

Thus the primal experience is also *self*-experience. When we discuss the developmental significance of the primal experience (Chapter 3), we will consider the ongoing significance of this correspondence in greater detail.

Creation of a New World View

The ego's "recognition" of the self is a necessary condition for creation of a new world view, for the intellectual instrument employed in the latter is created during the former. The third and last event in the primal experience of the new self in the world, occurring some weeks after the second step, is another rise in consciousness that accompanies the infant's creation of *a new world view*. Through the gradual, purposive shaping of exuberant self-motion, the infant forges a new intellectual instrument of assimilation, the *symbolic act*: "In the beginning was the deed!" Although these initial enactments are only expressive, they are quickly transposed to the cognitive domain when the movements assume a purposive character. The creation of a new world view begins at the moment when the infant applies and adapts this instrument toward the purpose of assimilating the world into its play and exploration.

At the beginning of her third month, Lucienne continues to enjoy self-motion.

> At 0;3(5) Lucienne shakes her bassinet by moving her legs violently (bending and unbending them, etc.), which makes the cloth dolls swing from the hood. Lucienne looks at them, smiling, and recommences at once. These movements are simply the concomitants of joy. When she experiences great pleasure Lucienne externalizes it in a total reaction including leg movements. (Piaget 1952: 157–8)

The simultaneous movement of her body and the dolls, which has been going on for weeks, suddenly takes on new meaning.

> The next day, at 0;3(6) I present the dolls: Lucienne immediately moves, shakes her legs, but this time without smiling. Her *interest* is intense and sustained and there also seems to be an intentional circular reaction. (ibid.: 158; italics added)

Lucienne experiences the results of "leg-shaking-doll-motion" as a *novelty*, thus creating for herself the life stimulus for the innate affect Interest–Excitement. A dialectical movement has occurred, from the world of expression to the field of consciousness that the phenomenologists call the noetic domain, which parents recognize in their children as cleverness. Motivated by Interest–Excitement, Lucienne becomes "aware" for the first time that there is a connection between her actions and the movements of the knick-knacks. The creation of a new world view is a cosmogonic event, and Lucienne will spend the rest of her infancy developing and differentiating this new perspective, moving the world through her arm shaking, hand clenching-and-unclenching, string pulling, leg shaking, foot kicking, head turning, body arching, etc. (ibid.: 147–209).

Piaget's observations make it clear that it takes only another day of exploration of this new phenomenon for the routine to become Familiar. From that point on Lucienne begins individual play with this scheme as the content.

> At 0;3(9) Lucienne is in her bassinet without the dolls. I shake the bassinet two or three times without her seeing me. She looks very interested and serious and begins again, for a long stretch of time, rough and definitely intentional shaking [exploration]. That evening I rediscover Lucienne in the act of shaking the hood spontaneously. She *laughs* at the sight [play]. (ibid., p. 158; italics added)

On this occasion, a dialectical movement takes place: from individual *exploration* to individual *play*. Accompanying this delightful dialectic, Lucienne's laughter marks her "recognition" of her new found symbolic capacity to be agent of her own pleasure, a sense of herself as "doer" which she is integrating into a new sense of self. (The reader can also observe a similar process of creation of a new world view in the case of Laurent: see Piaget 1952: 160–2.)

In the next observation of Laurent, we find him using, as an extension of his body, the rattle, that age-old toy which has often served to celebrate the creation of this new world view of the baby as agent.

At 0;2(27), the regular shakes Laurent gives the rattle reveal a certain skill [exploration] ... At 0;3(10), the operation lasts fully a quarter of an hour during which Laurent emits peals of laughter [play]. (ibid.: 161–2)

This is a further example of the beginning of the dialectic between two affect-behavior dynamisms that are archetypal, curiosity/exploration and play/fantasy. The spherical shape and the sound of the rattle, which in antiquity was known as the *sistrum* and was seen by parents both as an infant toy and as a protection for the child *against evil influences* (Harrison 1962: 17), is compelling to infant and watchful parent alike. As a nursery rhyme goes:

Dance, little baby, and mother shall sing,
With the merry gay coral, ding, ding-a-ding, ding.

A note to this play song states: "The baby's bell-bedecked rattle from which juts a sprig of coral ... is not so common today as it was in the nineteenth century" (Opie and Opie 1973: 60). Just so, many of the symbolic possibilities of play have become obscured in our time.

Because the developmental significance of the smile and the laugh as central milestones is central to our discussion, we next review the research which serves as the basis for this view.

Smile and Laugh

The fact that the infant's first laughs have drawn less attention than the first smiles is due to the mistaken view that the difference between the smile and laugh is only quantitative, one of degree of expression, and not qualitative, one of *kind* of expression. As part of our analysis of the primal experience, we consider the infant's first individual laughs, marking as they do the first "recognitions" of self, fully as significant an event as the same individual's first bright-eyed smiles, which we interpret as "recognitions" of the other. To be sure, laughter is quickly socialized, but it remains an individual form of expression, often one we engage in at a moment of self-recognition throughout our lives. Our view of the distinctive nature of the human laugh draws support from a series of studies, beginning with the evolutionary analysis of facial displays by the Dutch ethologist, J. A. R. A. M. Van Hooff.

Van Hooff (1972) notes that, whereas most authors "regard smiling and laughter as patterns that differ only in degree, smiling being a less intense form, a diminutive of laughter," a few authors "regard the movements as qualitatively different." The latter authors believe that a "comparison between the individual's relation to the environment during smiling and during laughing provides a basis for distinguishing between them." In smiling the "active directedness to the environment is maintained" [ego–other relation]; in laughter, on the other hand, there is "an abandoning of directed relationship to the environment [ego–self relation]." Van Hooff then embarked on a systematic study to test the hypothesis that "laughter and smiling could be conceived as displays with a different phylogenetic origin, that have converged to a considerable extent in *Homo*." His comparative analysis of the facial displays of the higher primates substantiated this notion and led to the following conclusions.

> When the distinguishing features of laughter and smiling are considered in relation to the comparative evidence, especially of the closely-related chimpanzee for which quantitative data have been presented here, the agreement is obvious. Laughter then fits neatly in the phylogenetic developmental range of the relaxed open-mouth display, a metacommunicative signal, designating the behaviour with which it is associated as mock-aggression or play. Smiling fits well as the final stage of the development of the silent bared-teeth display. Originally reflecting an attitude of submission, this display has come to represent non-hostility and finally has become emancipated to an expression of social attachment or friendliness, which is non-hostility par excellence. (Van Hooff 1972: 235–6)

Van Hooff's conclusions are echoed in studies of human smiles and laughter in infants, children, and adults.

Another study of the development of laughter in mother–infant communications demonstrated that *nondyadic* laughter is the predominant form exhibited by the infant in the first four months of life: "... analysis revealed that the frequency of isolated laughter for infants was significantly higher than coactive laughter at time 1 (4–17 weeks) ..." (Nwokah et al. 1994: 31). As a corollary to this finding, the investigators discovered that mothers were often startled by their infant's first laughs.

> Five infants produced their first laughter at 10 or 11 weeks of age, 4 infants from 13 to 16 weeks, and 4 infants from 17 to 21 weeks. This laughter was usually not expected by the mother, who then often commented on it: "Is that a laugh?" and "I know you're laughing." (ibid.: 27)

Thus, the mothers in this study readily distinguished between the smile and the laugh. The authors drew the following conclusions regarding individual laughter:

> Laughter, in this study, always occurred in an interpersonal setting, but most of maternal and infant laughter was nondyadic isolated

laughter rather than dyadic coactive or reciprocal. Laughter could, therefore, be viewed as a *personal expression* of increased intensity of pleasure, amusement, or excitement, regardless of whether the partner laughed or not. *The hypothesis that most laughter would be dyadic (reciprocal or coactive) was definitely not supported by the data.* (ibid.: 32; italics added)

In this study, then, the laughter of the infant is found to be an individual, not social, expressive form.

N. Blurton Jones studied the smile and the laugh in two- to five-year-old nursery school children. His review of the literature, as well as his own studies, supported the view that the smile and the laugh have distinctive meanings. He found an association of "laughing and open-mouthed smiles with running and jumping, hitting at others, wrestling and chasing in a temporal grouping of behaviour which he calls 'rough and tumble play'" (Blurton Jones 1972a: 280). Laughter evidently continued to accompany exuberant self-motion! Smiling, on the other hand, "loaded most conspicuously with talking, giving objects to children, receiving objects and pointing at things while looking at a child" (ibid.). Smiling, we note, continues to accompany *social* exchanges.

A more recent study of the smiles and laughter of nursery school children had a different focus, but arrived at the same conclusion.

A second result produced by the present set of observations was that laughing and smiling co-occurred *with somewhat different event patterns.* In general, laughter co-occurred more frequently than smiling with intentionally produced verbal-motor, silliness/clowning events, particularly when produced by the target child [self-expression]. (Bainum et al. 1984: 155; italics added)

Evidence in support of our thesis also appears in a study of the smile and laugh in adults.

Ethological data on 141 adult dyads support the hypothesis that the human smile had its origin in the silent bared-teeth submissive grimace of primates and that the facial expression accompanying laughter evolved from the relaxed open-mouth display of play. Affiliative smiling occurred in greeting and departure interactions, whereas frank laughter was almost exclusively seen in a recreational context. Convergence and learning may mask the original distinction, leaving the impression of a continuum of graded signals. (Lockard et al. 1977: 183)

Before leaving laughter, we should note that it also has a characteristic sonic (acoustic) signature, which in its simplicity is more characteristic of bird songs and animal calls than speech (Provine and Yong 1991). Presumably this is the way the child talks to itself in the moment of displaying its pleasure to others.

In the next chapter, we return to the unfolding of the primal experience and discuss its importance for psychological development throughout the stage of Infancy.

3

Realization in Infancy

Blessed indeed is the child who has a curious and playful mother.
——L. H. Stewart, 'A Brief Report: Affect and Archetype'

During the natural course of psychological development, the steps in constructing the primal experience are taken during the first weeks and months of life. Because their sequence is invariant, they seem to be the first major, postnatal realization of an innate ground plan. The developmental significance of the primal experience is suggested, as well, by a host of other findings.

In the first place, many observers have noted a major psychological transformation in the infant at about two to three months of age. For instance, in his discussion of the sense of an emergent self, Daniel Stern comments on this fact.

> This age of two months is almost as clear a boundary as birth itself. At about eight weeks, infants undergo a qualitative change: they begin to make direct eye-to-eye contact. Shortly thereafter they begin to smile more frequently, but also responsively and infectiously. They begin to coo ... Most learning is faster and more inclusive. Motor patterns mature. Sensorimotor intelligence reaches a new level ... Electroencephalograms reveal major changes. Diurnal hormonal milieu stabilizes, along with sleep and activity cycles. *Almost everything changes.* And all observers of infants, including parents agree on this ... (Stern 1985: 37; italics added)

In his discussion of the developmental and affective aspects of the infant's relationship experience, Robert Emde makes the following observation.

> After two months the infant can learn in a variety of ways, can accommodate and change behavior in a social situation, and can adjust to what is familiar, thereby completing learned activities so that *exploration of the new is possible* ... New parents often state that

beginning around two months their baby seems more human and less like a doll ... The social smile blossoms at about two months ... Social vocalization, or cooing in response to the face of another, begins within two weeks after the flowering of the social smile. Altogether, parents now begin to think of their baby as *playful*. (Emde 1989: 41–2; italics added)

From our perspective, Stern and Emde are describing the stepwise events of the unfolding primal experience.

In the second place, the phenomenon of the primal experience has cross-cultural validity. M. Konner refers to the pattern described by Stern and Emde at eight weeks of postnatal life as a "two-month" revolution and finds the same pattern in infants among the !Kung San, herder-gatherers of the African Kalahari Desert: "More importantly, such measures of social competence as social smiling and *en face* position rise markedly around this age."

Parallel development during this phase of infancy in an extremely different culture suggests a possibly universal developmental change. Development is continuous, but the transition at two to three months may have special importance as a uniquely human feature of the higher primate developmental plan, a possibly evolutionary adaptation. (Konner 1998: 185)

These facts support our view of the hereditary or innate nature of the observable stepwise pattern which seems to underlie the primal experience.

In the third place, the way the primal experience unfolds and develops in discrete stages proves out to be a paradigm for subsequent stages of development. As we will show in Chapters 4–7, each stage of symbolic development from Early Childhood through Early Adolescence begins with the same sequential differentiations of consciousness without variation: the ego's "recognition" first of other and then of self, followed by the creation of a new world view.

In the fourth place, the ego's "recognition" of other and self establish two important developmental channels, which we may describe as a social pathway and an individual pathway. These channels enable the infant to construct, throughout the stage of Infancy, socially sensitive feeling-toned complexes on the one hand and the structures of the ego-complex on the other. The parallel lines of development that we are here calling social and individual developmental pathways continue throughout subsequent stages of the child's psychological development. In the jargon of development, the relation between the pathways within a stage is one of reciprocal assimilation, whereas between stages it is one of hierarchical integration.

The developmental *dynamic* in both pathways, however, is the same: it consists of the dialectical relation between two innate affects, Interest–curiosity/exploration and Joy–play/fantasy, the motors respectively of cognitive and symbolic development. It is in and through this powerful developmental dialectic, activated for the first time during the unfolding of the primal experience, that an infant constructs the feeling-toned complexes and ego-complex to which we have just referred.

Each of the pathways, social and individual, is the locus of personal, cultural, and developmental experiences. In this formulation we are extending Winnicott's (1971) description of a "potential space" between (m)other and infant in three ways: (a) we have shown that this potential space between parent and infant is created as part of earliest step into the primal experience, the ego's "recognition" of the other; (b) we have shown that a similar space in the interior realm between infant and self begins its development once the second step toward the primal experience is taken, the ego's "recognition" of the self; and (c) we have added within both kinds of potential space, to Winnicott's personal and cultural levels, a symbolic level of development. It is at this level that the all-important symbolic mode characteristic of each stage emerges. Finally, natural objects or cultural artifacts may be introduced into the potential space of these two pathways as developmental, cultural, and interpersonal circumstances dictate.

SOCIAL AND INDIVIDUAL DEVELOPMENTAL PATHWAYS

We will illustrate the importance of keeping track of the social and individual pathways throughout the stage of Infancy by presenting an overview of psychological development during this stage. Our focus throughout this section is on the infant's construction of its feeling-toned complexes and its localization of the ego in the body.

Feeling-Toned Complexes

The basic premise which guides our understanding of complex formation is Jung's statement: *Every affective event becomes a complex.* A complex is a bit like Bohr's model atom. It has an affective nuclear element, composed of a factor determined by an experience with some other and thus causally related to the environment and an innate factor originating in the individual's disposition. Surrounding this nucleus are the layers of associations that have attached to the archetypal idea that the nucleus represents. The complex has also been described as a psychic "molecule" composed of three components: "sense-perception, intellectual components (ideas, memory-images, judgments, etc.), and feeling-tone" (*CW* 3: 79,38–9). During social exploration and play, an infant-other relational complex is being constructed; during individual exploration and play, an infant–self relational complex is being formed.

The infant's initial experience of innate affects, whether they originate in the parent or the self, is involuntary: As Jung says, "Emotion, incidentally, is not an activity of the individual but something that happens to him" (*CW* 9ii: 15,8–9). Experiments have shown that parents induce affects in their infants through the contagion of their own emotions as well as by activation of innate affects in the infant (Haviland and Lelwica 1987). In the former case, the environmental and innate nuclear elements are the same, for example, Joy and Joy, whereas in the latter case they may be different, e.g. Joy and Interest. It has also been shown that most parents make every effort to maintain positive affects in the infant, Interest–Joy–Surprise, and to avoid such "crisis" affects as Anger–Fear–Sadness–Shame/Contempt (Malatesta and Haviland 1982). When the latter do arise, parents and infants make immediate social and individual efforts to modulate them (Tronick 1989). (In psychotherapy, many therapists do the same.)

Localization of the Ego in the Body

The body, psychologically speaking, is the expression of individually conscious existence.

> So the identity with the body is one of the first things which makes an ego; it is the spatial separateness that induces, apparently, the concept of an ego. Later on it is mental differences, personal differences of all sorts, etc. (Jung 1977b: 285)

But it is in and through both social and individual exploration and play that localization of the ego in the body occurs. The initial *lack* of localization is demonstrated by the fact that during the first months of life infants do not know where to look when their hand is held outside their field of vision.

At the beginning of Infancy, in fact, the infant's body scheme appears from an archetypal perspective to be unbounded.

> The child's still undifferentiated body image is as large and undelimited as the cosmos. Its own sphere is so fused with the world and hence with everything that we call outside, that it may well be termed cosmic in scope. Only as its ego develops, does the child gradually come to differentiate its own body image, and concomitantly the world takes on clarity, as an object confronting the ego. (Neumann 1990: 12)

Piaget describes the localization of the ego in the body in similar cosmological terms as "a Copernican revolution," which begins in a world without substantive objects and is completed in one that does have permanent objects. At the completion of Piaget's sensorimotor period (our stage of Infancy) the child's own body is regarded as one object in a solid universe of coordinated objects, which includes the body as one of its elements.

Winnicott refers to the developmental process whereby the infant achieves identity with the body as *personalization*, defined as the indwelling or inhabitation of the ego in the body. He explains:

> The term *personalization* was intended to draw attention to the fact that the in-dwelling of this other part of the personality in the body, and its firm link with whatever is there which we call psyche, in developmental terms represents an achievement in health. (Winnicott 1972: 7)

The environmental provisions which are necessary for personalization are, according to Winnicott, a secure parent–infant relation and, more particularly, adequate *handling*. Winnicott states that optimal handling occurs when parents hold and handle the infant in a natural way *as a whole person*. One way that optimal handling occurs, we suggest, is when parents play baby games with their infants. This is one of the vital functions provided by those baby games which involve physical contact between parent and infant as reciprocal agents.

A DEVELOPMENTAL HIERARCHY OF NURSERY RHYMES, BABY GAMES, AND PLAY SONGS

One of the best guides to the natural process of psychological development during Infancy, as we have already indicated in several places, are the nursery rhymes, baby games, and play songs that comprise the oral literary tradition of earliest childhood. Many of these are traditional, and can be found in collections such as those by Opie and Opie (1973) and Baring-Gould and Baring-Gould (1962). These rhymes, games, and songs serve to shape the waking dream of the infant, providing a symbolic impetus to drive development forward. For instance, the hand-clapping, hand-rubbing, palm-pecking, and hand-tossing game of 'Pat-a-cake, pat-a-cake, baker's man' provides a symbolic mirror for that numinous moment when the infant begins to join and separate its hands in front of its face, all the while studying this novel achievement with great joy and interest. The universality of such games and their accompanying verbalizations is supported by the impressive cross-linguistic similarities in even the metrics of nursery rhymes, a fact which surely points to their origin in our common humanity.

Gayatri Chatterjee has presented a review of Bengali nursery rhymes in the light of his thoughts on socialization of children. The pioneers in collecting these rhymes, what the author refers to as "complete cultural products," are R. Tagore and J. Sarkar. Chatterjee notes with interest that "Sarkar chose to begin with two verses that celebrate the bond of affection between parent–child and delineate parental affection, that is given outward manifestation and verbalization" (Chatterjee 1999: 65). And he presents the preface to Sakar's collection which is written by R. Trevedi:

> My friends might not find any sound theory, any truism, or any joy in these verses. But I hope that all those, who have not yet been chained by the strict rules of the universe, of Nature, who have not yet turned joyless, mirthless, who find everything in the world interesting, amusing, natural, everything spontaneous chaotic, free and frolicsome. I hope this book will increase their *joie-de-vivre*. (ibid.: 76)

Chatterjee suggests that the nursery rhyme gives the child a "very complex narrative, vocabulary and sound pattern" (ibid.: 69).

> Social reality is mixed and married with imagination and fantasy, and at times with desires and wild-wishing of all kinds. It creates an environment where socialization can take place in a complex and composite manner. (ibid.: 67)

For the infant, the nursery rhyme is a formal supplement to the spontaneous expressions of "motherese." He concludes his study with the following thoughts:

> The world of the nursery rhyme opened up for a child a *real world*: a world of societal, cultural, and political reality and diversity. "Real" does not mean that everything about it is easily understood, easily represented. This world is shrouded in myths and mysteries, tinged with desires and fantasies. A world that one approaches both objectively and subjectively. (ibid.: 82)

What holds all the elements of the nursery rhyme – locale, class, social structure, rites and rituals, history – together is, in Chatterjee's view, the creative imagination and the energy underlying it. In my view, the creative imagination is not only central but purposive, shaping the waking dream of Infancy into symbolic images that drive sensorimotor development, as well as other emerging ego-attributes, forward.

This point becomes clearer when the focus is upon the games that accompany common nursery rhymes. From the collections in Opie and Opie and Barring-Gould and Barring-Gould mentioned above, I have selected a developmental hierarchy of games (C. T. Stewart 1981, C. T. Stewart and L. H. Stewart 1981) to identify key phases of psychological growth during the waking dream of Infancy.

Extremity Games

By Extremity games, I mean Arm ('Arm over'), Hand ('Pat-a-cake'), Finger ('Dance, Thumbkin, dance'), Leg ('Leg over leg'), Foot ('Shoe a little horse'), Toe ('This Pig went to Market') games. These are among the earliest games which parents play with their infants and fall into the category referred to by Escalona (1968) as *gentle play*. When parents use the infant's body as a field for exploration, as a playing field for Extremity games and spontaneous play, they are making positive contributions to the infant's construction of socially-oriented feeling-toned complexes and the secure localization of the ego in the body. When infants explore and play with their extremities on their own, they are engaging in similar constructive and localizing activities, but in the individual pathway.

This differentiation of ego-consciousness through body exploration and play is mirrored, I and others believe, in myths and legends which portray the creation of the world, i.e. the birth of consciousness from the whole body, or part of the body, of a primal being. One example of such an all-encompassing world-soul is the Indian primal man, Purusha.

> The moon was born from his mind, from his eye was born the sun; from his mouth Indra and Agni; from his breath Vayu was born. From his navel grew the atmosphere; from his head the sky; from his feet the earth; from his ear the directions. Thus the worlds are made. (*CW* 5: 651,417)

From a psychological perspective, Purusha, an image of the self, symbolizes both the primal psychic state and the primal energy emerging from that state. These are the basis for a *psychological* cosmogony originating in our dreaming about and our revelatory apprehension during waking of the body as the originary ground of primal experience.

Carl Schuster, after reviewing the ethnographic accounts of birth from *limbs, joints, fingers, toes, head,* etc., concludes as follows: "Perhaps such legends about birth from the limbs are to be explained as fragments of a cosmogonic myth, according to which the world in general and mankind in particular originated from parts of a primordial cosmic giant" (Schuster 1956/1958: 86). Schuster also recounts the fate of a culture-hero, who, dismembered and eaten except for one finger, appeared the next morning, the single finger being sufficient to assure regeneration of the whole body. In psychological terms, such corpogenic myths refer to the birth of consciousness from the individual's or parents' exploration and play with his or her own body. The psychological cosmogony is accompanied by the progressive construction of a realistic body scheme. In such contexts, the thumb appears frequently as a special libido symbol, that is, as a symbol of boundless energy.

One personification of the thumb that we are familiar with is the Tom Thumb of fairytales. Jung, however, has located a passage from the Katha Upanishad which refers to the primordial being, Purusha, as a *thumbling*: "That Person in the heart, maker of past and future, no bigger than a *thumb*, burning like a flame without smoke, maker of past and future, the same today and tomorrow, that is Self" (*CW* 5: 179,124; italics added). In Egyptian mythology, a child is nourished by sucking on the *thumb* of a god. This may be the prototype antecedent of the following peculiar nursery rhyme, with its uroboric configuration.

> Old Father Greybeard,
> Without tooth or tongue,
> If you'll give me your finger
> I'll give you my thumb.

Fingers are often magical. When Rhea was giving birth to Zeus, she pressed her fingers into the soil to ease her pangs and gave birth to the Dactyls, five females from her left hand and five males from her right hand. The names of the sisters was a well-guarded secret, but the names of the brothers were known, the *thumb* being called Heracles.

In *The Story of the Human Hand*, Sorell presents the following statements regarding the uniqueness of the human thumb.

> Isaac Newton once remarked that, in the absence of any other proofs, the thumb alone would convince him of God's existence. And the French writer Malcolm de Chazal made the acute comment "the fingers must be educated – the thumb is born knowing." (Sorell 1968: 89)

These notions are expressed in the legend of the Celtic hero, Fionn, and his "thumb of knowledge."

The story of Fionn's acquisition of his supernatural "thumb" is as follows.

> To learn the art of poetry he went to Finneces, who for seven years sought to capture a salmon which would impart supernatural knowledge to him – the "salmon of knowledge" – and after he had caught it, he bade Fionn cook it, forbidding him to taste it. When Finneces inquired whether he had eaten any of it, Fionn replied, "No, but my thumb I burned, and I put it into my mouth after that"; whereupon Finneces gave him the name Fionn, since prophecy had announced that Fionn should eat the salmon. He ate it in fact, and ever after, on placing his thumb in his mouth, knowledge of things unknown came to him. (Macculloch 1964: 166)

"When Fionn sought supernatural knowledge, he chewed his thumb or laid it on his tooth, to which it had given this clairvoyant gift; or again, the knowledge is already in his thumb" (ibid.: 166–7). Scott has shown that "this curious tradition regarding Fionn has its counterpart in traditions relating to the Norse Sigurd as well as in those which concern the Welsh Taliesin" (Scott 1930: 1).

Laurent's "Thumb of Knowledge"

In the twentieth century, there are quite similar echoes in Piaget's scientific observation of his own children. As the following records show, Laurent had a "thumb of knowledge," which contributed to the development of consciousness of his arm, hand, nose, and eyes at the earliest phases of formation of a body-ego.

When he is one month old, Laurent learns to suck his thumb. As a direct result of his exploration of his face before and after thumb sucking, Laurent learns how to hold his nose and rub his eyes: "Thus at 0;2(17) Laurent babbles and smiles without any desire to suck, while holding his nose with his right hand" (Piaget 1952: 93). Laurent's smiles indicate his recognition of his nose and/or holding-the-nose. And, as a direct result of thumb sucking, Laurent learns to rub his eyes.

At 0;2(18) both his eyes close before he scratches his right eye. At 0;2(19) he turns his head to the left as his left hand is being directed toward his eye. Then he rubs both eyes simultaneously with both hands. At 0;2(20) he makes fists in order to rub his eyes, again closes his eyes beforehand and *smiles with joy*; there is no connection with stretching. (ibid.; italics added)

Laurent's smiles, again, indicate his recognition of his eyes and or eye-rubbing. At this point nose-holding and eye-rubbing schemes have been fully constructed as structures of his emerging body ego. This ego is localized in the body, the beginning of its personalization.

Once these schemes have become familiar, they can go on to become the *content* of Laurent's individual play.

At 0;2(21) he holds his two fists in the air and looks at the left one, after which he slowly brings it toward his face and rubs his nose with it, then his eye. A moment later the left hand again approaches his face; he looks at it and touches his nose. He recommences and *laughs five or six times in succession* while moving his left hand to his face. He seems to *laugh* before the hand moves, but looking has no influence on its movement. He *laughs* beforehand but begins to smile again on seeing the hand. Then he rubs his nose. (ibid.: 97; italics added)

Laurent's individual laughs mark his "recognition" and integration, in and through exuberant play, of nose-holding and eye-rubbing as new aspects of *himself*.

Although each of these observations depict Laurent's progressive differentiation of consciousness in the developmental pathway we have termed "individual," they were recorded in an intersubjective context, that is under the sympathetic and watchful eye of his loving father, Piaget. We have no doubt that this fact translates into a richer actualization by Laurent in his individual efforts at ego-development. We can also see more clearly from these observations how parents engagement of their infants in Extremity games will have positive, reciprocal effects on both social and individual development.

When Laurent learns to suck his big toe, and then discovers his legs, knees, feet, and other toes, a similar developmental process was set in motion. This, too, is a rich locus of body-ego fantasy that can be enriched by the parental engagement of their infants in lower Extremity games. The mythical prototype of a "toe of knowledge" is found in the vision of *The Infant Krishna Floating on the Cosmic Ocean* (see cover of the paperback edition of this book) and *The Birth of Vishnu* (frontispiece to Neumann's *The Origins and History of Consciousness*).

Tickling games follow naturally from Extremity games.

Tickling Games

In a typical Tickling game, such as 'There was a little mouse', the parent's finger circles the palm of the infant's hand, marches up the arm, and tickles the infant in the mouse's home, the armpit. These gestures are accompanied by the melody and lyrics of the play song.

When parents play Tickling games, they are not only having fun but are also contributing to the infant's development of feeling-toned complexes and to personalization. (Simultaneously, infants are transforming their parents' bodies into fields for exploration and play.) To illustrate these facts, we analyze a mother playing seven episodes, over a four-minute period, of 'I'm gonna get ya' with her three-month-old infant (Stern 1977: 2–5).

At the beginning of the observation, mother and infant exchange "monitoring" glances: both the innate and environmental contributions to the nucleus of the infant mother-complex are the affect Interest. Then, they exchange smiles: both innate and environmental Joy are added to the nucleus of the mother-complex.

> The mother now greets the infant with a series of "hellos," successively longer and more stressed: "Well hello! ... heelló ... heeelloóoo!". The baby is delighted and his body resonates, almost like a balloon being pumped up. The mother pauses; they watch each other expectantly; suddenly the infant smiles. The mother, eyes alight, says: "Oooooh ...

ya wanna play do ya ... yeah? ... I didn't know if you were still hungry ... no ... nooooo ... no I didn't ..."

The affective intonations, the musical melodies, of the mother's "motherese," and the infant's "delight" become environmental and innate elements in the nucleus of the mother-complex.

Melodic contours, that is, affective expressions, are the primary units of parental speech to infants, are preadapted, are unconscious, and are universal (Papousek 1992). In addition, infants are preadapted, through the capacity for perception of expression, to discriminate and process the affective contours of parental melodies.

Game 1

As a potential social play space has been mutually constructed, the stage is set and the Tickling game begins.

Mother looms in frowning, eyes bright, and her mouth on the edge of a smile. She says, "This time I'm gonna get ya," and carries out the finger-tickle-march. The baby smiles and squirms.

Mother's pretend anger, excitement, and joy, and the infant's joy and fear (squirming) are incorporated into the nucleus of the mother-complex. When the mother settles in her chair and looks away, the infant emits a captivated "aaah." This rapturous "aaah" is an indication of the numinosity, the intensity, of the innate affects of Interest and Joy at the center of the developing mother-complex.

Games 2–7

An overview of the infant's emotional experiences during the next six games is as follows. In games 3, 4, 5, and 6, the infant is bathed in the affects Interest and Joy, originating in mother and self, and occurring at various levels of intensity. These positive affects become additional environmental and innate elements in the nucleus of the developing mother-complex.

In game 2 the mother begins unexpectedly, and the infant's experience is dominated by the innate affect Surprise. The life stimulus the Unexpected, originating in the mother, and the reorienting affect Surprise, evoked in the infant, become nuclear elements in the feeling-toned mother-complex.

In games 4, 5, and 6, in response to the mother's looming and pretend threats, the infant experiences various intensities of the affect Fear, which is integrated as an innate element in the mother-complex, along with the maternal behaviors that evoked them.

In games 2, 5, 6, and 7 there was face and/or gaze aversion by the infant. These behaviors are attempts at affect modulation, which means that crisis affects have exceeded optimal developmental levels, and the infant is indicating, "I don't like what just happened." Through these behaviors the crisis affects are successfully integrated as nuclear elements in the developing infant's mother-complex.

Game 7 was marked by a play disruption, at which time the infant frowned. We can speculate that the frown expresses the activation of the innate affect Anger, stimulated by mother's intrusiveness. If so, mother-Intrusiveness and infant-Anger are integrated as nuclear elements to the mother-complex.

We can conclude that such a simple Tickling game as 'I'm gonna get ya' illustrates the fact that all games are symbolic systems which serve to evoke powerful emotions within their containing structures: "The universal games constellate emotions or sets of emotions which are equilibrated through the process of playing the games" (L. H. Stewart 1987a: 37). Such games are among the primary ways that all of the innate emotions, the primary motivational system in humans, enter the growth process so that their developmental potential can be realized. The symbolic form and rules of each type of game are configured so that playing the game evokes and modulates a pattern of emotions specific to its particular structure: games of Chance evoke and modulate Fear–Terror; games of Physical Skill evoke and modulate Sadness–Anguish; games of Strategy evoke and modulate Anger–Rage; Central-Person games evoke and modulate Shame/Contempt–Humiliation/Loathing. Thus, opportunities for the activation, constructive use, and modulation of all of the innate affects lie between the covers of any nursery rhyme collection.

We should note that in myth and legend, tickling and laughter appear in both a positive and a negative light. The laughter of a god may create the divine cosmos.

And God laughed seven times Cha Cha Cha Cha Cha Cha Cha,
and as God laughed, there arose seven gods. (CW 5: 65n8,45)

We may speculate that the seven gods are the seven innate affects, which color all of one's symbolic apprehension of the universe.

Mythical perception is always impregnated with these emotional qualities. Whatever is seen or felt is surrounded by a special atmosphere – an atmosphere of joy or grief, of anguish, of excitement, of exultation or depression. Here we cannot speak of "things" as a dead or indifferent stuff. All objects are benignant or malignant, friendly or inimical, familiar or uncanny, alluring and fascinating or repellent and threatening. We can easily reconstruct this elemental form of human experience, for even in the life of the civilized man it has by no means lost its original power. If we are under the strain of a violent emotion we have still this dramatic conception of all things. They no longer wear their usual faces; they abruptly change their physiognomy; they are tinged with the specific color of our passions, of love or hate, of fear or hope. (Cassirer 1944: 76–7)

The laughter of parents does create a numinous affective universe for their infants.

Tickling, on the other hand, is a mechanism for the origin of humankind and of consciousness.

In South Australia ... there is apparently a belief in the creation of men from excrement which was moulded and then *tickled*, this causing the image to *laugh* and become alive. (Dixon 1916: 274; italics added)

In the above example of a mother playing 'I'm gonna get ya' with her infant, we observed how she repeatedly enlivened him by evoking Joy and Excitement.

Among the aborigines of South-East Australia, the Gourgourgahgah laughs every dawn as soon as the morning star is paled and this wakes up the world, that is, gives rise to consciousness. When frog swallows the waters of the world, the life-giving libido, the aborigines of Western Victoria are saved from eternal drought by eel's ability to evoke laughter: "When the eel wiggled and writhed, the frog first smiled, and then laughed, and, as he opened his mouth, the waters burst forth."

In Slavic mythology, on the other hand, a dark side of tickling appears.

In Polish superstition the Dziwozony are superhuman females with cold and callous hearts and filled with passionate sensuality. They are tall in stature, their faces are thin, and their hair is long and dishevelled. They fling their breasts over their shoulders, since otherwise they would be hindered in running; and their garments are always disarranged. Groups of them go about the woods and fields, and if they chance upon human beings, they tickle the adults to death, but take the young folk with them to be their lovers and playmates. (Macculloch 1964: 264)

In Finno-Ugric and Siberian myth and legend, it is a male Forest spirit, variously named Targeldes, Ovda, Shurale, and Obyda, who shrieks or roars with laughter, and tickles people to death (Holmberg 1927). Finally, to limit our examples to just one more provocative amplification, in Slavic mythology it is the souls of children who have died unbaptized, been drowned by their mothers, or born of mothers who have met a violent death, that attract people by laughing and giggling and then proceed to tickle them to death.

In psychological terms, a "violent death" means the overwhelming of the nascent ego by primal affects. Thus, sensitive parents instinctively modulate their Tickling games and protect their infants from an excess intensity of the affects which accompany such a simple, and yet vital, nursery game as 'Tickle ye'.

Another group of baby games which tickle the funny bones of infants are Knee Rides.

Knee Rides

Knee rides, such as "Ride a Cock Horse to Banbury Cross," are nursery games linking two components, (a) a play song to be sung, while (b) "galloping" a baby on one's knee. Like the Tickling games, they are social realities, symbolic systems, which have been passed from one generation to the next, for how long nobody knows. If like some toys, they were originally employed at the cultural level of ritual, and, subsequently, were transferred to the personal level in order to enrich child-rearing, they may be very old indeed.

Schuster has identified an ancient mythical substratum from many parts of the world in which there is "the birth of human beings from arms or fingers, more commonly the legs, and most commonly from the *knees*" (Schuster 1956/1958: 82).

> However these myths may vary in details, their basic relationship to each other is hardly open to question. Birth from the knees or legs is generally preceded by a swelling of the affected parts, analogous to that preceding normal birth from the womb. Often both knees are involved: sometimes a male child springs from one knee and a female from the other ... (ibid.: 84)

In addition, the primitive idea of the whole body as a kinship chart is widespread and deeply embedded in linguistic usage: "... the fact remains that the name of at least one bodily part is used in the terminology of kinship throughout all or most languages of the Indo-European family: namely, that for the *knee*" (ibid.: 100). After surveying the homonymy of the Indo-European roots for "knee", "beget", and "know", Meillet (quoted by Schuster) "concluded that there was originally but one verbal root, meaning 'know', and that this came to mean 'beget' by being used ... 'to know as ones own' or 'to recognize as legitimate, with a child as the implied object'" (ibid.: 101). He and other linguists then postulated that "the homonymy of the roots for 'knee' and 'beget' rests in the final analysis, upon the early existence of a *rite of legitimation, or filiation* performed by the father, in which he recognized the new-born infant as his own by placing it upon his *knee* ..." (ibid.). (Fathers have been found to play more vigorous bouncing games with their babies than mothers.) This ritual of filiation is also reflected in Germanic rites of adoption, where the child was placed upon the knee of the adoptive parent.

In the Near East, a Hittite myth dealing with the exploits of the god Kumarbi, concerns the birth of a stone monster following the god's impregnation of a mountain with his own seeds (Gaster 1952). When a huge boulder shape like a human baby was born, goddesses carried it tenderly to Kumarbi and placed it on his *knee*. The joyful Kumarbi lifted the child in the air, *dandled* it upon his lap, and then placed the child upon his *knee* and gazed into its stony, unsmiling face: "Baby," he said, "I must give you a name. You shall be called Ullikummi" (ibid.: 117). In the West, when the great hero Odysseus was an infant, he was named while sitting on the knee of his maternal grandfather, Autolycus.

That there is close symbolic relation between the knee and the thigh, both seen as containers of the fluid of life, helps explain such mythic parallels as (a) the rebirth of Dionysos from the thigh of Zeus, (b) the Hindu legends of the birth of Aurva out of the left thigh of his mother Vamoru and of Nishada out of the left thigh of the prince Vena, (c) the legend, in an old French poem that St. Anne, mother of the Virgin Mary, and grandmother of Jesus, was born direct from the thigh of her father Phanuel, and (d) the myth that the Egyptian king Wn'is "issued from both the thighs of the Nine Gods and was carried in the womb of the goddess Shmt" (Onians 1951: 82–3).

Applying all this to the birth of the symbolizing capacity in the primal experience, we can conclude, first of all, that Knee rides provide parents and their infants with opportunities for joyful social play, during which the infant continues his construction of parental-complexes and body-scheme. Second of all, Knee rides connect parents and infant alike with their ancestral past: "Those born in this way [from the knee/thigh] are generally imagined as 'the first people'; and the limbs from which they spring are those of an Ultimate Ancestor" (Schuster 1956/1958: 82). Last of all, Knee rides serve to acknowledge and celebrate one of the infant's major steps toward human upright posture, sitting up. One can hardly imagine a sterner test of the infant's stabilization of the sitting posture than a Knee Ride. And in the constant physical adjustments made by the infant during the game, we can discern further steps in the infant's localization of the ego in the body.

'Peek-a-Boo'

'Peek-a-boo' is perhaps the best known game of infancy. It appears during a remarkable phase of development which extends from about nine to twelve months. This seminal period of sensorimotor maturation includes the following achievements: (a) first coordinations of ends-means behaviors, the beginning of empirical intelligence; (b) the beginnings of construction of permanent objects; (c) a major step in the differentiation of subject and object and attribution of agency to the other and self; (d) the creation of gestural and vocal elements of a protolanguage; and (e) continuing construction of parental-complexes and the body scheme. Playing the universal game of 'Peek-a-boo' has the signal advantage of acknowledging each of these achievements, while at the same time integrating them into a structural whole, as a new sense of the self. Parents, of course, need not intellectually know these facts for 'Peek-a-boo' to work its magic.

The following game of 'Peek-a-boo' between Piaget and his daughter makes, in my opinion, a direct contribution to the continuing construction by Jacqueline of socially oriented feeling-toned complexes.

> For example, at 0;8(14) Jacqueline is lying on my bed beside me. I cover my head and cry "coucou"; I emerge and do it again. She burst into peals of laughter, then pulls the covers away to find me again. Attitude of expectation and lively interest. (Piaget 1954: 50)

By now, we can expect that the state of interaction Jung has described as unconscious identity and Piaget refers to as adualism is lessening, and some of the personal features of the parents are becoming known to the infant.

> With the awakening of ego-consciousness the participation gradually weakens, and consciousness begins to enter into opposition to the unconscious, its own precondition. This leads to differentiation of the ego from the mother, whose personal peculiarities gradually become more distinct. (CW 9i: 188,102)

In the following behavior we can see how 'Peek-a-boo' makes an indirect contribution to the construction of the body scheme.

> At 0;11(3) Lucienne hides her feet under a coverlet, then raises the coverlet, looks at them, hides them again, etc. Same observations at 0;11(15) with a rattle which she slips under a rug to bring it out and put it under again endlessly. Same observations on Jacqueline between 11;0 and 1;0. (Piaget 1954: 172)

Given these facts, it is not surprising when we encounter, in various contexts, the image of the *veiled lady*.

When an adult patient has the following dream, "The veiled figure of a woman seated on a stair" (CW 12: 64,54), which is followed shortly after by a visual impression, "The veiled woman uncovers her face. It shines like the sun" (ibid.: 67,57), we are ready to conjecture that the 'Peek-a-boo' phase of infant development has been reactivated.

Is there a better mythological expression of the mother's way of drawing her child into the startling new world we have described than the Veil of Maya? Maya's illusions draw the individual into life because they are "real," i.e. she spins fantasies with real things (even a simple cloth). Prior to the 'Peek-a-boo' phase the infant is still enclosed in his or her own psyche, as in a waking dream. Thus, Maya symbolizes not just the anima, as the hidden presence behind illusory projections, but also the mother in her world-building character.

In the Near East, the Mother-goddess of the Aramaeans in the late period was Atargatis, who is depicted wearing a veil falling to her waist. Gilgamesh found Siduri (a west Semitic name of Ishtar) sitting in a cave covered with a veil. In Greece, at Eleusis, the initiate was veiled and, when this veil was removed, the initiate encountered the veiled Demeter. Neith is a sky-goddess of great antiquity, known throughout Egypt, who was viewed as "the mother who brought forth the sun." (Was she also responsible for its occasional eclipse?) She is originally a creative goddess who is represented as having woven the universe as a weaver weaves cloth. In the temple of Neith at Sais, her statue, which was taken to also represent Athena and Isis, is *veiled* and bears the following inscription: "I am all that has been, and is, and shall be, and my robe has never yet been uncovered by mortal man" (Hastings 1926/1969, Zimmer 1938, Langdon 1964, Eliade 1987). When we discover in folklore the recurrent theme of the magic veil which renders its wearer *invisible*, we may conjecture that this motif originates in the 'Peek-a-boo' phase of development. Its survival into the stories and myths of later childhood and adult religious motifs suggests the unmasking quality of the symbolic play we know as 'Peek-a-boo', its power to uncover the latent in the mother archetype that governs the earliest facilitation of symbolic development itself.

In the next phases of development, the infant will go on to discover *invisible aspects of its own body*.

'Brow Bender' and 'Tae Titly'

During this last phase of Infancy, the infant is busy consolidating the localization of the ego in the body and thereby completing the construction of a complete body-scheme. One aspect of this process is the infant's ability to identify, in and through social exploration and play, certain "invisible" parts of its own body, that is, the parts it cannot naturally see. It is through the discovery of the hair and forehead, for instance, that the child's grasp of the correspondence between his or her own face and that of others is completed.

At 1;0(16) J. discovered her forehead. When I touched the middle of mine, she first rubbed her eyes, then felt above it and touched her hair, after which she brought her hand down a little and finally put her finger on her forehead. (Piaget 1962: 55–6)

One game which mirrors these achievements is 'Brow Bender', which has the following lyrics.

> Brow bender,
> Eye peeper,
> Nose dreeper,
> Mouth eater,
> Chin chopper, Knock at the door,
> Ring the bell,
> Walk in ...
> Take a chair
> Sit by there,
> How d'you do this morning?

Opie and Opie give the following instructions to accompany the words.

As the words are repeated, a finger is laid successively on the baby's forehead, eyes, nose, mouth, and chin. While saying "knock at the door," the chin is tickled; "ring the bell," the hair or ear is pulled; "lift the latch and walk in," the baby's nose is raised and a finger is popped in the mouth. (Opie and Opie 1973: 103)

The relation between this game and the child's discovery of the invisible parts of its face is self-evident.

The fullest version is found in the Scottish 'Tae Titly', which begins with the toe and ends at the top of the head.

> Tae titly,
> Little fitty,
> Shin sharply,
> Knee knappy,
> Hinchie pinchy,
> Wymie bulgy,
> Breast berry,
> Chin cherry,
> Moo merry,
> Nose nappy,
> Ee winky,
> Broo brinky,
> Ower the croon,
> And awa' wi' it.

In this nursery game, parents celebrate the infant's completion of the body-scheme at the conclusion of Infancy.

The following observation shows, however, that there are still limitations in the child's awareness of the body.

> At 1;6(13) Jacqueline descends into a deep and narrow ditch (she disappears into it to the middle of her thighs) and tries to get out. She puts her left foot on the edge but cannot hoist herself. Keeping her left foot on the bank, she bends over and grasps her right foot with both hands as though to bring it up to meet the first foot. She makes a series of real attempts and becomes red with effort. After this she gives up and climbs out on her stomach. But as soon as she emerges from the ditch she redescends and resumes her attempts. This time she places her right foot first and grasps the left one with both hands, obviously pulling. (Piaget 1954: 228)

This reminds us of the level of consciousness of the collective figure, the trickster archetype.

> He is both subhuman and superhuman, a bestial and divine being, whose chief and most alarming characteristic is his unconsciousness. Because of it he is deserted by his (evidently human) companions, which seems to indicate that he has fallen below their level of consciousness. He is so unconscious of himself that his body is not a unity, and his two hands fight each other. (CW 9i: 472,263–4)

Jacqueline's limitation is due to her inability to represent imaginatively to herself the totality of the bodily movements she would like to perform. This limitation will be overcome when the child enters Early Childhood and achieves the capacity for representation. Or as the rhyme says, "Bo-peep, bo-peep, now's the time for hide-and-seek."

EGO-FUNCTIONS AND CULTURAL ATTITUDES

As the infant is forming parental-complexes and localizing the ego in the body, he or she is also constructing ego-functions and symbolic cultural attitudes. In the last section of this chapter we will illustrate two of these achievement, the development of the ego-function Thinking and that of the culturally sensitive Aesthetic Attitude.

Ego-Function Thinking

Jung's definition of the ego-function Thinking is as follows.

> Thinking is the psychological function which, following its own laws, brings the contents of ideation into conceptual connection with one

another ... The term "thinking" should, in my view, be confined to the linking up of ideas by means of concepts, in other words, to an act of judgment, no matter whether this act is intentional or not. (*CW* 6: 830,481)

L. H. Stewart describes the origin of the ego-function Thinking in the innate affect Anger as portrayed in Table 8 (see also Table 3, Column 7).

Table 8: Ego-Function Thinking

Inborn Image	Life Situation	Innate Affect	Noetic Domain	Ego-Function
Chaos	Restriction of Autonomy	Anger–Rage	Quantitative Ordering	Thinking

Our analysis of Laurent's construction of the Thinking function begins when he is six months old. Piaget has established an experimental situation to determine when Laurent first achieves empirical intelligence, ends-means coordination.

For instance at 0;6(0) I present Laurent with a matchbox, extending my hand laterally to make an obstacle to his prehension. Laurent tries to pass over my hand, or to the side, but he does not attempt to displace it. As each time I prevent his passage, he ends by storming at the box while waving his hand, shaking himself, wagging his head from side to side, in short, by substituting magic-phenomenalistic "procedures" for prehension rendered impossible. (Piaget 1952: 217)

The experimental situation may be likened to a game of strategy, which fosters the development of reason.

Whether checkers, chess, (or) go ... the outcome of the game is determined by the rational choices one makes. By playing the game, we learn to bear a sustained, intensely concentrated focus. Irritable impulses that come up tend to get channeled into the symbolic attack of the game. Those who like to play games of strategy are usually good thinkers ... (Chodorow 1991: 154)

When Laurent "ends by storming at the box," chaotically we would add, it is evident that he is expressing the innate affect Anger.

A study by Stenberg and co-workers of the effects of repeated biscuit removal, we would say Restriction of Autonomy, on the facial expression of anger by thirty seven-month-old infants discovered that "the capacity to express anger is well developed by 7 months of age: facial patterning was detected reliably in the absence of contextual information, and repeated frustration increased the amount of anger shown" (Stenberg et al. 1983: 178).

The experiment continues with the same reactions throughout the month, on 0;6(8), 0;6(10), 0;6(21), etc. On 0;7(10), Laurent sets aside the obstacle, but not intentionally. It seems reasonable to assume that during this period there was more "storming."

The moment when Laurent achieved his first act of empirical intelligence, that is, coordination of end and means, is described in the next observation.

Finally, at 0;7(13) Laurent reacts quite differently almost from the beginning of the experiment. I present a box of matches above my hand, but behind it, so that he cannot reach it without setting the obstacle aside. But Laurent after trying to take no notice of it, suddenly tries to hit my hand as though to remove or lower it; I let him do it to me and he grasps the box. – I recommence to bar his passage, but using as a screen a sufficiently supple cushion to keep the impress of the child's gestures. Laurent tries to reach the box, and, bothered by the obstacle, he at once strikes it, definitely lowering it until the way is clear. (Piaget 1952: 217)

Piaget makes a functional comparison between empirical and conceptual intelligence: "In effect, the subordination of means to ends is the equivalent, on the plane of practical intelligence, of the subordination of premises to conclusions, on the plane of logical intelligence" (ibid.: 238). The latter corresponds to Jung's "linking up of ideas by means of concepts." Thus, I understand Laurent's behavior on 0;7(13) as a moment in the construction and differentiation of the ego-function Thinking.

With the correspondence between Piaget's description of Laurent's acquisition of empirical intelligence and what Jung and Stewart describe as the development of the ego-function Thinking in mind, let us examine the interactions between Molly and her mother. Stern presents the following interactions as examples of a "form of intolerable overstimulation."

Molly's mother was very controlling. She had to design, initiate, direct, and terminate all agendas. She determined which toy Molly should play with, how Molly was to play with it ... when Molly was done playing with it, and what to do next ... The mother overcontrolled the action to such an extent that it was often hard to trace the natural crescendo and decrescendo of Molly's own interest and excitement. (Stern 1985: 196)

Stern describes the reactions of the research group to this type of interaction.

> Most experienced viewers who watch these televised interactions between Molly and her mother find themselves getting a tense feeling most often described as a knot in the stomach and slowly realize how *enraged* they are becoming. (ibid.; italics added)

Stern also describes Molly's adaptation to her mother's pattern of behavior.

> She gradually became more compliant. Instead of actively avoiding or opposing these intrusions, she became one of those enigmatic gazers into space. She could stare through you, her eyes focused somewhere at infinity and her facial expression opaque enough to by just uninterpretable, and at the same time remain in good contingent contact and by and large do what she was invited or told to do. (ibid.)

Stern says: "At some point in her development, anger, oppositionalism, hostility, and the like will be sorely needed to rescue her" (ibid.: 197).

To this interpretation, I add one qualification: If one views the behavior of the mother as the life-stimulus Restriction of Autonomy, and considers the "anger" felt by the research team as correctly reflecting Molly's natural emotional response to this stimulus, then it also follows that during these observations Molly is structuring the ego-function Thinking. In order, therefore, to assess the overall significance of this type of interactive pattern for Molly's present and future development it is important to take this fact into consideration. Perhaps she will develop an intellectual's capacity to see through the confines of a would-be definitive argument and it may take a parent like Molly's to produce an adult with a truly superior Thinking function. Without this perspective, one runs the risk of omitting the natural process of differentiation of the ego-functions, through an overemphasis on the pathogenic aspects of the mother–infant interaction.

To conclude our analysis of the development of thinking, we want to turn to an additional observation of Laurent's behavior at 0;7(13).

> At 0;7(13), after learning to remove an obstacle to gain his objective, T. began to enjoy this kind of exercise. When several times in succession I put my hand or a piece of cardboard between him and the toy he desired, he reached the stage of momentarily forgetting the toy and pushed aside the obstacle, bursting into *laughter*. What had been intelligent adaptation had thus become play, through transfer of interest to the action itself, regardless of the aim. (Piaget 1962: 92; italics added)

Thus, on the same day Laurent constructs his first means-ends scheme, he plays with this scheme, in order to integrate it into a new sense of self. The dialectical process between exploration and play is again apparent; Laurent's laughter expresses his "recognition" of his new intellectual achievement.

Studies of the differentiation in Infancy of the other ego-functions – Feeling, Sensation, Intuition – are yet to be undertaken.

AESTHETIC ATTITUDE

Jung defines an attitude as a readiness of the psyche to act or react in a certain way.

> To have an attitude means to be ready for something definite, even though this something is unconscious; for having an attitude is synonymous with an *a priori* orientation to a definite thing, no matter whether this be represented in consciousness or not. The state of readiness, which I conceive attitude to be, consists in the presence of a certain subjective constellation, a definite combination of psychic factors or contents, which will either determine action in this or that definite direction, or react to an external stimulus in a definite way. (*CW* 6: 687,414–15)

Then, in language strongly reminiscent of William James in *The Principles of Psychology*, Jung identifies emotions as the determinants of attitudes.

> The presence of a strongly feeling-toned content in the conscious field of vision forms (maybe with other contents) a particular constellation that is equivalent to a definite attitude, because such a content promotes the perception and apperception of everything similar and blacks out the dissimilar. It creates an attitude that corresponds to it. (ibid.: 415)

Further, Jung contrasts cultural attitudes derived primarily from the outer, societal collectivity in which any possible individual is immersed to individual cultural attitudes, which are creative centers in the personality, arising from deep within the psyche of individuals that resonate with and introduce new contributions to collective culture. He specifically names the religious and philosophical attitudes, but his remarks apply to other types of cultural attitudes (e.g. aesthetic, social, scientific, and psychological as well):

> A religious or philosophical attitude is not the same thing as belief in a dogma. A dogma is a temporary intellectual formulation, the outcome of a religious and philosophical attitude conditioned by time

and circumstances. But the attitude itself is a cultural achievement; it is a function that is exceedingly valuable from a biological point of view, for it gives rise to incentives that drive human beings to do creative work for the benefit of the future age and, if necessary, to sacrifice themselves for the welfare of the species. (*CW* 4: 555,241)

Jung's notion of attitudes as categories of the cultural imagination was taken up and elaborated by the Jungian analyst and theoretician Joseph Henderson (1984), who both established a psychological basis for the common cultural attitudes he identified as basic, viz. the Religious, Aesthetic, Philosophical, and Social cultural attitudes, recognized the Psychological attitude as the emergent standpoint from which Jung's and his own point of view takes its vantage. Henderson was particularly careful to demonstrate the clinical usefulness of a conception of cultural attitudes. Louis H. Stewart took the position soon after Henderson published his material that Henderson's cultural attitudes originate in the various archetypal affects identified by Tomkins and others (Table 3, Row 7).

As an illustration of this view, my brother Lou and I presented the following description of the construction by Jacqueline Piaget of an Aesthetic Cultural attitude during stages IV, V, and VI of the sensorimotor period.

> 0:9(9) She was looking at a celluloid parrot; when it was made to swing she imitated this movement.
> 0;10(7) She watched a brush and cardboard box swinging in the same way and waved her hand.
> 1:2(25) She saw a lamp swaying from the ceiling and swayed her body saying "Bim bam."
> 1;3 She learned to balance on a curved piece of wood which she rocked with her feet in a standing position.
> 1;4 She adopted the habit of walking on the ground with her legs apart, pretending to lose her balance, as if she were on the board, and laughed heartily, saying "Bimbam."
> 1;6 She swayed bits of wood or leaves and kept saying Bimbam. (L. H. Stewart and C. T. Stewart 1981: 48)

Piaget noted that in the behavior of observation 1;6 Jacqueline is using the term "Bimbam" as "a half generic, half symbolic schema referring to branches, hanging objects and even grasses" (Piaget 1962: 96). For my brother and me, there was a quite aesthetic sensibility shaping the choice of this picturesque and onomatopoetic word. We summarized Jacqueline's construction of an Aesthetic Attitude as follows:

We see in this example not only evidence of the practical form of an expressive category, but in addition an illustration of a seizure of consciousness: Usener's "momentary God," which through being named leads to simultaneous developments in the mythical image and in the concept; Bimbam, the hemistitch of prototypical poetic meter in nursery rhyme, and a classificatory concept of living form. (L. H. Stewart and C. T. Stewart, 1981: 48–9)

It would be very helpful if someone would undertake to study the developmental foundations in Infancy of the Philosophic, Social, and Religious Attitudes, but this important work remains yet to be undertaken.

SUMMARY

I would like to close this chapter with a brief, stepwise summary of the way in which the primal experience functions to organize psychological development throughout the stage of Infancy.

During the first step of the primal experience, which is ego–other "recognition," a supraordinate maternal symbol is constellated in the infant and projected onto the parent. (This is Kohut's idealized parental-imago.) This projection establishes a vital, emotional infant–parent bond, so that the parent becomes for the infant a primary object of psychic attention. The symbolic bond so produced persists throughout Infancy and serves as one basis of the infant's *social* developmental pathway. (The other basis for this pathway is, of course, the symbolic parent–infant bond which is established when the Divine Child is projected onto the infant by his parents, who convey through the projection that any amount of development is possible for their smart, multifaceted, talented baby.) The mother archetype has a special purchase on an infant's imagination because it is a totality symbol, composed of the building blocks – primal images and innate affects – for *all of the psychic functions*. In a process of constructive integration throughout the first year of life, the infant utilizes these pluripotential images and affects for building the socially-oriented feeling-toned complexes, the ego-functions, and the creative cultural attitudes of the ego-complex. (Neumann (1954) first described this process for analytical psychology using the terms fragmentation of archetypes, exhaustion of emotional components, rationalization, and secondary personalization, and Fordham (1979) speaks of the infant's healthy deintegration of the primal self into more meaningful "deintegrates.") For our purposes, it seems easiest to imagine that, as development proceeds, the archetype of Infancy, the mother imago, is naturally depotentiated and a space is created for the emergence of World Parents, which are the archetypes governing of the following stage of Early Childhood.

What follows in normal development is the first ego–self "recognition." We need to recall that at childbirth symbols of the Divine Child have been constellated in the parents and projected onto the infant to stay in place for most of the first two years of life. (It is reasonable to speculate that the parents' construction of their symbolic mode of Infancy, the Divine Child, also follows the three-step pattern of the primal experience.) In addition to establishing a vital emotional parent–infant bond, in which the child becomes a primary object of parental psychic attention, the projection of the Divine Child activates the infant's collective unconscious. An axis is formed between the infant's nascent ego and the center of its total personality, the self. (This is the basis of Kohut's grandiose self.) This infant–self bond, which is a bridge between the ego and the self's own energized, autonomous, developmental ground plan, persists throughout Infancy as the foundation for its *individual* path of psychological development. This is the context in which archetypal images and affects of the self appear to serve as the building blocks for all the structures and functions of the ego-complex. It should be added that it is only in such a context that they could become available to the infant for its individual constructive activities. As we will see throughout this book, the social and individual developmental pathways potentiate each other.

The third step in the primal experience is the creation of a new world view. That step is marked by the beginning of the infant's application of a new intellectual instrument of assimilation, the symbolic act, and by its use of symbolic behavior to begin to reach out to its environment, which if we are truly raising citizens of the world will eventually extend to the four corners of the globe.

4

The Beginning of Make-Believe in Early Childhood

> They too animate their dolls and toys, and with imaginative children it is easy to see that they inhabit a world of marvels.
> ——C. G. Jung, *Symbols of Transformation*

The stage of development we shall analyze in this chapter extends from about one and a half to three and a half years and is referred to by developmental psychologists as Early Childhood. Psychoanalysts call this the Preoedipal Period, and Erikson has defined its psychosocial, existential crisis as one of Autonomy versus Shame and Doubt. The Jungian analyst Erich Neumann calls this the Magic-Phallic stage. The mode of the symbolic process which emerges at this stage is *Pretend* or *Make-Believe*. The new instrument for the assimilation of experience, constructed by the child at the beginning of this stage, is the *symbolic scheme*. As we will show, its emergence exhibits the same invariant sequence in the differentiation of consciousness that we have observed in our discussion of primal experience at the beginning of Infancy (Chapter 2).

Our analysis of Early Childhood focuses not only on the emergence of "pretend" at the beginning of this stage, but also on what we call the *interiorization* of the symbolic process that characterizes the previous stage of Infancy. If the Infant is primarily a "doer," the Child becomes a "knower" once three conditions are met, all contingent on interiorizations. These are (1) advent of the permanent object, (2) the appearance of representative thought, and (3) the capacity for make-believe. It is this third we will discuss now.

DEVELOPMENT OF THE SYMBOLIC PROCESS: PRETEND

In our discussion of the invariant, sequential differentiation of consciousness at the beginning of Infancy (Chapter 2), from recognition of other, to awareness of self, to construction of a new view of the world, all of which we referred to as the "primal experience," we indicated that a three-step pattern was actually the paradigm at each subsequent stage of development in the emergence of the symbolic process from Early Childhood through Adolescence. To illustrate the content of this sequence at the beginning of Early Childhood, we draw upon the moving observations by Piaget of his own daughter, Jacqueline, and by the teacher Annie Sullivan of the blind, deaf, mute child, Helen Keller.

Jacqueline

(1) "Recognition" of the Other

In the unfolding of the primal experience, we have seen that the provision by the parents of a positive affective *temenos* (a sheltered, containing space) during the difficult early period of non-recognition serves as the primary environmental influence conditioning all further differentiation of consciousness (Chapter 2). Parents make a similar provision for the emergence of make-believe. Studies have shown that mothers regularly engage their children in symbolic play well before their children reach the level of development when they can pretend on their own: "In the context of their homes, all mothers directed pretend play to their children at twelve months of age, although pretend play had barely emerged in some children and not at all in others" (Haight and Miller 1993: 42).

We can assume, therefore, that for some time before this observation of her play by Piaget, Jacqueline's mother had been engaging in symbolic play in front of her daughter.

> At 1; 1(20) J. scratched at the wall-paper in the bedroom where there was the design of a bird, then shut her hand as if it held the bird and went to her mother: "*Look* (she opened her hand and pretended to give something). – What have you brought me? – *A birdie.*" (Piaget 1962: 119)

In this infant observation, we are able to see Jacqueline's "recognition" of her mother's capacity for make-believe. The mother's interested, playful response serves as another source of encouragement for Jacqueline's symbolic development. We can contrast this enabling mother's behavior with responses of indifference, misunderstanding, rejection, ridicule, ignoring, or cooptation that some parents unfortunately bring to the fantasy lives of their children. From an archetypal perspective, it appears that Jacqueline's mother is an ideal facilitator of fantasy; in mythological language, she has become the Mistress of the Beasts, one of the aspects of the Great Mother. In this role she is still well ahead of her daughter. Although Jacqueline is aware that the "birdie" is not real, she is not yet really aware of her own capacity for pretend. The differentiation of this level of self-consciousness occurs only two months later.

(2) "Awareness" of Self

The next step in symbolic developmental transformation occurs when Jacqueline believes she is by herself.

> In the case of J., who has been our main example in the preceding observations, the true ludic symbol, with every appearance of awareness of "make-believe" first appeared at 1;3(12) in the following circumstances. She saw a cloth whose fringed edges vaguely recalled those of her pillow; she seized it, held a fold of it in her right hand, sucked the thumb of the same hand and lay down on her side, *laughing hard*. She kept her eyes open, but blinked from time to time as if she were alluding to closed eyes. Finally, *laughing* more and more, she cried "*Nene*" (Nono). (ibid.: 96; italics added)

Here, Jacqueline engages in her first observed individual act of pretend play: her sleep ritual is the content. Her laughter expresses her pleasureful *self-awareness* of the birth of her newly differentiated capacity for make-believe. "Nene," a *verbal scheme*, is not only an additional expression of Jacqueline's now-sophisticated awareness of make-believe but also an indication of the emergence of her linguistic *representative* capacity. Clearly a new level of the ego-complex is starting to form.

In this observation of Piaget's, Jacqueline's sleep ritual, created when she was four months old and the content of her practice play at nine months (see Interiorization below), appears for the first time in the form of what we can call a *symbolic scheme*. She will go on to employ this symbolic scheme in her first steps toward the creation of a new world view.

(3) Construction of a New View of the World

Over the next few months, Jacqueline progressively dissociates the symbolic scheme of her sleep ritual from its material content, first using the collar of her mother's coat and then the tail of her rubber donkey to represent the pillow. In this process the symbolic scheme becomes mobile, that is, increasingly under ego control: that enables Jacqueline, at a certain moment, to consciously project the scheme into the world.

> And from 1;5 onwards she made her animals, a bear and a plush dog also do "Nono." (ibid.)

By projecting her own actions of expressive self-motion to make her crib toys move, Jacqueline's sister, Lucienne, in a previous observation, also created a new world view. Now with a similar act of projection, Jacqueline has herself become Mistress of the Beasts, interiorizing the symbolic function carried for her by her mother.

With pretend now under Jacqueline's control, she is able to transform her world. She will rapidly expand her use of symbolic schemes to create a complete magical world of make-believe. She begins by "pretending" additional actions of her own and then improvises the actions of others. A further differentiation in her use of symbolic schemes occurs when she begins to *become* the other: the cleaning lady, her father, a tree, her mother, her sister, and a cat. She also commences to use physical objects – shells, milk, a stone – as symbols to represent other things. She begins, moreover, to construct whole symbolic scenes with her dolls. Such scenes are the rudiments of fantasy narratives, which are characteristic of the next stage we will be looking at in Chapter 5, the Preschool Period.

Jacqueline now lives in an animated world where the moon runs, the wind sings, and the leaves that have fallen from trees dance.

At 2;1(0) she said: "*Moon running*" when walking in the evening along the lake (illusion of being followed by the moon). (ibid.: 250–1)

At 2;5(8): "*You can hear the wind singing. How does it do it?*" (ibid.: 251)

At 2;10(13): "*Do they like dancing* (dead leaves)?" (ibid.)

The possibilities for cosmic experiences abound, in this magically animated symbolic world.

Helen Keller

Helen Keller was one and a half years old when the catastrophic illness occurred that left her blind, deaf, and mute. When she was nearing her seventh birthday as a nearly unsocialized child, Anne Sullivan became her teacher. One month later, Anne recorded the following events (as reported by Cassirer), which portray the development of the representative function in the linguistic sphere.

(1) "Recognition" of the Other

Although Helen's development of the representative function characteristic of Early Childhood was delayed chronologically until her seventh year, its emergence follows the same sequence in terms of the differentiation of consciousness as we see with children whose development is on schedule.

This morning, while she was washing, she wanted to know the name for "water." When she wants to know the name for anything, she points to it and pats my hand. I spelled "w-a-t-e-r" and thought no more about it until after breakfast ... (Later on) we went out to the pump house, and I made Helen hold her mug under the spout while I pumped. As the cold water gushed forth, filling the mug, I spelled "w-a-t-e-r" in Helen's free hand. The word coming so close upon the sensation of the cold water rushing over her hand seemed to *startle* her. She dropped the mug and stood as one transfixed. A new light came over her face. (Cassirer 1944: 34; italics added)

Helen's experience of the primal affect Surprise–Startle marks an experiential moment of disorientation-reorientation, which is followed by a new level or breakthrough of ego-consciousness: "a new light came over her face." Helen has discovered the force of the capacity for symbolic linguistic representation in Anne, even though she is not yet aware of this capacity in herself. Anne can define a sensory experience as rich as that of cold, fresh water with the word she spells out on Helen's hand.

(2) "Awareness" of Self

But Helen's recognition of her *own* capacity for the use of linguistic signs, in formal language, her self-reflective awareness of the ego's representative function, follows immediately: "She spelled 'water' several times" (ibid.: 34). Her creation of a new world view immediately follows in this cascade of unfolding interiorization of the symbolic function.

(3) Creation of New View of the World

Helen's capacity for symbolic assimilation now returns to the place where it began, that is, to Anne, and then extends into the rest of her immediate environment.

Then she dropped on the ground and asked for its name and pointed to the pump and the trellis and suddenly turning round she asked for my name. I spelled "teacher." All the way back to the house she was highly excited, and learned the name of every object she touched, so that in a few hours she had added thirty new words to her vocabulary (ibid.)

Cassirer comments on the revolutionary nature of the world-relationship that Helen has created for herself upon discovering the representative function of language.

The decisive step leading from the use of signs and pantomime to the use of words, that is, of symbols, could scarcely be described in a more striking manner. What was the child's real discovery at that moment? Helen Keller had previously learned to combine a certain thing or event with a certain sign of the manual alphabet. A fixed association had been established between these things and certain tactile impressions. But a series of associations, even if they are repeated and amplified, still does not imply an understanding of what human speech is and means. In order to arrive at such an understanding the child had to make a new and much more significant discovery. It had to understand that *everything has a name* – that the symbolic function is not restricted to particular cases but is a principle of *universal* applicability which encompasses the whole field of human thought. In the case of Helen Keller this discovery came as a sudden shock. She was a girl seven years of age who, with the exception of defects in the use of certain sense organs, was in an excellent state of health and possessed of a highly developed mind ... Then, suddenly, the crucial development takes place. It works like an intellectual revolution. *The child begins to see the world in a new light* [italics added]. It has learned the use of words not merely as mechanical signs or signals but as an entirely new instrument of thought. A new horizon is opened up, and henceforth the child will roam at will in this incomparably wider and freer area. (ibid.: 34–5)

Developmental transformations such as this are based on the following principle: "*It is not that something different is seen, but that one sees differently*" (CW 11: 891,546).

Helen's behavior (as described by Anne) on the day following her discovery of the world of linguistic symbols certainly indicates that she is now seeing the world differently:

The next morning she got up like a radiant fairy. She has flitted from object to object, asking the name of everything and kissing me for gladness ... Everything must have a name now. Wherever we go, she asks eagerly for the name of things she has not learned at home. She is anxious for her friends to spell, and eager to teach the letters to everyone she meets. She drops the signs and pantomime she used before, as soon as she has words to supply their place, and the acquirement of a new word affords her the liveliest pleasure. And we notice that her face grows more expressive each day. (Cassirer 1944: 34)

This description of Helen's continuing symbolic development captures the magical quality of her experience, beginning with her emergence from sleep looking like "a radiant fairy." This accords with Jung's view that the development of ego-consciousness is itself a numinous experience, governed by archetypes and the symbolic process.

With these two examples of the development of pretend at the beginning of Early Childhood in mind, we look more closely at the process of interiorization in Infancy which is a necessary condition for this transformation.

INTERIORIZATION OF THE SYMBOLIC PROCESS: INFANCY

As we have indicated, each stage in the development of the symbolic mode requires that interiorization of the mode of the previous stage already be accomplished. Interiorization, which can be defined as the dissociation of the process of the symbolic mode from its specific learned content, is accomplished in and through play itself. It is best to describe play (an outer behavior) as the face with which fantasy (an inner experience) shows itself to the world and by the formulaic phrase play/fantasy. The dynamism of play/fantasy needs to be studied in relation to its dialectical twin, also Janus-faced: curiosity/exploration. In a manner similar to play/fantasy, curiosity and exploration are the inner experience and the outer behavior respectively of this dynamism. In what follows, we present a detailed analysis of the dialectical spiral between these two dynamisms as it occurs at the beginning of Infancy. That will provide a basis for tracking the symbolic mode's seamless progression throughout the rest of this stage.

Just Babbling

The "babbling" period of development corresponds with Extremity and Tickling games (Chapter 3). Under optimal circumstances, infants are enveloped in the melodic intonations of their parents' voices from birth, heard in "motherese," "fatherese," lullaby, and call-and-response play songs. Thus, infants are already enclosed in a world of pure affective sound when they begin to sing.

Exploration (to Play)

In the following observation Piaget's subject, Laurent, is actively engaged in exploring, constructing, and differentiating various cognitive auditory-vocal schemes.

> At 0;2(7) Laurent babbles in the twilight [says goodbye to the day and hello to the night] and at 0;2(16) he does this on awakening early in the morning [says goodbye to the night and hello to the day] often for half an hour at a time. (Piaget 1952: 79)

This observation conveys the likelihood that the motivation for Laurent's babbling begins with an activation of the affect Interest–Excitement, which occurs initially in response to light changes at the close or beginning of day. But soon Interest–Excitement is kept alive when he experiences the sound of his own voice as the life stimulus, which produces novel sounds. This novelty sustains the motivational context of Interest–Excitement, allowing that affect/behavior to develop its own dynamism.

Our interpretation in the above observation is also based on our knowledge of the establishment in the infant of a precocious circadian rhythm. Twenty-four-hour temporal organization, that is, the location of sleep predominantly at night and awake states in the daytime, becomes evident between the fourth and sixth days of life (Sander 1988). Given this fact, it does not require too great a stretch of the imagination to believe that Laurent's babbling expresses his internal circadian experience of the numinous transitions from light to darkness, and darkness to light. In all peoples and in all religions, creation appears as the creation of light: "Thus the coming of consciousness, manifesting itself as light in contrast to the darkness of the unconscious, is the real 'object' of creation mythology" (Neumann 1954: 6).

Through sustained playful repetition of his auditory-vocal schemes, Laurent comes to "recognize" them, either spontaneously or when they are imitated. At 0;2(5) Laurent is observed to emit the sound *aa*. Three weeks later, Laurent imitates this sound after it is produced by his father.

> At 0;2(25) I made the sound *aa*. There was a long, ineffective effort, with his mouth open, followed by a faint sound. Then a broad smile and regular imitation. (Piaget 1962: 9)

The "broad smile" marks the moment of "recognition" of the auditory-vocal scheme *aa*. A movement from exploration to play then follows.

Exploration to Play and Back

As the schemes are now experienced under the rubric of the life stimulus that we can call the Familiar, the affect Joy and its behavior/inner-state dynamism play/fantasy are activated. Laurent begins to play with the intonations of his voice and to create an expressive or symbolic world of pure sound.

> At 0;3 [Laurent] played with his voice, not only through interest in the sound, but for "functional pleasure," laughing at his own power. (ibid.: 91)

Laurent's delighted playing with the vocal-auditory schemes he has constructed leads, first of all, to their integration as new aspects of the self and its agency; Laurent's laughter marks his self-reflective awareness of this new level of ego identity. At this level of development, dissociation of form and content is limited to the transposition of the schemes out of the cognitive and into an expressive context.

In and through his playful babbling, Laurent is discovering the *expressive intonations* of each babble. These intonations are expressions of emotion through the vocal channel. As researchers have noted, "The infant's musical rhythm seems to be closer to folk music and jazz improvisation than to the classical Western music" (Papousek and Papousek 1981: 192). Further interiorization will occur during such musical play. In addition, the intonational patterns developed by infants during the first year, for example, "calm cooing," are similar to intonations of affirmations in adults (Tonkova-Yampol'skaya 1973). By the completion of Infancy, the child will have achieved a whole new level of melodic development.

> At approximately eighteen months, children's singing undergoes a qualitative change. Whereas earlier vocalizations consisted of continuous blends, children now begin producing discrete pitches. They have added to their system the most basic elements necessary for singing as it is defined in Western culture and at this point can embark upon the twin tasks of rhythmic and melodic organization. (McKernon 1979)

In his early babbling, however, Laurent is not bent on becoming an accomplished musician. He starts by creating a world of pure sound which initiates the harmony of the spheres and provides the vocal foundation for all his future articulations of myth, poem, and song.

In and through this playful babbling, Laurent produces novel sounds which capture his interest. The developmental rhythm will now move from play back to exploration. Prior to the following observation, Laurent had become interested in the sound of his own laughter.

> At 0;2(26) he reproduces the peals of his voice which ordinarily accompany his laughter, but without laughing and out of pure phonetic interest. (Piaget 1952: 79)

Laurent's exploration of the sounds and intonations of his laughter, "out of pure phonetic interest," indicates that the contrary dialectical movement, from play back to exploration, has also occurred. The new phase of exploration of vocal-auditory schemes occurs at a higher level of development, for the dialectic we have described, from exploration to play and back, has the form of a *spiral*.

Gestural Names

In our discussion of the primal experience in Chapter 2, we described the infant's creation of a new world view through recognizing that movements of its body were effective in moving the crib and the toys attached to it. This view of the world as responsive to the infant's agency is expanded over the next few months as the infant uses movements of its whole body, as well as movements of its head, arms, hands, legs and feet to literally shake, rattle, and roll the world. The adaptation of each of these behaviors into the construction of cognitive schemes, which Piaget refers to as "secondary circular reactions," is motivated by the affect Interest–Excitement and its inner/outer dynamism, curiosity/exploration.

Once the infant has adapted, repeated, and recognized these action schemes as occasioning the movements he finds so interesting, they become the content of integrative and creative play. The "pleasure of being the cause" is thus added to "functional pleasure," pleasure that the cognitive scheme "works."

In and through this play, yet a further step in the interiorization of the symbolic process occurs. The behavior through which this more subtle interiorization manifests is referred to by various psychologists in different ways. Piaget calls it motor "recognition," the psycholinguist Roger Brown (1973) "nomination," and the linguist M. A. K. Halliday (1975) the "gestural" element in the infant's "protolanguage." It is manifest in the following observation of Piaget's subject Lucienne:

> At 0;5(3) Lucienne tries to grasp spools suspended above her by means of elastic bands. She usually uses them in order to suck them, but sometimes she swings them while shaking herself when they are there ... She manages to touch but not yet to grasp them. Having shaken them fortuitously, she then breaks off to shake herself a moment while looking at them (shakes of the legs and trunk), then she resumes her attempts at grasping. (Piaget 1952: 186)

Piaget offers the following explanation for Lucienne's behavior:

> Everything transpires as though the subject, endowed for a moment with reflection and internal language, had said to [herself] something like this: "Yes, I see that this object could be swung, but it is not what I am looking for." But, lacking language, it is by working the schema that Lucienne would have thought that, before resuming [her] attempts to grasp. In this hypothesis, the short interlude of swinging would thus be equivalent to a sort of motor recognition. (ibid.)

Lucienne's use of the scheme for bodily, gestural naming can only occur, we believe, because it has already been dissociated from its original content and is thus available to the infant for other applications. In such ways the interiorization of the symbolic process continues.

Encore

As a second order of business, the infant also displaces the circular reactions from instrumental to interpersonal contexts, to construct what is referred to by Piaget as "procedures to make interesting spectacles last." Brown knows such behaviors by the term Recurrence, which means to him that they form a request rather than a comment. Halliday also sees it as a vocal regulatory element in the infant's protolanguage; i.e. "Do that again!" The following example of such development in the ability to prolong pleasurable schemes occurs at about the time of the Knee Ride period (Chapter 3).

We find Jacqueline, at six months, continuing to explore auditory-vocal schemes, at first in the individual pathway.

> At 0;6(25) J. invented a new sound by putting her tongue between her teeth. It was something like *pfs*. (Piaget 1962: 19)

When her mother overhears her, she invites Jacqueline into the social pathway for vocal exploration and play. Jacqueline accepts the invitation.

> Her mother then made the same sound. J. was delighted and laughed as she repeated it in he turn. Then came a long period of mutual imitation. J. said *pfs*, her mother imitated her, and J., watched her without moving her lips. (ibid.)

Her father can hardly wait to get in on the fun.

> Then when her mother stopped, J. began again, and so it went on. Later on, after remaining silent for some time, I myself said *pfs*. J. laughed and at once imitated me. (ibid.)

In the next observation Jacqueline uses *pfs* in an attempt to induce her father to repeat his babbling. She wants an encore.

> At 0;6(26) J. frequently made, during the day, the sounds *bva, bve* and also *va* and *ve* without anyone imitating her. On the next day, however, at 0;6(27), when I said "*bva, bve*," etc. to her, she looked at me, smiled, and said: "*pfs, pfs ... bva*." Thus instead of at once imitating the model given to her, J. began by reproducing the sound she had become used to imitating two days earlier. (ibid.: 20)

Pfs has thus become a "device for making something interesting continue to happen." There has in other words been a dissociation of *pfs* from its content, that is, an interiorization of it. Fully belonging to her now, it has become available to Jacqueline as an instrument for regulating communication with her parents. These observations also show the way in which the reciprocal relation between the social and individual uses of a symbol facilitates ego development.

Freedom of Expression

In our analysis of the 'Peek-a-boo' phase of Infancy (Chapter 3), we commented on the "mobility" of cognitive schemes. It is this mobility that allows the infant to combine, dissociate, and recombine the schemes to create the first goal-directed (ends-means) behaviors. This emergence of empirical intelligence is again predicated on the dissociation of cognitive schemes from their content; that is what their "mobility" means.

In the following observation of the play of Piaget's subject, Jacqueline, we find her enjoying her newfound freedom of expression.

> At 0;9(3) J. was sitting in her cot and I hung her celluloid duck above her. She pulled a string hanging from the top of the cot and in this way shook the duck for a moment, laughing. The involuntary movements left an impression on her eiderdown: she then forgot the duck, pulled the eiderdown towards her and moved the whole of it with her feet and arms. As the top of the cot was also being shaken, she looked at it, stretched up then fell back heavily, shaking the whole cot. After doing this some ten times, J. again noticed her duck: she then grasped a doll also hanging from the top of the cot and went on shaking it, which made the duck swing. Then noticing the movement of her hands she let everything go, so as to clasp and shake them (continuing the preceding movement). Then she pulled her pillow from under her head, and having shaken it, struck it hard and struck the sides of the cot and the doll with it. (Piaget 1962: 93)

Piaget refers to Jacqueline's behaviors as "a happy display of known actions." But they are also evidence of the continuing interiorization, in and through play, of the symbolic process – we can see how there has been further dissociation of the schemes from their content.

Jacqueline's play with her pillow, for instance, points her in a different direction. For she is now playing with her sleep ritual itself, even though this is not a new adaptation, but one she constructed when she was in her fourth month.

> As she was holding the pillow, she noticed the fringe, which she began to suck. This action, which reminded her of what she did every day before going to sleep, caused he to lie down on her side, in the position for sleep, holding a corner of the fringe and sucking her thumb. This, however, did not last for half a minute and J. resumed her earlier activity. (ibid.)

By removing her sleep ritual from its usual context, bed time, Jacqueline has taken another step in the continuing dissociation of form and content. Piaget refers to such differentiation of the expressive domain as "ritualisation" of a scheme and considers it a precursor to true symbolic play.

All that is needed for the ludic ritual to become a symbol is that the child, instead of merely following the cycle of his habitual movements, should be aware of the make believe, i.e., that he should "pretend" to sleep. (ibid.: 93–4)

Given this observation, it is not surprising that the content of Jacqueline's first act of make-believe was her sleep ritual.

Verging on Pretend

This period of interiorization corresponds with the "Brow Bender" and "Tae Titly" phase of development described in Chapter 3. Two new cognitive schemes are constructed, referred to by Piaget as "tertiary circular reactions," an effort to grasp novelties in themselves, and "discovery of new means through active experimentation." The ability to engage freely in such behaviors is predicated on further dissociation of cognitive schemes from their content. We find a parallel dissociation in the infant's play behavior, that is, in the interiorization of the symbolic process.

When she is fifteen months old, Jacqueline engages in the ritualization of yet another scheme, much as she did at nine months with the sleep ritual:

At 1;3(11) J. asked for her pot and laughed a lot when it was given to her. She indulged in a certain number of ritual movements, playfully, and the game stopped there, to be taken up again the following days. (ibid.: 94)

Her laughter reflects her growing awareness of her symbolic capacity, for it is on the next day that she engages in her first act of pretend play.

Our analysis of the interiorization of the symbolic function during Infancy has taken us to the threshold of Early Childhood. In the next section I will analyze the development of the ego-complex during this stage.

DEVELOPMENT OF THE EGO-COMPLEX

Neumann (1990) has identified a universal myth, the Separation of the World Parents, as portraying, in projection, the psychology of his Phallic-Magic stage, which we call Early Childhood. This mythologizing projection begins with the primordial female and male locked in such a close embrace that the world is kept in darkness. In some versions of this world-wide myth, there is not enough room for humans to walk upright. It is the task of a hero to separate the primordial pair, which he accomplishes sometimes by lying on his back and kicking them apart, so that they are transformed into the supportive earth and the overarching sky. Here is a Hindu version of the story:

> In the beginning this world was Soul (Atman) alone in the form of a person. Looking around, he saw nothing else than himself. He said first: "I am." ... He was, indeed, as large as a woman and a man closely embraced. He caused that self to fall (*pat*) into two pieces. Therefrom arose a husband (*pati*) and a wife (*patni*). (Neumann 1954: 105)

Once the heroic psyche has separated the World Parents, there is now both darkness and light, as well as room enough to walk, i.e. a space for ego-development. In the child psyche, this transformation of early self-awareness is experienced as an accentuation of the polarization of the world into opposites: real/pretend; mother/father; girl/boy; good/bad; night/day; above/below; left/right; and today/tomorrow, etc.

This application of cosmogonic myth to the process of early ego development is not so far-fetched as it might seem to our normal adult consciousness. Jung has suggested that the creative fantasies of children are closer to myth than conceptual thought.

> The naive man of antiquity saw the sun as the great Father of heaven and earth, and the moon as the fruitful Mother ... Thus there arose a picture of the universe which was completely removed from reality, but which corresponded exactly to man's subjective fantasies. It needs no very elaborate proof to show that children think in much the same way. They too animate their dolls and toys, and with imaginative children it is easy to see that they inhabit a world of marvels. (*CW* 5: 24,21)

Parent-Complexes

Jacqueline's subjective fantasies at the beginning of Early Childhood confirm the views of Neumann and Jung. In one of Jacqueline's mythic reveries, for instance, an image associated with her father assumes the proportions of a god of the daytime sky.

> At 1;8(12) J. was looking through the window at the mist forming on the mountain top (200 yards away) and cried: "*Mist daddy smoke,*" alluding to the smoke of my pipe. The next day, in the same situation, she merely said: "*Mist daddy.*" ... From 1;9 to 1;10 she constantly said: "*Clouds daddy*" or "*Mist daddy*" whenever she saw mist. (Piaget 1962: 245–6)

On another mythic occasion, the moon appears as the goddess of the nighttime sky.

At 1;10(1), on seeing the moon, she spontaneously said "*lady*," without laughing and without the comparison ever having been suggested to her either by words or pictures. Moreover, she added "*bell*," referring to the one hung over the door of the chalet. (ibid.: 221)

Jacqueline, now a child of the sun and the moon, creates spontaneous myths of origin, artificialism (the notion that the natural world has been created by humans), and animism, which Piaget indicates are half-way between imaginative symbolism and the exploratory investigation that is proper to cognitive intelligence (ibid.: 245–54).

The symbolic apprehension of the parents at the beginning of this stage also forms the foundation for the child's continuing construction of personal parent-complexes. As with all complexes, the parental images and associated complexes that cluster around them, are feeling-toned. The following observations indicate a few of the steps taken by Jacqueline in constructing personal parent-complexes on the foundations of the archetypal images we have just described. She pulls her back and pretends to be her "Daddy," she pretends to be "Mummy," asks her father to kiss her, and kisses him! This development culminates when she objectifies their relationship: "At about 2;9, she enacted conversations between her parents: '*Yes, my dear ... No, John*'" (ibid.: 128). By the time Jacqueline has reached the completion of this stage, her parents have shed their mythical envelopes and are experienced not only as persons but also in an ongoing symbolic relationship which she can imagine and, in fantasy, direct.

Memory

At the beginning of Early Childhood the child has difficulty in distinguishing between perceptions and memories. That is because memories are also "perceived."

At 1;3(9) Lucienne is in the garden with her mother. Then I arrive; she sees me come, smiles at me, therefore obviously recognizes me (I am at a distance of about 1 meter 50). Her mother then asks her: "Where is papa?" Curiously enough, Lucienne immediately turns toward the window of my office where she is accustomed to seeing me and points in that direction. A moment later we repeat the experiment; she has just seen me 1 meter away from her, yet, when her mother pronounces my name, Lucienne again turns toward my office. Here it may be clearly seen that if I do not represent two archetypes to her, at least I give rise to two distinct behavior patterns not synthesized not exclusive of one another but merely juxtaposed: "papa at his window" [memory-image] and "papa in the garden" [perceived image]. (Piaget 1954: 64)

When Jacqueline is nearly three years old she is still apt to refer to herself by her first name, but she has difficulty in recognizing herself in a photograph taken at an earlier age. In other words, Jacqueline does not experience continuity in her identity over time. By the end of Early Childhood, however, memory has become continuous, which is attested to in part by the child's consistent use of the personal pronoun "I" in referring to herself. We should look beyond memory, however, to account for this development.

Impersonal to Personal Pronouns

A significant manifestation of the growth of the ego-complex is to be found, as many psychologists have noticed, in the child's use of personal pronouns when referring to him or herself. The style of self-reference develops from the impersonal pronoun "You" (or first name) at the beginning of the stage of Early Childhood to the personal pronoun "I" at its completion: This is true for both English- and French-speaking, and sighted and blind children (Huxley 1970; Fraiberg and Adelson 1973; Halliday 1975). Jung has commented on the meaning of this development.

> I wouldn't call the ego a creation of mind or consciousness, since, as we know, little children talk of themselves first in the third person and begin to say "I" only when they have found their ego. The ego, therefore, is rather a find or an experience and not a creation. We rather might say the empirical existence of an ego is a condition through which continuous consciousness becomes possible. For we know that the sort of impersonal consciousness observed in little children is not continuous but of a dissociated and insular character. (Jung 1973b: 254–5)

As she nears the completion of Early Childhood, however, Jacqueline is so identified with her ego that she consistently uses the personal pronoun "I" in self-reference, even when trying to conceal her identity: "One day when I saw her lying down and went up to her, J. called out: '*Go away, I'm Marceline*'" (Piaget 1962: 128). Jacqueline's identification with her ego-personality makes it possible for her to playfully assume the identity of her cousin, Marceline (whom she had never met but only heard about), and still remain securely "I" in referring to herself.

Feeling-Valuation as a Function of the Ego

Feeling is defined by the Jungian theory of psychological "types" of consciousness as that ego-function which assigns a positive or negative *value* to every content of consciousness. Therefore it is perhaps best called "feeling-valuation." Feeling is considered by Jung to be a rational function of judgment and discrimination, like Thinking, and so quite unlike the irrational perceptual functions of consciousness, Sensation and Intuition. The content of Feeling valuation involves the assignment of particular feelings, that is discriminating feeling valuations which, when the function is under conscious control, can be distinguished from innate affects and complex-emotions by their lack of physiological concomitants and unconscious pressure to act on the feelings involved.

As do all of the ego-functions, the Feeling function begins to develop in Infancy and continues to do so throughout the life cycle. The innate affect which seems to be the cornerstone for the construction of the ego-function of feeling is Shame/Contempt (L. H. Stewart 1987b: 150–4). This affect, in turn, is activated when an efficient symbol emerges that combines the infant's experience of the life-stimulus Rejection with the primal image Alienation. Jung has emphasized the importance of this life stimulus for development of the feeling function:

> Disappointment, always a shock to the feelings, is not only the mother of bitterness but the strongest incentive to a differentiation of feeling. The failure of a pet plan, the disappointing behaviour of someone one loves, can supply the impulse either for a more or less brutal outburst of affect or for a modification and adjustment of feeling, and hence for its higher development. (CW 14: 334, 248)

The result of such disappointments is often an early moral judgment, that is, a positive or negative feeling valuation.

In what follows, I will interpret Piaget's analysis of the development of Jacqueline's moral judgment during Early Childhood as describing, in the terminology of analytical psychology, the differentiation of the ego-function Feeling. Piaget starts by describing the family atmosphere within which his observations were made.

> Jacqueline has never been punished in the strict sense of the term. At the worst, when she makes a scene, we leave her alone for a little while and tell her we shall come back when she can talk quietly again. She has never been given duties as such, nor have we ever demanded for her that sort of passive obedience without discussion which in the eyes of so many parents constitutes the highest virtue. We have always tried to make her understand the "why" of orders instead of laying down "categorical" rules. Above all, we have always put things to her in the light of cooperation: "to help mummy," to "please her parents," to "show her sister," etc. – are for her reasons for carrying out orders that cannot be understood in themselves. As to rules that are unintelligible to very little children, such as the rule of truthfulness, she has never even heard of them. (Piaget 1965: 178)

Although the Piaget's have done their best in this enlightened Swiss educational fashion to minimize Jacqueline's experience of Rejection, their natural authority cannot be completely abrogated.

> But in ordinary life it is impossible to avoid certain injunctions of which the purport does not immediately seem to have any sense from the child's point of view. Such are going to bed and having meals at given hours, not spoiling things, not touching things on daddy's table, etc. Now, these commandments, received and applied before being really understood, naturally give rise to a whole ethic of heteronomy with a feeling of pure obligation, with remorse in case of violation of the law, etc. (ibid.)

Piaget's first observation illustrates the fact that "during the early years, a child will often regard his own clumsiness from a purely objective point of view, even to his own detriment."

> J., at about 2 years old, is playing with a shell I have lent her. The shell is very fragile and breaks the first time it is dropped. J. is dismayed, and I have the great difficulty in persuading her it is not her fault. (ibid.: 182)

Piaget comments: "In the early stages, it is only the result that counts" (ibid.). The "result counts," I believe, because Jacqueline, through the yet autonomous activity of the shame inducing ego-function Feeling, assigns a *negative* value to her behavior, that is she *rejects herself*. In other words, she becomes "alienated" because she is shamed and this self-evaluation is a feeling judgment visited upon herself. Piaget's success in persuading Jacqueline "it is not her fault," which is grounded in his loving acceptance of her, will in turn remove her shame and lead to a *positive* revalorization of herself, a judgment that also requires the activity of the ego-function Feeling. It also supports the development of her conscious control of the Feeling function.

In the next example, Jacqueline exerts her autonomy and appears to intentionally execute the behaviors that concern her parents.

> For example, one evening I find Jacqueline, aged 2;6(15), in bed, spoiling a towel by pulling out the threads one by one. Her mother had already often told her that it is a pity to do that, that it makes holes, that you can't mend the holes, etc. So I say to J.: "Oh, but mummy will be sad." J. answers calmly and even with an ill-concealed smile: "*Yes. It makes holes you can't mend.*" ... I continue my lecture, but she obviously is not going to take me seriously. Still hiding her amusement with difficulty, she suddenly says to me "*Laugh!*" in so comic a tone, that in order to keep a straight face I quickly change the subject. J.,

very conscious of her powers of seduction, then says to me "*My little darling Daddy,*" and the incident ends. (ibid.: 178)

I interpret Jacqueline's use of her "powers of seduction" as an attempt to avert the approaching alienation from her father, that is, if he laughs they are once again a loving community and she is relieved from making a negative self-evaluation. The observation continues:

The next morning, however, J. wakes up full of it. Her first words refer to what happened the night before. She thinks about the towel and asks her mother whether she isn't sad. So in spite of the first reaction showing such charming disrespect, my words had told and the command had brought about the usual consequences. (ibid.)

By morning the father's judgment has stirred up Jacqueline's own. There has been a symbolic activation of Shame/Contempt and a measure of self-rejection and "alienation" has occurred, although this is largely projected onto the supposedly disappointed ("sad") mother. Piaget continues.

The evening of the same day, J. begins to pull the threads out of the towel again. Her mother repeats that it is a pity. J. listens attentively but says nothing. A moment later she is calling out and cries till someone comes to her: she simply wanted to see her parents again and make sure that they bore her no grudge. (ibid.: 178–9)

Clearly in Heinz Kohut's terms, a merger has broken down between her and her parents, and a painful state of shame and alienation has emerged. When Jacqueline cries out and gains acceptance from her parents, however, this facilitates a renewed positive revalorization of herself, again through the ego-function Feeling, which can choose to address the shame in a healthy way. Piaget comments:

We have here an example of a command bringing about, with or without apparent respect, a well-marked feeling of duty and wrong. Now it seems obvious to us that such feelings are set up before the child has any clear consciousness of moral intention, or at any rate before it can distinguish between what is "done on purpose" (an action carried out knowingly and in voluntary defiance of the command) and what is "not done on purpose." A child of two and a half spoiling a bath towel has obviously no intention of doing harm. It is simply making an experiment in physics. (ibid.: 179)

In these observations, we see how a child of two and a half years old can be overwhelmed by the feeling-judgment at the core of the experience

Shame, even under circumstances of minimal rejection by the parents. Jacqueline is not only making sure that her parents "bore her no grudge," but also is attempting to atone for her behavior, in order to overcome her own sense of "alienation." These attempts at atonement, like the sentence passed on her character, are directed by the activity of the ego-function Feeling. And its use fosters its development. (Piaget also gives examples concerning "food and the rules connected with it," which take place when Jacqueline is two years and ten months old (ibid.: 181–2).)

In a further example of the differentiation of the ego-function Feeling through symbolic play, the plastic compensatory nature of this function is evident:

At 2;7(15) a friend of her mother went for a walk with them. J. who did not care for the presence of a third person, expressed frankly what she felt: "*She's naughty ... she can't talk.... don't like people to laugh,*" and especially "*I don't understand what they're saying.*" Then, as soon as the walk was over, J. accepted her, put her beside her in the bath, then in her bed, talked to her, and went for the walk again with her (all in imagination). (Piaget 1962: 133)

We can explain this sequence in terms of the mobility of ego schemes in Early Childhood. At the time of the walk, Jacqueline was experiencing the life stimulus Rejection, and "alienation" followed; she then acted through the ego-function Feeling to assign a negative value to her mother's friend. After the walk is over, however, Jacqueline has a compensatory change of heart about that construction. Through the continuing activity of the ego-function Feeling, which is increasingly under conscious control, she reestablishes a positive attitude toward her mother's friend. Furthermore, in this example we observe not only the dialectical process between everyday reality and pretend, which is a motor for the differentiation of all ego-schemes, including the valuation function Feeling, but also the *self-healing* function of play. A minor narcissistic wound in which too-negative evaluations of self and other predominate can be ameliorated through the creation of a "utopian relationship," in which reciprocal positive evaluations rule. That is one of the functions of the imaginary companion, to whom the child is apt to turn with increasing frequency in the Preschool Period.

5

The Invisible Friend in the Preschool Period

The treasure is also the "companion" – in all probability a close analogy to the lonely ego who finds a mate in the self ... This is the theme of the magical travelling companion ...
——C. G. Jung, *Psychology and Alchemy*

The stage of development we analyze in this chapter, extending from three to four to six to seven years, is referred to by developmental psychologists as the Preschool Period. This is also the period psychoanalysts refer to as the "Oedipal Period proper," with its crisis of Initiative versus Guilt (Erik Erikson's formulation of the conflict behind the "Oedipus Complex"). The Jungian analyst Erich Neumann interestingly described it as the Magic-Warlike stage. All of these formulations suggest that attempts at self-assertion and heavy internal conflicts characterize this period of development, and so we can understand that the child's imagination needs to be especially resourceful. The *symbolic* process at the beginning of this stage involves a tension within the *imaginary companion*, who functions as an ego-ideal that knows how to cope with the challenges and as the shadow, which represents both the past outgrown infantile identity and any other traits which are currently unacceptable. A new instrument for the assimilation of experience that originates in the dialectic between these two aspects of the imaginary companion, the ego-ideal and shadow, is the *symbolic narrative*.

A survey of studies of the imaginary companion over the last century reveal both agreement and diversity among the views of the researchers (Hurlock and Burstein 1932; Bender and Vogel 1941; Ames and Learned 1946; Sperling 1954; Nagera 1969; Manosevitz et al. 1973; Manosevitz et al. 1977; Taylor et al. 1993; Taylor 1999). Most of the students of the phenomenon have found that imaginary companions appear at three to four years and persist until their disappearance at six to seven years. The majority of these invisible friends were of the same sex and age as their real companions. The incidence of this phenomenon, on the other hand, has varied greatly from study to study, with a spread from 10 to 100 percent among the children studied. Some authors have thought the imaginary companion is normal and adaptive, whereas others have viewed the appearance of such a figure as at best defensive, and usually indicative of more severe present or future psychopathology. There has tended to be agreement among the researchers that the imaginary companion is invented, that is, conceived intentionally, and not discovered in a dream or fantasy as a product derived from the developmental unconscious. None of the studies concluded that this symbol was stage-specific. Ames and Learned stand out in viewing the imaginary companion as "one part of a total 'imaginative gradient,' any or all parts of which may quite normally occur in any one child" (Ames and Learned 1946: 165–6). It is our view that the imaginary companion is *the* characteristic symbolic mode of the Preschool Period of development and, in this sense, is neither invented nor constructed but discovered, out of an ongoing pool of creative fantasy experience.

Parents start very early to mirror a child's psychological development through nursery rhymes, fairytales, legends, myths, and other cultural forms. This process begins in Infancy and continues without interruption through Adolescence. The unfolding of the unconscious developmental process so "reflected" gradually becomes a *conscious*, as well as unconscious experience, which means that it becomes vitally important to the daily preoccupations of the developing child. One parental provision which enhances symbolic development at the Oedipal stage is the *bedtime story*.

The emergence of the imaginary companion exhibits the same sequential pattern that we observed at the beginning of Infancy and Early Childhood: the ego's "recognition" of the other, and of itself in relation to that other, which is followed by the creation of a new world view.

DEVELOPMENT OF THE SYMBOLIC PROCESS: EGO-IDEAL AND SHADOW IN THE IMAGINARY COMPANION

Let us revisit Piaget's subject Jacqueline, who was studied when just entering this exciting period of transformation, and then go on to observe the same process in Kathie, a blind child.

Jacqueline

(1) Recognition of a New Other

When Jacqueline is three years old, she explores her father's reactions to her mock questions.

At 3;8 J. at the sight of a picture asked: "*What's that?* – It's a cowshed. – *Why?* – It's a house for cows. – *Why?* – Because there are cows in it, there, do you see? – *Why are they cows?* – Don't you see? They've got horns. – *Why have they horns? ...*" etc. As a matter of fact, though in such cases the first question may be serious, the others become more and more just questions asked for the sake of asking and to see how long answers will be forthcoming. (Piaget 1962: 118)

A month later, Jacqueline starts to test her father's reactions to more adventurous stories which are populated with mythical beasts.

At 3;9 J. often made up stories merely to contradict or to put ideas together as she pleased. She was not at all concerned with what she was saying, but merely with the combination as such: "*Are those wings?* (an elephant's ear). – No, elephants don't fly. – *Yes, they do, I've seen them.* – You're joking. – *No, I'm not. It's true. I've seen them.*" ... And another day: "*I saw a pig washing itself. I'm not joking, I saw it. It was doing like this ...*" etc. (ibid.)

This research observation portrays Jacqueline's creative "recognition" of her father's willingness to listen to her and thus to support her telling of stories with archetypal, imaginary or mythical beasts as central characters. This interaction between Jacqueline and her father is not unlike the exchange of the symbolic "bird" between Jacqueline and her mother at the beginning of Early Childhood (Chapter 4). At this stage the child is beginning to show more autonomy and initiative, and, for the first time, even a real agency in taking the lead in the storytelling. A disaffirming response by a parent to such an upwelling of creativity can have a dampening effect on any further development and conscious manifestation's of this new form of the symbolic function. This dampening effect can extend along a continuum from the child's merely shifting the context of storytelling to more sympathetic listeners, to a more or less complete block. Sometimes it results in the defensive, rather than natural, turn to an imaginary companion, as the only other Self who can support a symbolic fantasy life.

(2) Awareness of New Possibilities in the Self

Two months after the story of the flying elephants and the bathing pig, Jacqueline encounters the "aseau."

At 3;11(20) she invented a creature which she called the "aseau," and which she deliberately distinguished from "oiseau" (bird) which she pronounced correctly at this age. J. imitated it and took its place. She ran about the room flapping her wings (her outstretched arms) to suggest flight. But she also crawled on all fours, growling: "It's a kind of dog" and at the same time it was "like a big bird." Its form varied from day to day: it had wings, legs, it was "huge," it had long hair (J. said to her mother: "You've got hair like the aseau"). It had moral authority: "You mustn't do that" (tear a piece of paper): "Aseau will scold you." Two days later J. tried to eat nicely so that Aseau should not scold her. (ibid.: 129–30)

As I have said, Jacqueline did not, in my view, invent the aseau, but rather discovered this mythical beast, which in turn is about to invent and construct Jacqueline, that is, guide her development, moral and otherwise.

Piaget reports sympathetically that "this strange creature which engaged her attention for about two months was a help in all that she learned or desired, gave her moral encouragement in obeying orders, and consoled her when she was unhappy" (ibid.: 130). In this statement, we can see that the "aseau" contains the dynamic seeds of the ego-functions Thinking and Feeling, as well as the self-soothing function of the ego. We also notice that the environment around Jacqueline was not at all hostile to her fantasy life.

Then, a transformation begins. The creature disappears: "At 4;0(7) her aseau had died." It reappears, however, and undergoes further differentiation of form:

At 4;0(17) he "*turned into a dog, and then afterwards he turned* back *into an aseau.*" As J. made more and more discoveries about zoology, Aseau acquired all the possible attributes: he was an insect, etc. (ibid.)

In addition to exhibiting its protean transformational skills, the "aseau" in this observation becomes associated with a classificatory scaffold, which in Jungian terms suggests again its role in the differentiation of the ego-function Thinking.

Then, a miraculous final transformation occurs: the "aseau" assumes human form!

Subsequently, at about 4;1(15), Aseau was replaced by a girl who was a dwarf (cf. obs. 84), then by a [young black woman] to whom she gave the name "Cadile." Cadile turned into "Marecage," a symbolic companion and she also was associated with everything new, amusing or difficult. Although Marecage was a [woman], she was usually represented by a walking stick, a spade, etc. (ibid.)

That the "aseau" has become "Marecage" means that at the completion of Early Childhood and the beginning of the Preschool Period, a new mode of the symbolic process, the "imaginary companion," has been discovered.

I say discovered, because the dog who is also a bird is an archetypal image. In its legendary, historical form, the mythical beast formed from bird and dog is the *senmurv*.

> The senmurv, whose name is thought to mean "dog-bird," seems to have been a creature of two natures and two worlds, the only connecting link or means of communication between heaven and earth. He is described as having wings that darken the skies, and if anything it is the bird half of his nature that predominates, but he also has teeth, and the female suckles her young. In art, particularly of the Sassanian period, his component parts seem to undergo a change, for although he has wings and flies, it is his tail that is the tail of a bird, while his head and paws are alike. (Lum 1951: 50)

The senmurv is thought to be either a direct ancestor, or an indirect ancestor through the gryphon, of the sphinx, that mythical signifier of the Oedipal Period.

Jacqueline's "aseau" belongs as well to the familiar folklore motif of helpful animals, which we encounter again and again in fairytales. These animals are noted for a sagacity and knowledge superior to humans. For instance, if the child's attitude toward the parents is too dependent, then it may be compensated in dreams by powerful animals or monsters, which in this context can still be considered helpful, because they provide an energy that is linked with the child's efforts at psychological growth. This interpretation of them does not contradict Neumann's view that the mythologem characteristic of this stage is the dragon fight, which portrays the child's struggle for independence from the World Parents of the previous stage. (Even the terrifying Sphinx who must be conquered is in a certain sense "helpful," helpful to the individuation of Oedipus.)

(3) Construction of a New World View

A task for the child from the beginning of Infancy is to create a new relationship to the world, in which the baby begins to move the world with its actions. This is often referred to as the emergence of the developing child's *agency*. With the onset of Early Childhood, the child begins to function as an agent of his or her own self-experience by securely employing a symbolic scheme to assimilate the world. At the beginning of the Preschool Period, the child creates yet another new world-relationship by consciously employing an even more powerful instrument of assimilation, *symbolic narrative*. The preschool child actively draws upon the newly appropriated gift of storytelling to assimilate the world into a developing psychological life.

The day after her symbolic companion first assumed human form, Jacqueline reacted to an unexpected death in her community in the following manner.

> Expecting to see again a dwarf whom she had seen several times before in a village, J. learned that she was dead. She immediately told a *story* [italics added] about a little girl dwarf who met a boy dwarf: "*Then he died, but she looked after him so well that he got better and went back home.*" (Piaget 1962: 132)

This illustrates both Jacqueline's use of symbolic narrative to assimilate a traumatic event in the world and her achievement of a new level of structure, and even language, in her stories.

In their study of the development of *plot structure* in children's fantasy-narratives, G. J. Botvin and B. Sutton-Smith found that under three years of age, several characters are listed with only the implication of action and at three years of age, narratives contain a series of events. The first plot structures appear at about four to five years of age.

> Narratives at this level are short but structurally symmetrical. They are characterized by the presence of one nuclear dyad. Although these narratives may have action elements either before or after the nuclear dyad, no elements occur between the initial and final terms of the dyad. a) An astronaut went into space (Departure). He was attacked by a monster (Villainy). The astronaut got his spaceship and flew away (Villainy nullified). (Botvin and Sutton-Smith 1977: 379)

Jacqueline's symbolic narrative at the beginning of her fourth year has a similar structure: "*Then he died* [Villainy] *but she looked after him so well that he got better and went back home* [Villainy nullified]."

The child's ability to construct fantasy narratives is strongly conditioned by environmental influences. When adults *tell* stories to five year old children, they increase the children's narrative fluency.

> Thus, listening to maternal story telling can have an immediate effect on a child's narrative skill, especially on the number of clauses in the story and the use of evaluative devices. Maternal story telling may therefore be an important source of the child's acquisition of narrative skills. Maternal story telling may be a form of "motherese" appropriate for the development of narrative skill. (Harkins et al. 1994: 255)

When children listen to fairytales, the archetypes in the tales activate images from the listener's collective unconscious, which are expressed in the drawings children make afterwards (Walker and Lunz 1976).

When adults *listen* attentively to children tell stories, they also increase the children's narrative skills.

> If you keep asking children to make up stories for you and show some delight at the stories they tell; and if you keep coming back and asking for more stories, then the stories get better and better. There appears to be clear signs of an increase in their narrative competence just because you have been a good and a rewarding listener. Children also progress from telling you stories to wanting to write their own stories. (Sutton-Smith 1975: 82)

We have already seen the great psychologist Piaget's willingness to listen and record his daughter's mythic symbolic narratives.

Jacqueline's imaginary companion, "Marecage" becomes the central figure in a total of eight recorded symbolic narratives: this figure accompanied Jacqueline from four years and one month to five years and eight months of age.

Kathie

Kathie was a blind child who was delayed in developing "pretend." Her first recorded episode of symbolic play occurred when she was three years and three months of age.

> Later in the session, Kathie was walking around the room when she discovered the sink in the nursery. We did not tell her what it was. She climbed in and examined the sides and faucets with her fingers. One of us said, "What is it?" and, after a moment, she said firmly, "It's a sink!" Kathie curled up inside it. She was unmistakably pretending that the sink was a bed and said, in a mother's intonation, "Night-night, have good sleep, night-night. Go sleep in the sink." She closed her eyes, then opened them mischievously, and went through the whole routine again, with some variation. (Fraiberg and Adelson 1973: 549–50)

In an observation recorded fifteen months later, when Kathie was four and a half years old, there is still little differentiation in her pretend play: "Our observations of Kathie's doll play paralleled in all significant ways the doll play of sighted children at two to three years of age" (ibid.: 552).

What is of particular interest, however, is that despite this delayed onset the sequence – pretend, then imaginary companion – is maintained. In fact, in spite of her delay in the achievement and differentiation of pretend, Kathie's development of an imaginary companion was chronologically on time.

Around the same time, Kathie acquired an imaginary companion she called "Zeen." Kathie carried on conversations with Zeen in two voices. When addressed by a friendly adult, Zeen was willing to extend the conversation. At lunch, when the observers were having coffee, E. A. asked what Zeen would like. Kathie, in an animated voice, said, "Here he comes. He's driving up the driveway driving a car. He has to go home to make a cup of tea." It was Zeen who spilled the macaroni all over the kitchen floor, Kathie told her mother righteously when she herself was caught in the act. (ibid.: 552–3)

In this observation, "Zeen" exhibits elements which will contribute both to the formation of Kathie's "ego-ideal," whose particular competence is in the area of perceptual and motor coordination Jung calls "sensation," as seen, for instance, in his driving, as well as her clumsy "shadow," as is acted out, for example, in Zeen's spilling the macaroni.

Now we will turn our attention to a retrospective analysis of the process of interiorization of the symbolic process during Early Childhood.

INTERIORIZATION OF MAKE-BELIEVE CREATES THE IMAGINARY COMPANION

In comparing the play of Infancy with that of Early Childhood, Piaget has demonstrated (1) that play is assimilatory in its development at both stages, and (2) that play and intelligence interact at each moment of assimilation. Here is a typical observation that demonstrates the dialectic between exploration and play: "... what she said when playing with her dolls at about 2;11(15) is an inextricable medley of scenes from real life [integration] and imaginary episodes [creativity] ..." (Piaget 1962: 128).

About nine months after her first creative transformation of her sleep ritual, Jacqueline has progressed to the point when she can pretend any actions of her own, pretend any actions of others, can "become" the other, and can direct any object to become any other object. The symbol, as Piaget says, has been "constituted in its generality."

Each event in this rapid but extensive expansion of the world of make-believe (the word-for-word transcription of Jacqueline's conversation with her dolls comes to several pages) is also a development of the symbolic scheme of pretend itself, quite apart from its particular content. It is this dissociation of the symbolic scheme from its particular content that marks the beginning of interiorization of pretend. Once schemes cease to belong exclusively to the unconscious and become more and more under the control of the ego, they become much more plastic and mobile. As the deployability of the symbolic schemes at Jacqueline's disposal increases, the following sort of behavior results:

A fortnight earlier J. [now 2;8] had met, when she was away, a cousin whom she had not mentioned since. Suddenly everything became "Cousin Andree": the cat, the lid, herself, her mother, her dolls, etc. She talked about her all day long and made her do everything: go for walks, have meals, etc., down to the most intimate details, without in the least troubling about resemblances. (ibid.)

As a plastic symbol, "Cousin Andree" is freely deployed, with little attention to its original boundaries as a fixed content of fantasy linked to a single image in the unconscious. In the next observations still further dissociation between symbolic schemes and their content occurs, this time in terms of a dissolution of literalizing fantasies about relatives.

At 2;9, the freely deploying behavior appears in relation to the symbolic figures, "Marceline," a cousin, and "Miss Jerli," her grandmother's greengrocer. The only content transposed to "Marceline" and "Miss Jerli" from their real counterparts is based on what Jacqueline has heard about them from adults (she has never even met Miss Jerli). With the dissociation of the broader symbolic form from the limitations of known content, whether in the unconscious or outer reality, "Marceline" and "Miss Jerli" clearly stop being rigidly fixed images and are able to approach the status of *imaginary companions*.

As the process of interiorization continues, Jacqueline, is finally able, at three and a half years, to free the symbolic scheme from *all* content by introducing imaginary characters into her play. The "aseau" is about to arrive.

DEVELOPMENT OF THE EGO-COMPLEX: EGO-IDEAL AND SHADOW

From a structural perspective, it seems appropriate to link the imaginary companion with the Freudian ego-ideal. (In Jungian terms this would be the "light" shadow, a figure carrying the subject's repressed unconscious aspirations.) Our illustration of the effect of such an introject on the ego-complex can be seen if we return to the fate of "Marecage." As we mentioned earlier, Piaget has provided us with a series of observations spanning the Preschool Period, in which Jacqueline created symbolic narratives with "Marecage" as the protagonist. We can now usefully group two of these observations under the headings "Ego-Ideal" and "Shadow".

Ego-Ideal

At 4;6 the "Marecage" cycle helped J. not to mind being laughed at, and being frightened when she thought she was lost. The two scenes were reproduced in detail, with Marecage as character. (Piaget 1962: 133)

Shadow

J., at 4;6(23), was walking on a steep mountain-road: "Mind that loose stone." "Marecage (obs. 83) once trod on a stone, you know, and didn't take care, and she slipped and hurt herself badly." (ibid.: 134)

Additional observations of "Marecage" presented by Piaget clearly demonstrate what Jung would call the compensatory functions of this imaginary companion (ibid.: 133–5).

DEVELOPMENT OF PEER RELATIONSHIPS

In parallel to Jacqueline's developing relation with her invisible friend, we find an advance in her capacity for social relationships with her peers. Although exploration and play with the parents continues during this stage and remains crucial to the development of a flexible creative process, interaction with other children now increases: "Mothers were children's major play partners through thirty-six months; at forty-eight months children played about equally with mothers and other children (i.e. siblings and other child playmates)" (Haight and Miller 1993: 38).

At the completion of Early Childhood, however, Jacqueline's social play with her sister is still undifferentiated. That is, she can engage without anxiety in social play with this important peer only so long as the roles they take up are identical. (For instance, she has them play at being two sisters reading books or flying in an airplane.) Later, by the end of the Preschool Period, that is, when Jacqueline is about to enter school, she is capable of developing complementary roles in complex games with her peers.

As is to be expected, the content of the symbolic narratives in these episodes of sociodramatic play derives from the child's everyday world. A Jungian way to say this is that during peer exploration and play of this stage, *personal peer-complexes* are being constructed. These peer-complexes become the foundation stones for social attitudes, which are refined through exploration and play with classmates during Middle Childhood. The adaptive significance of developing such internalized structures will not be lost on parents, teachers, and therapists dealing with school-age children who have not been able to achieve this level of social interiority.

DEVELOPMENT OF THE EGO-FUNCTIONS: INTUITION

According to Jung's typology of ego-functions as elaborated in *Psychological Types* (1921 [1974a]), the ego adapts to reality by means of four "functions of consciousness," thinking, feeling, sensation, and intuition. Intuition is the ego-function which uses the unconscious to mediate perceptions of subjective or objective data. Intuition draws upon the archetypes to focus on the *possibilities* in a given situation. It is the source of the individual's "lucky hunch," the origin of which cannot exactly be explained, because a magical omniscience in the unconscious has been tapped into. When we focus on what is unknown, we bring Intuition into play: "Whenever you have to deal with strange conditions where you have no established values or established concepts, you will depend on that faculty of intuition" (CW 18: 25–6,15).

In L. H. Stewart's theory of the development of the ego-function Intuition, *the Unknown* is that life stimulus which combines with the primordial image, *the Abyss*, to form a symbol which is the efficient cause of the innate affect Fear–Terror (see Table 3, Column 5). (This is perhaps the earliest intuition of the world, the sense a child gets, beyond any direct experience to support it, of the potential danger of the world.) Fear, in other words, is the building block for the development of Intuition.

A good illustration of the differentiation of ego-function Intuition during the Preschool Period consists of excerpts from the confrontation Jung's patient Anna (CW 17: 1–79,8–35) made with the Unknown. This came in the midst of her speculations concerning the origin of babies. In the course of her efforts to understand where babies come from, the primal image of the Abyss and its compensatory image, the Holy Mountain, were evoked. Fear, a characteristic innate affect, accompanies these images. Even the life-giving womb was intuited as a terrifying abyss in which the child could still be lost.

Anna

Anna's confrontation with the unknown began when she was three years old.

> For some time she had been in the habit of asking her mother whether she would ever have a real live doll, a baby brother, which naturally gave rise to the question of where babies come from. As such questions were asked quite spontaneously and unobtrusively, the parents attached no significance to them, but responded to them as lightly as the child herself seemed to ask them. Thus one day she was told the pretty story that children are brought by the stork. Anna had already heard somewhere a slightly more serious version, namely that children are little angels who live in heaven and are then brought down by the said stork. This theory seems to have become the point of departure for the little one's investigating activities. (CW 17: 6,9)

Anna has the following conversation with her grandmother.

> "Granny, why are your eyes so dim?"
> "Because I am old."

"But you will become young again?"
"Oh dear, no, I shall become older and older, and then I shall die."
"And what then?"
"Then I shall be an angel."
"And then you will be a baby again." (ibid.: 5,9)

Jung notes that this conversation results in Anna's first answer to her question.

The child found here a welcome opportunity for the provisional solution of a problem ... From the conversation with the grandmother it could be seen that this theory was capable of wide application; for it solved in a comforting manner not only the painful thought of dying, but at the same time the riddle of where children come from. Anna seemed to be saying to herself: "When somebody dies [Villainy] he becomes an angel, and then he becomes a child [Villainy nullified]" ... In this simple conception there lie the seeds of the reincarnation theory, which, as we know, is still alive today in millions of human beings. (ibid.: 6,9–10)

As Jung understands, the instrument used by Anna is a symbolic narrative [my interpolations], which carries the philosophic "seeds of the reincarnation theory."
    Anna is four years old when her baby brother is born.

Anna threw a rapid glance at her rather wan-looking mother and then displayed something like a mixture of embarrassment and suspicion, as if thinking, "What's going to happen now?" She evinced hardly any pleasure at the sight of the new arrival, so that the cool reception she gave it caused general disappointment. For the rest of the morning she kept very noticeably away from the mother; this was the more striking, as normally she was always hanging around her. But once, when her mother was alone, she ran into the room, flung her arms round her neck and whispered hurriedly, "Aren't you going to die now?" (ibid.: 10,11)

Jung interprets Anna's unsettling behavior toward her mother as arising out of the dilemma the child's fantasy is up against:

Something of the conflict in the child's soul is now revealed to us. The stork theory had obviously never caught on properly, but the fruitful rebirth hypothesis undoubtedly had, according to which a person helps a child into life by dying. Mama ought therefore to die ... Mama did not die. With this happy issue, however, the rebirth theory received a severe setback. How was it now possible to explain little brother's birth and the origins of children in general? There still remained the stork theory, which, though never expressly rejected, had been implicitly waived in favour of the rebirth hypothesis. The next attempts at explanation unfortunately remained hidden from the parents, as the child went to stay with her grandmother for a few weeks. From the latter's report, however, it appears that the stork theory was much discussed, there being of course a tacit agreement to support it. (ibid.: 11,11–12)

When Anna returns home from her grandmother's, her mistrust of her parents is apparent.

Mother: "Come, we'll go into the garden."
Anna: "You're lying to me. Watch out if you're not telling the truth."
Mother: "What are you thinking of? Of course I'm telling the truth."
Anna: "No, you're not telling the truth."
Mother: "You'll soon see whether I'm telling the truth: we are going into the garden this minute."
Anna: "Is that true? You're quite sure it's true? You're not lying?" (ibid.: 15,14)

In spite of her mother's reassurances, Anna develops nocturnal and daytime *fears*.

We should mention that the Messina earthquake had just occurred, and this event was much discussed at the table. Anna was extraordinarily interested in everything to do with it, getting her grandmother to tell her over and over again how the earth shook and the houses tumbled down and how many people lost their lives. That was the beginning of the nocturnal fears; she could not be left alone, her mother had to go to her and stay with her, otherwise she was afraid that the earthquake would come and the house fall in and kill her. By day, too, she was intensely occupied with such thoughts; when out walking with her mother she would pester her with such questions as "Will the house be standing when we get home? Will Papa still be alive? Are you sure there's no earthquake at home?" At every stone in the road she would ask if it was from the earthquake. A house under construction was a house destroyed by the earthquake, and so on. Finally she used to cry out at night that the earthquake was coming, she could hear it rumbling. Every evening she had to be solemnly promised that no earthquake would come. (ibid.: 19,16–17)

The parents' mystifying behaviors (among them, the mother's remaining alive) have served as the life stimulus for a fantasy exploration of the Unknown. Once the primal image, the "Abyss," i.e. "earthquakes," is constellated, the affect Fear–Terror is evoked with it, and the child can voice her fears. The parents' attempts to reassure Anna go awry.

> Various ways of calming her were tried, for instance she was told that earthquakes only occur where there are volcanoes. But then she had to be satisfied that the mountains surrounding the town were not volcanoes. This reasoning gradually led the child to an intense and, at her age, unnatural craving for knowledge, until finally all the geological pictures and atlases had to be fetched from her father's library. For hours she would rummage through them looking for pictures of volcanoes and earthquakes, and asking endless questions. (ibid.: 19,17)

It is likely that the "volcano" was constellated, and then seized upon by Anna, in part because it carries an image compensatory to that of the Abyss. Archetypally, a volcano is an image of the "Holy Mountain," whose fiery outbursts are purposive, in contrast to the dizzying, chaotic depths of the Abyss. Nevertheless, the fact that the mountain appears in the form of a "volcano" suggests a disintegrating disturbance within the developmental process we are tracing. (The child is beginning to realize that the sacred womb has in fact erupted a child.) At this juncture the parents decide that "the mother ought to tell the child the truth about her little brother at the first favourable opportunity." This opportunity presented itself soon afterward:

> Anna again inquired about the stork. Her mother told her that the story of the stork was not true, but that Freddie grew inside his mother as the flower grows out of the earth. At first he was very little, and then he grew bigger and bigger like a plant. The child listened attentively without the least surprise and then asked:
> "But did he come all by himself?"
> "Yes."
> "But he can't walk yet!"
> At this point she interrupted herself and exclaimed, "No, I know the stork brought him down from heaven!" Then, before the mother could answer her questions, she dropped the subject and again asked to see pictures of volcanoes. (ibid.: 22,17–18)

The helpful effects of this demystification by the mother soon became evident: "The evening following this conversation was calm" (ibid.: 18). What finally seemed to have resolved Anna's fears, however, was a *symbolic narrative* in which an "imaginary brother" played the central role.

> For some three months the children had been spinning a stereotyped fantasy of a "big brother" who knew everything, could do everything,

and had everything. He had been to all places where they had not been, was allowed to do all the things they were not allowed to do, was the owner of enormous cows, horses, sheep, dogs, etc. Each of them has such a big brother. The source of this fantasy is not far to seek: its model is the father, who seems to be rather like a brother to Mama. So the children too must have an equally powerful brother. This brother is very brave, he is at present in dangerous Italy and lives in an impossibly fragile house which does not fall down. For the child this is an important wish-fulfilment: the earthquake is no longer dangerous. In consequence the fear and anxiety were banished and did not return. The fear of earthquakes now entirely disappeared ... Even the photograph of a volcanic eruption no longer held any attraction for her. (ibid.: 29,20)

In summary, Anna was a child who suffered a temporary disturbance in the differentiation of the ego-function Intuition as a consequence of her parents' *mystifying* behaviors. This disturbance is manifested in the symbolic image of the Abyss, which in turn is associated with the destructiveness of the earthquake and the volcano. This last, however, is actually a compensatory image from the unconscious concealing the idea of the Holy Mountain, carrying a god's will and not only chaotic destruction. This sacralization of course did not prevent and may even have enhanced the activation of the innate affect Fear, for a god is terrible as well as loving. When the parents intervene by telling Anna the realistic truth about the origin of a baby like her brother Freddie, new fantasy structures appear that provide a trusting foundation for a return to parent–child relatedness. It is reasonable to assume that the symbolic narrative that emerges (with imaginary "big brother" as hero), enabled Anna to return to her normal developmental pathway.

6

The Social Realm in Middle Childhood

The city is a maternal symbol, a woman who harbours the inhabitants
in herself like children.
——C. G. Jung, *Symbols of Transformation*

The stage we analyze in this chapter, which is referred to by developmental psychologists as Middle Childhood, extends from approximately
the sixth year through the eleventh year of life. Psychoanalysts refer to
it as the Latency Period, characterized not by any struggle with sexuality
but instead what Erik Erikson refers to in near-Adlerian terms as a crisis
of Industry versus Inferiority. Erich Neumann, however, has described it
more colorfully in Jungian archetypal terms as the Solar-Warlike stage,
and indeed many warlike games emerge at this time. The mode of the
symbolic function which emerges at the beginning of this stage is the
social realm, which brings to life identifications with the deeds of *action*
heroes and heroines, present and past, real and fictional, who serve as
role models in the struggle for the ego's ascendancy. The new instrument
for the assimilation of experience at this stage is the *symbolic community*.

The emergence of this symbolic mode and instrument exhibits the
same invariant sequence in the differentiation of consciousness that we
have observed at the beginning of Infancy, Early Childhood, and the
Preschool Period.

THE SOCIAL REALM

In Western societies, the symbolic developmental transformation which
marks, at one and the same time, the completion of the Preschool Period
and the beginning of Middle Childhood usually coincides with the child's
entry into elementary school. One study of the influence of parents on
the child's transition to school drew the following conclusions: "Results
indicated that the length of time in [parent–child] physical play was
favorably related to social adjustment in school" (Barth and Parke 1993:
173). It is reasonable to assume that other forms of social play and games

between parents and their children have similar effects, facilitating the child's successful adaptation to truly social functioning.

Our demonstration of the emergence of the social realm and the symbolic community will begin with observations of Piaget's subject, Jacqueline, which will provide living proof of how archetypal symbols provide an impetus to development, as it has been described by Jung:

> The marked predominance of mythological elements in the psyche of the child gives us a clear hint of the way the individual mind gradually develops out of the "collective mind" of early childhood, thus giving rise to the old theory of a state of perfect knowledge before and after individual existence. (*CW* 4: 520,225)

We continue with studies of children's sand play worlds by R. Bowyer (1970) by L. Jones (1982) and a survey by D. Cohen and S. A. McKeith (1991) of children's symbolic "countries."

Jacqueline

(1) Recognition of the Social Other

As the Preschool Period draws to its close, the child continues to believe in the universal or absolute nature of its own consciousness, which is centered in a definable ego at the center of that consciousness. Relativization of individual ego-consciousness occurs through "recognition" of the separate ego-consciousness of another, and that is the first step in the development of the symbolic process at the beginning of Middle Childhood. Through play, the child establishes a coordinated relationship between the newly differentiated other and self, thus forming a "realm" of two.

The following observation shows us that, as her Preschool Period draws to a close, Jacqueline indeed believes in the universality of her own consciousness.

> At 5;6(21) she was turning round on herself: "*This moves the grass. –* I don't see how. *– It's because I'm turning; then it turns too.*" (Piaget 1962: 259)

This reminds us of the infant's belief that if a movement of its body happens to coincide with the movement of an object, that the former is the "cause" of the latter. Two months later, however, Jacqueline begins to express doubts that her consciousness and that of her father are really the same.

> At 5;8(24) J. turned round faster and faster until she was giddy and then said to me: "*Can you feel it turning?*" – Why? – *Because I turned.*

Why don't we feel it when somebody else turns? – What do you think? – *Oh, I really can't find that out* (pause)." (ibid.)

Before continuing with Piaget's observation, let us recall what Jung has pointed out, that when one is faced with a question for which there is no conscious answer, as when Jacqueline exclaims, "Oh, I really can't find that out," the unconscious provides a symbolic reply:

> If, therefore, my cognitive process comes to a stop at one point or another this does not mean that the underlying psychological process has also stopped. Experience shows that it continues regardless ... Wherever the inquiring mind comes up against a darkness in which objects are only dimly discernible, it fills the gap with previous experience or, if these are lacking, with imaginative material, that is with archetypal or mythical material. (Jung 1976a: 327–8)

When Jacqueline can't fill the gap with previous experience, her attempt to answer the question, "Why don't we feel it when someone else turns?", takes a spontaneous, mythological detour. We continue with the observation of 5;8(24):

> "*It's 'hand.'* – What? *When I turn, it's 'hand' that makes the air turn, and when you turn very fast, it flies, everything flies, 'hand' flies into the air. You see, when I do that* (gesture of moving the air with her hand), *the air comes, and when I do that* (pushing away), *it goes away. 'Hand' makes the air rise.* – Then why do you say it doesn't turn for me when you turn? – *It's blue 'hand,' it's your 'hand.'* – What does that mean? – ..." A moment later, spontaneously: "*I know what blue 'hand' and white 'hand' are. 'Hand' is when it moves. Blue 'hand' is when it doesn't move. When I do that with my hand* (moving it), *I'm doing white 'hand,' and that moves the trees and the clouds and all the air, and when I do that* (gesture of raising something from the ground), *it raises the air and then it's all blue.* – And what is it that we can see now, blue 'hand' or white 'hand'? – (Looking at the sky) *It's white 'hand,' it's full of clouds. It's the air that has gone up, that's moving. And when you raise it, it's all blue and it doesn't move any more.*" Then she began to run, without speaking, turning round and said: "*Look at my hand (beating the air), I'm doing white 'hand,' it makes me run very fast. You're not moving, that's blue 'hand.' There* (pointing to my motionless arm), *you can't see anything. Now, look* (running and then stopping), *that's blue 'hand,' I'm not running now.*"(Piaget 1962: 259–60)

Jacqueline's attempt to answer her unanswerable question, therefore, appears in her turning to the mythologem of "blue hand" and "white hand." There is a lapse of seven months from the emergence of this mythical realm to Jacqueline's achievement of the new level of ego-consciousness she has been constructing.

> At 6;3(10) J. was whirling round as in the preceding observation but she no longer believed in the objective results: "*You can feel it going round, but things aren't really moving.*" (ibid.: 260)

Piaget points out that this differentiation corresponds at the "operational level" to the infant's construction of the permanent object at the "sensorimotor level." He summarizes the current developmental process as follows.

> In the case of "hand," on the contrary, in spite of the initial egocentrism of this preconcept, J. gradually succeeds in dissociating two distinct points of view as her thought begins to be socialised. She becomes aware of her own point of view, i.e., that of the subject whirling round and thus producing "white hand" (involving the movement of objects situated within its range) and the point of view of the adult observer, i.e., of the motionless subject who is in "blue hand," and who consequently cannot see anything turning. This co-ordination of viewpoints later enables her to abandon her subjective belief in the reality of movements provoked by her own activity. (ibid.: 261–2)

What he means is that through a new set of symbolic operations, Jacqueline now understands that she and her father actually experience different states of consciousness and that their separate, individual points of view are both available for coordination. "Hand" has become a social realm, within which father ("blue hand") and Jacqueline ("white hand") are contained cooperatively as inhabitants.

The above observation may also be understood as an *interpersonal* interaction between Jacqueline and her father that implies a new level of consciousness for Jacqueline. Her father's sympathy toward the rather obscure content of her fantasies would seem to ensure that the ability to operate with the aid of abstractions will reach an optimal level. I wish to suggest, however, another interpretation of this material, that emphasizes the symbolic, rather than logical, development involved.

In conversations with her parents during the three months before she discriminates what "hand" can and cannot do, Jacqueline has been discussing the origin of stones, the sun, the moon, ponds in the woods, light, water, and rain. During the month before the observation, she has been asking how air is made and making air herself.

> At 5;7(11): "*Can air be made? ... Can you make air?*" The same day: "*The air in the sky is blue, but the air by the house isn't blue. – That's right. – Then how do they make air? – I don't really know.*" The same evening:

"*But tell me really how they make air.*" At 5;7(22) she was by herself in a room, walking up and down and clapping her hands. Then she went into the next room, still clapping, and came up to me, saying: "*I'm making fresh air.*" (ibid.: 259)

This is a most creative synthesis! From the symbolic perspective, the events involving "white hand" and "blue hand" may be seen as belonging to the mythologem that Jung has referred to in *Mysterium Coniunctionis* as the discrimination and synthesis of psychic opposites: "white hand" seems to describe what Jung calls Luna or feminine consciousness – characterized by the color white, moving air, Eros – while "blue hand" refers to Sol, or masculine consciousness – color blue, still air, Logos or *pneuma*, which for Jacqueline is more uncanny, more unconscious. Together they combine to make "fresh" air, an alchemical image of *coniunctio*. We might have expected that the masculine "blue hand" would be the more dynamic, the source of air or wind in motion. It is in fact, however, the hermaphroditism of having *both* principles "at hand" that is likely to be responsible for the energy at the heart of Jacqueline's conception of herself as being able to "make" fresh air.

But we have historical evidence for these hermaphroditic ideas: namely, it is a very universal idea that the creator of the world was a hermaphroditic being. Almost every mythology contained this idea of the original being – that it created itself by means of itself, being both father and mother ... Therefore, this concept of the wind, or the spirit, is uncertain in its character: it can be either masculine or feminine. (Jung 1988: 1076)

Thus, "blue hand" and "white hand" may be viewed as the masculine and feminine elements of a developmental totality, a symbol of the alchemical creativity of mind itself in the latency age child. Furthermore, one month before this observation Jacqueline had come to the conclusion that clouds, which are elements of "white hand," are water and are made by the sky. Both wind and water are not only symbols for the creativity of the life-spirit, they are also basic "elements" in natural philosophies around the world.

Earth is not moving, not spirit, but wind and water are. In astrology, for instance, the sign for Aquarius (a spiritual sign) has been taken from the Egyptian sign for water. Originally it had a denser part and also a more ethereal part, the upper part being the more spiritual. (Jung 1984: 222)

Through this archetypal interpretation of "white hand" and "blue hand" we gain a deeper understanding of how creative fantasy serves to motivate symbolic development. If we interpret this archetypal image of air-making as simultaneously a differentiation and a conjunction of cosmic opposites, then we can expect a "birth" as the issue of their coming together. This new entity appears in the ego's "recognition" of the self, which will occur for Jacqueline both on the same day and one month later (see later in this chapter).

Another development occurring at this stage is the explanatory function of language, which also contributes to the child's realization of the relativity of its own ego-consciousness and may actually attest to the power of that realization.

> At about the age of seven the child becomes capable of cooperation because he no longer confuses his own point of view with that of others. He is able both to dissociate his point of view from that of others and to coordinate these different points of view. This is apparent from conversations among children. True discussions are now possible in that the children show comprehension with respect to the other's point of view and a search for justification or proof with respect to their own statements. Explanations between children develop on the plane of thought and not just on the level of material action. (Piaget 1967: 39)

This may explain the mounting complexity of children's ways of accounting for each other's experience in their conversations at this stage. When consciousness was absolute there was no need for explanations.

(2) Dawning Awareness of the Social Self

The new aspects of self which the child discovers at this juncture are interrelated – self as member both of a "peer" community and of a wider, "school and city" community. Jacqueline's recognition of herself as "peer" is evident in the following observation of three friends, one of which is her imaginary companion, "Marecage."

> At 5;8(24): "*I've got two friends, Marecage and Julia. Marecage has two friends, Julia and Jacqueline. Julia has two friends, Marecage and Jacqueline. That makes three little friends.*" (Piaget 1962: 232)

In this observation, we can see how the transition from invisible to visible friends is made. Soon "Marecage" will disappear from Jacqueline's conscious life, interiorized as Ego-Ideal/Shadow, even as her friendship with her real-life friend Julia will blossom. This observation occurred on the same day as "hand" and one month before the following dream, which clearly expresses Jacqueline's dawning "recognition" of herself as a "student" who is "alone" only when she is not keeping up with her peers.

At 5;9(24): "*I dreamt I was going to school all by myself in the tram* (she laughed with pleasure at this idea). *But I missed the tram and walked, all alone* (more laughter) [nuclear dyad 1]. *I was late, and the mistress sent me away, and I walked home all by myself* [nuclear dyad 2]." (ibid.: 178)

Jacqueline's laughter is generated not only by the mischievous elements in the dream, but also by her "recognition" of a new sense of self as apart from her peers. The interpolations placed in the observation by myself point to the dyads involved and are there to show that the plot structure of the dream is characteristic of the advance in fantasy-narrative at the beginning of Middle Childhood.

At the beginning of the Preschool Period the characteristic fantasy narrative generally has only one plot structure or nuclear dyad, which usually takes the form of "lack" – "lack liquidated" or "villainy" – "villainy nullified." At the beginning of Middle Childhood, there emerges a more complicated plot structure consisting of two nuclear dyads (Botvin and Sutton-Smith 1977). In the above dream, Jacqueline "liquidates" the "lack" of a tram by an adventurous walk to school and "nullifies" the teacher's "villainy" by a confident walk home. With a symbolic community as the firm fantasy base for her explorations, she is now ready to venture forth into her real community. The emergence of two dyads at this juncture is another indication of the shift in awareness from absolute consciousness – one dyad, to the relativity of consciousness – two dyads.

Eventually symbolic transformation at the beginning of Middle Childhood leads to a new world-relationship.

(3) Construction of a Social World View

At this point the child possesses a new instrument for the assimilation of experience in the form of the symbolic community. The next step in the symbolic developmental transformation of Middle Childhood is taken when, as at other stages of development, the child applies this new instrument to create a genuinely new world view. Thus, a few months after the "student" dream, Jacqueline discovers a symbolic "village" in her individual play.

Later, it was a whole village, "*Ventichon*" that gradually grew up [note that "Vent" in French means wind]. J.'s whole life was connected with this place and its inhabitants. Reproduction of reality was the main interest, but elements of compensation could be observed ("*At Ventichon they drink a whole glass of water*" and not just a little in the bottom of a glass), and also protective transpositions: the inhabitants had a special costume (a veil over the face to protect them from adult indiscretions) and certain passwords: "*Ye tenn*," when going into a house (they were kept out if they pronounced it badly), "*to-to-to*" when going up certain stairs, etc. (Piaget 1962: 137)

Private languages and secret passwords, perennial emblems of the latency age child's secret club, become during this stage essential elements in the child's vernacular. Piaget also described the symbolic communities discovered by Lucienne and Laurent (ibid.: 140).

In a study of the development of the symbolic play of eight- to ten-year-old children, using the Lowenfeld World Technique, R. Bowyer identified the following pattern as characteristic of this age group.

There is now one scene, e.g. a town or village – but with stratification that is not quite unified or interdependent – one level for animals, carefully fenced in rows of fields – one level for the street and traffic – and another row of buildings. (Bowyer 1970: 29)

These findings were confirmed and elaborated in L. Jones's developmental study of children's Sand Worlds during Middle Childhood.

Clear human neighborhoods become characteristic and clear human and animal dyads remain so. Implied and clear human families, clear animal families, and implied animal communities may be significant to this stage. (Jones 1982: 178)

In both these studies, "Town," "Village," "Neighborhoods," and "Communities" serve as symbolic collectives that seem to correspond to Jacqueline's "Ventichon."

In *The Development of Imagination*, D. Cohen and S. A. MacKeith (1991) present their collection of no less than fifty-seven "paracosms," which is the term they have invented to refer to the "spontaneous imaginary worlds of children." Of these imaginary "countries," 72 percent were discovered and elaborated by children between seven and twelve years of age, i.e. in the stage of Middle Childhood. These paracosms are, in my judgment, examples of social "realms," elaborated in the course of normal symbolic development at this stage. The particular types of symbolic communities within this constellation are individually variable: *Heroines All* is set in an imaginary school; *Coneland* has a mythical setting; *Mohawks and Wolves* is set on an island; *Awentishland* and *Rull* are the imaginary countries of two playmates. Paracosms formed an integral part of the child's life throughout Middle Childhood and on occasion continued into Early Adolescence.

Team sports also begin to develop during Middle Childhood because the child now has a symbolic "team" image upon which a personal, feeling-toned, team-complex can be constructed.

INTERIORIZATION: IMAGINARY COMPANION TO SOCIAL REALM

The developmental dialectic between archetypal affects of Interest–curiosity/exploration and Joy–play/fantasy offers the mechanism of interiorization of the symbolic process, which continues on its seamless course during the Preschool Period, taking both social and individual byways. In the following examples, it is easy to see how the child's affective "interests" in the everyday world provide the content of the social and individual play.

The Social Pathway

At the completion of Early Childhood, social play with peers is particularly bound by its content: "At 3;9(2) J. said to L.: '*Let's be two sisters reading a book, shall we?*' and both of them sat down (L. was 1;4) and each looked at a book" (Piaget 1962: 138). Two months later, at 3;11(26), at the time when Jacqueline encounters the "aseau," she begins to differentiate roles and dissociate form and content by trying to arrange a shop game with her sister, but treats her like a doll (ibid.). Just six months later, at 4;5(13), Jacqueline's active role playing has become much more flexible, when she is able to arrange parts with her sister, no longer treating her like a doll (ibid.: 139); it exhibits further dissociation of form and content in achieving a life of its own, and, in this regard, is comparable to the previous observations of "Miss Jerli" and "Marceline" during their interiorization as symbolic capacities in Early Childhood (Chapter 4). In a final observation from this stage, Jacqueline demonstrates that role playing is now a symbolic form dissociated from its content and entirely under her socialized ego's control: "At 4;7(23), when J. was playing with a girl of ten, she adapted herself perfectly to all her games of meals, families, etc. ..." (ibid.). When social role play is interiorized at the completion of the Preschool Period, it becomes a basis for the emergence of the new elements of the symbolic process during Middle Childhood, the social realm and the symbolic community.

Individual Pathway

In the following observations, Jacqueline is seen actively constructing a personally relevant social community on the already constellated symbolic foundation of social role play.

From about 5;6 onwards, J. spent her time organising scenes dealing with families, education, weddings, etc., with her dolls, but also making houses, gardens, an often furniture. At 6;5(12), using interlocking bricks and rods she built a big house, a stable and a woodshed, surrounded by a garden, with paths and avenues. Her dolls continually walked about and held conversations but she also took care that the material constructions should be exact and true to life. (ibid.: 137)

Many other examples of interiorization in the individual pathway abound throughout Piaget's *Play, Dreams and Imitation in Childhood*.

DREAMS, THOUGHTS, NAMES

The interiorization of the symbolic process during the Preschool Period is also evident in dreams, thoughts, and names.

Dreams

At the beginning of Early Childhood, dreams are still perceived as real events occurring in the room at night. By the beginning of the Preschool Period, dreams have become imaginary events that occur at night in the circumambient air, that is, they are experienced as pictures external to the child, like living illustrated storybooks. By the end of this stage and the beginning of Middle Childhood, dreams are finally located as "in one's head." It is at this time that these involuntary nocturnal fantasies begin to show a more definite collective structure.

Thoughts

Near the end of the Preschool Period, thoughts are still conceived to originate in the body. At 6;7(4), Jacqueline finds ideas in her "tummy," and her "mouth" helps her to think (ibid.: 256). Interiorization is not complete until thoughts are located "in the head" and simple "reflection" emerges.

> Reflection is nothing other than internal deliberation, that is to say, a discussion which is conducted with oneself just as it might be conducted with real interlocutors or opponents. One could then say that reflection is internalized social discussion (just as thought itself presupposes internalized language). (Piaget 1967: 40–1)

The internal potential space that has been constructed, to formulate this development in the language not just of Piaget but also that of Winnicott, may be filled with social daydreams that alternate in content between real and symbolic communities.

Names

At the beginning of the Preschool Period, names are assumed to be located in their objects. At 3;6(7), when asked where names are, Jacqueline points to the world around her. The name of a spider is in its nest. At the completion of this stage, on the other hand, names and the operation of naming are subjective phenomena. At 6;9(15), Jacqueline does not even remember her earlier view that the names were in the things themselves and laughs at such childishness when reminded of it. It is obvious to her now that you can't see names, you *know* them. From the perspective we have been following in this chapter, they have become interiorized. (The specific observations of dreams, thoughts, and names can be found in Piaget 1962: 255–6.)

DEVELOPMENT OF THE EGO-COMPLEX

Action Heroes and Heroines

The "hero" and "heroine" are according to Jung, inborn "images," that is, empty archetypal forms, which, when constellated into the field of consciousness, attain phenomenal presentation as compelling symbols, gathering the ego's interest by drawing upon the available interesting conscious representations of hero-figures that abound in children's stories and games. As these traditional sources attest, the hero or heroine is a symbol of the greatest value that we recognize.

> The hero is always the embodiment of man's highest and the most powerful aspiration, or of what this aspiration ought ideally to be and what he would most gladly realize. It is therefore of importance what kind of fantasy constitutes the hero-motif. (*CW* 10: 100,47–8)

During the development of the ego-complex, it is the increasing activity of the ego and the intensity of its libido that stimulates the unconscious to form symbols of heroes or heroines. They are appropriate to the stage of Middle Childhood because they are images of the transcendent capacity to get things done in a social context, and, in so doing, to overcome failure to live up to the socialized ego-ideal. The symbols of heroic figures both condition and represent the urge and the compulsion to self-realization (see Henderson 1964: 110–28). The most common symbolic exponent of the developing ego during Middle Childhood is the *action hero* or *heroine*. The classical action hero is Heracles, with his twelve labors, but he is also Robin Hood, Superman, and Captain Marvel. Contemporary action heroines range from the Wonder Woman of my generation to the contemporary slayer of vampires, TV's Buffy (Dougherty 1998), a feminine creation. In Joseph Campbell's (1956) classification of types of hero, the action hero figures are examples of the hero or heroine as Warrior. Heroes and Heroines always live in socially sophisticated mythical realms, for instance, Batman lives in Gotham.

The task of the hero or heroine, as dreams, myths, fairytales, and popular culture perennially declare, is the fight with evil, typically in the form of the dragon. Evil is usually personified as a shape-shifting demonic trickster, protean in its manifestations, as the characters in *Batman* reveal – Cat Woman, the Joker, etc. Presumably the trickster represents an earlier stage of development toward which the ego must remain suspiciously vigilant less regression to less socialized forms of behavior assume ascendancy. On the other hand, the chance to do battle with the regressive tendencies of the unconscious, the "dragon" the hero must slay, is an opportunity for the ego to display its socialized mastery of primitive yearnings.

> The activity of the hero in the fight with the dragon is of the acting, willing, and discriminating ego which, no longer fascinated and overpowered, and abandoning its youthful attitude of passive defenses, seeks out the danger, performs new and extraordinary deeds, and battles its way to victory. (Neumann 1954: 318)

For the child entering Middle Childhood, the "dragon" is both the spirit of the regressive pull to home and family and the emerging shadow of fear of school, neighborhood, and community: "The conquest of fear is therefore the essential characteristic of the ego-hero who dares the evolutionary leap to the next stage ..." (ibid.: 312). The symbolic image works because it "always brings with it a certain influence or power by virtue of which it either exercises a numinous or fascinating effect, or impels to action" (CW 7: 109,70). The libidinal charge of hero and heroine "symbols" give hope to all who inhabit the school and community playgrounds. Finally, in mythology "the birth of the hero or the symbolic rebirth coincides with sunrise, for the growth of the personality is synonymous with an increase of self-consciousness" (CW 17: 318,184).

The stories told by children from age four to twelve follow a progression from fear and flight to confrontation and dominance, which appears to portray the development and strengthening of the ego-complex during Middle Childhood.

> There is a progression from a first stage, where the protagonist is overwhelmed with fear before a threatening monster (ages four-to-five); to a second stage, where he tries to run away or throw something at the monster (ages six-to-seven); to a third stage, where he confronts the monster and nullifies it temporarily by kicking it out the window or by some other action (ages eight-to-nine); and a fourth stage, where the central character permanently does away with the threat and ends up stronger than at the beginning of the story (ages ten-to-eleven). Like the hero tales in folklore, the protagonist in these level four stories is generally transformed to a higher status, such as kingship, toward the end of the tale" (Abrams and Sutton-Smith 1977: 36–7)

But if the monster of regressive unconsciousness is, in the end, finally defeated, the trickster is not. Rather, part of social development is the healthy integration of the trickster capacity. In parallel with the above progressive series the child's development is also reflected in the stages of the *trickster* tale, which clearly show a sophistication of this originally primitive figure:

> At five years of age there is ... one tale type that could be called the *stage of physical clumsiness*. The six-to-seven year-olds relate a slightly more advanced slapstick clown story, which we call the *stage of moronic defeat*. At around seven-to-eight years, there emerges a *stage of the unsuccessful trickster*; where the use of trickery by the protagonist makes its appearance. The *stage of the successful trickster* ... seems to occur between nine and eleven years of age, but may occur earlier ... (ibid.: 38–9)

The Literature of Middle Childhood

J. A. Appleyard has made a rough typology of what seven- to twelve-year-old-children read: (1) they read factual books to discover information about the world they live in and (2) virtually all of the fiction they read is what can be loosely be called adventure. Although Appleyard assumes that the interest in heroes and heroines displayed by children in Middle Childhood is solely due to sociocultural influences, he does not fail to acknowledge the relevance to social development.

> Like the whole enterprise of learning one's way in the adult world (the journey, after all, is the major motif of romance), it involves the fundamental question of whether a child will turn out to be competent and therefore successful or defeated and fearful of evil forces. The continually reenacted victory of the heroes and heroines of juvenile narratives reassures the young reader that the adventure of traveling into the world and meeting its challenges can have a happy ending. (Appleyard 1990: 63)

A. H. Dyson has described the uses children in elementary school make, when given the opportunity, of Greek myths and superhero images drawn from popular culture to compose and enact stories within the classroom (which is teacher-governed) and playground (which is peer-governed). Dyson describes the children's use of these cultural symbols as material for story construction and social affiliation. Considering that in the classroom the children had a wealth of literature to choose from, Dyson thought it significant that it was most often the Greek myths that found their way to the playground. Here is her explanation for the lasting power of these cultural archetypes for children raised in the West:

Like the superhero stories, the Greek myths offer consistent characters whose qualities and exploits become familiar as they appear and reappear in story after story. Moreover, these stories touch directly on themes central to children's imaginations and their desires ... Good guys and bad guys, great quarrels, and grand rescues, marriage, births, and deaths – all are powerful playground fare. This may account for the ease with which the superheroes and the family dramatists took to this material, for their assumptions that they could play with it. (Dyson 1996: 493)

Both the Appleyard and Dyson studies point to the dialectic relation between the everyday social world and the social realms of heroes and heroines. Neither, however, acknowledge the part played by the inborn archetypal image of the action hero or heroine, which this author feels is the actual basis for the child's reading and playground interests.

Construction of "Community" as Symbol and Complex

As we mentioned earlier in this chapter, Piaget records over a five-month period, from 6;7(4) to 7;0(7), Jacqueline's differentiation and development of her symbolic community, "Ventichon" (Piaget 1962: 137–8). In these observations the dialectic between Jacqueline's world of everyday reality and the imaginal realm, that is between exploration and play, is apparent. Through this dialectical process Jacqueline is constructing a real community on a symbolic foundation. That it takes the form of architectural complexes suggests the structuring and differentiation of the complexes of her own psyche, which are increasingly serving her socialization.

As Piaget's son, Laurent, entered Middle Childhood, he also discovered a social realm: "T. [Laurent] made himself a country called 'Six-Twenty Balls,' which underwent differentiation and development" (ibid.: 140–2). Shortly after discovering "Six-Twenty Balls," Laurent became interested in cartography, both mythical and real.

But from the age of seven onwards, T., after drawing the various aspects of Six-Twenty Balls, began to make maps of the country. Its name became Siwimbal, and it had in it towns called Bergai, Mir, Blanker, Sogar, etc. Numerous adventures took place (journeys, animal stories) and T. peopled Bergai with schoolchildren like himself with whom he had imaginary relations. (ibid.: 140)

We are immediately reminded of the "paracosms" described by Cohen and McKeith. A year later, we find Laurent is continuing the dialectic between symbolic and realistic maps, but treating the former as if they were real countries.

After the age of eight T. eliminated the imaginary characters, but put increased care and ingenuity into the drawings of his maps, and into extending Siwimbal. He made cartographic models with as much attention to detail as though they were maps of real countries, in which he was beginning to be interested. (ibid.: 141)

Then, Laurent creates a symbolic community in which its inhabitants are drawn from real life, but are owners of districts in the fantasy country. These districts have been introduced into Siwimbal from realistic maps.

At 8;2 and 8;3 he divided his time during an illness between making the most complete planispheres, and drawing in detail districts of Siwimbal. In addition he distributed to his sisters and friends particular districts of the country which had varied climates (a bathing resort with a tropical climate to one, a piece of arctic territory to others, and so on), and gave detailed descriptions of them by transposition of those parts of the globe that he was then actually studying with intense interest. (ibid.)

In the next observation, another step is taken toward the creation of real countries on the symbolic base of Siwimbal.

Later on, at about the age of nine, their place was taken by real maps, though there were occasional returns to the imaginary ones. But a curious transitional stage occurred, in which his drawings were very exact from the point of view of physical geography, but in which the frontiers were changed, e.g., Switzerland included part of northern Italy and a corridor running along the Rhone down to the Mediterranean. Germany was reduced to its simplest form, and so on. (ibid.)

We note here that the last aspect of the mythical realm to be interiorized, so that realistic countries may supervene in Laurent's preoocupations, are their borders. Finally, when Laurent was ten years old, "the maps became quite objective." This indicates the degree to which Laurent, as he nears the completion of Middle Childhood, has, like his sister, constructed a real, feeling-toned community, that is a fully operational social complex constructed on the symbolic foundation we have already traced.

Of course, at the new level of social interaction with classmates, teachers, and adults in the real community of Middle Childhood, every affective event becomes a complex. Thus "peer," "teacher," and "member of the community" are feeling-toned social complexes which during this stage are constructed, differentiated, hierarchically integrated, and reciprocally assimilated alongside the original "family" and the current "symbolic community" complexes.

Will

The last psychological development of Middle Childhood we will examine in this chapter is that of the *will*. Will, the capacity to deploy libido in the ego's service, is one of the key dynamic factors that determine human behavior. There are, however, different definitions of this psychological phenomenon, which in turn correlate with different views as to its ontogenesis.

Erikson considers will as one virtue in a developmental series of attained psychological virtues. He associates will with certain qualities of human ego-strength. He defines will as follows:

> Will, therefore, is the unbroken determination to exercise free choice as well as self-restraint, in spite of the unavoidable experience of shame and doubts in infancy. Will is the basis for the acceptance of law and necessity, and it is rooted in the judiciousness of parents guided by the spirit of law. (Erikson 1964: 119)

Erikson assigns the developmental rudiments of will to that early stage of childhood development that is characterized by the crisis of confidence in self that he calls Autonomy versus Shame or Doubt.

> It is during the second and third year that the child must yield to newcomers. It is now the task of judicious parenthood to honor the privileges of the strong and yet protect the rights of the weak. It will gradually grant a measure of self-control to the child who learns to control willfulness, to offer willingness, and to exchange good will. (ibid.)

Erikson identifies Law as the social institution which guides parents in their task of judiciousness. I believe that the ego strength that Erikson considers the norm in latency, *industriousness*, also requires activity of the will.

Piaget, focusing on the development of mental capacities, compares the equilibria achieved in thought and feeling during Middle Childhood: "The mental instruments which will facilitate logical and moral coordination are the operation in the field of intelligence and the will in the field of affectivity" (Piaget 1967: 41). Thus, he defines the will as a regulator of energy in the field of autonomous moral feelings. This explains his view that the will is a late-appearing function of the ego that develops during Middle Childhood.

> Thus, affectivity from, seven to twelve years is characterized by the appearance of new moral feelings and, above all, by an organization

of will, which culminates in a better integration of the self and a more effective regulation of affective life. (ibid.: 54–5)

Piaget considers the social institution which conditions development of the will as "the game with rules," especially rules transmitted by older to younger children and from peer to peer.

Jung, interestingly, also conceives of the will in energic terms.

I regard the will as the amount of psychic energy at the disposal of consciousness. Volition would, accordingly, be an energic process that is released by conscious motivation ... The will is a psychological phenomenon that owes its existence to culture and moral education, but is largely lacking in the primitive mentality. (CW 6: 844,486)

Whereas Piaget limits the effect of the will to the moral sentiments, Jung considers the will capable of modifying, to a certain degree, *any* of the conscious functions of the ego.

Psychological functions are usually controlled by the will, or we hope they are, because we are afraid of everything that moves by itself. When the functions are controlled they can be excluded from use, they can be suppressed, they can be selected, they can be increased in intensity, they can be directed by will-power, by what we call intention. (CW 18: 27,16)

Although Jung does not specify a stage in which the development of the will is primary, he considers it a task of later childhood and youth.

It is of the greatest importance for the young person, who is still unadapted and has as yet achieved nothing, to shape his conscious ego as effectively as possible, that is, to educate his will. Unless he is a positive genius he cannot, indeed, should not, believe in anything active within him that is not identical with his will. He must feel himself a man of will, and may safely depreciate everything else in him and deem it subject to his will, for without this illusion he could not succeed in adapting himself socially. (CW 16: 109,50)

Jung conceives of the will itself as *regulated by reflection*; this correlates with Piaget's assignment of the beginning of reflection to Middle Childhood. Jung states above that the environmental influences which condition the development of the will are cultural and moral education.

Now if development has proceeded optimally and on time, the moral agencies ego-ideal and shadow were interiorized at the completion of the Preschool Period. With the development of the will in Middle Childhood, a new basis for psychic realization is established that permits a socialized moral imagination. A healthy dialectic between the shadow and the opposing will become the conditions for the actualization of socially responsible but also personally creative behavior during this stage.

> Seen from the one-sided point of view of the conscious attitude, the shadow is an inferior component of the personality and is consequently repressed through intensive resistance. But the repressed content must be made conscious so as to produce a tension of opposites, without which no forward movement is possible. The conscious mind is on top, the shadow underneath, and just as high always longs for low and hot for cold, so all consciousness, perhaps without being aware of it, seeks its unconscious opposite, lacking which it is doomed to stagnation, congestion, and ossification. Life is born only of the spark of opposites. (*CW* 7: 78,53–4)

In *The Marriage of Heaven and Hell*, William Blake (1977) refers to the "spark of opposites" in the following passage: "Without Contraries is no progression. Attraction and Repulsion, Reason and Energy, Love and Hate, are necesary to Human existence." In mythical projection this creative tension of opposites appears in the form of Lucifer's rebellion against God, a story which takes the deep dialectic of Middle Childhood to its ultimate extreme, as opposed aims within the Self, essential to all psychological creativity.

> The shadow and the opposing will are the necessary conditions for all actualization. An object that has no will of its own, capable, if need be, of opposing its creator, and with no qualities other than it's creator's, such an object has no independent existence and is incapable of ethical decision. At best it is just a piece of clock-work which the Creator has to wind up to make it function. Therefore Lucifer was perhaps the one who best understood the divine will struggling to create a world and who carried out that will most faithfully. For, by rebelling against God, he became the active principle of a creation which opposed to God a counter-will of its own. (*CW* 11: 290,196)

The danger in this willful vision of creative agency is the individual's tendency to *identify* with his willpower, "Where there's a will there's a way!", and, through this one-sidedness, to be cut off from the unconscious roots of his being, the healthy base. Symbolic development has to wrestle with this paradox from now on.

In summary, we can say that most psychological theories agree that the will is a measure of the free energy available to ego-consciousness, that it is capable of regulating all of the activities of ego-consciousness, that its first major phase of development occurs during Middle Childhood, that its development is conditioned by environmental influences, and that either an overdeveloped or underdeveloped will may be a source of psychological difficulties. Finally, will seems to be an image of the conscious appropriation of symbolic development itself, which therefore runs the risk of ignoring the contribution of the unconscious even to will's own emergence.

7

Rehearsals of Identity in Early Adolescence

> Whatever the shortsighted and doctrinaire rationalist may say about the meaning of culture, the fact remains that there is a culture-creating spirit.
>
> ——C. G. Jung, *Development of the Personality*

In this chapter we will analyze the stage of development known to most of us as Adolescence, extending from eleven to twelve to sixteen to seventeen years of age. The initial period of this entry into the stage of sexual maturation and new educational challenges is referred to by developmental psychologists as Early Adolescence. Psychoanalysts, following Erikson, have seen it as a stage of psychosocial maturation characterized by a crisis of Identity versus Identity Diffusion. Erich Neumann has referred to it in Jungian terms as the Solar-Rational stage, because the archetype of the (solar) hero is drawn upon to organize the personality. The mode of the symbolic function which emerges at the beginning of this stage is the *cultural attitude*, which brings to life identifications with the deeds and presumed psychologies of culture heroes and heroines, present and past, real and fictional. A new instrument of assimilation of experience also appears: *the symbolic form*. The emergence of both a new symbolic mode and a new symbolic instrument of assimilation are dramatic, but they exhibit the same invariant three-step sequence in the differentiation of consciousness that we have observed in our discussion at the four previous stages of development: recognition of other, awareness of self, and a new view of the world.

DEVELOPMENT OF THE SYMBOLIC PROCESS

Cultural Attitude

In traditional societies, the initiation rite is the primary environmental influence conditioning adolescent development.

We do find, even at the most primitive level, certain drastic measures at all those moments in life when psychic transitions have to be effected. The most important of these are the initiations at puberty and the rites pertaining to marriage, birth, and death. All these ceremonies, which in primitive cultures ... are observed with utmost care and exactitude, are probably designed in the first place to avert the psychic injuries liable to occur at such times; but they are also intended to impart to the initiand the preparation and teaching needed for life. (CW 16: 214,97)

Eliade was among the first to contrast initiation rites in traditional and contemporary societies: "It has often been said that one of the characteristics of the modern world is the disappearance of any meaningful rites of initiation" (Eliade 1958: ix). Neumann points out that under these circumstances the individual must discover an *individual* path into the collective.

But when the collective no longer possesses values, that is to say, when a crisis in values has occurred, the individual lacks a collective orientation. He falls sick because of a problem for which there is no longer a collective answer and a collective procedure for reaching a settlement. He then becomes involved in a conflict from which no institution is any longer in a position to set him free, but for which he must suffer and experience an individual solution in the living process of his personal destiny. (Neumann 1973: 31–2)

As a consequence of the relative absence of other initiation practices in contemporary Western societies, psychological treatment often assumes this function. Jung could even say:

The only "initiation process" that is still alive and practised today in the West is the analysis of the unconscious as used by doctors for therapeutic purposes. This penetration into the ground-layers of consciousness is a kind of rational maieutics in the Socratic sense, a bringing forth of psychic contents that are still germinal, subliminal, and as yet unborn. (CW 11: 842,514–15)

The Jungian analyst and theoretician, Joseph Henderson, tested this hypothesis in his analytical practice for thirty years and concluded that an initiation motif exists in the collective unconscious. Henderson (1967) devotes Chapter VIII of *Thresholds of Initiation* to a discussion of the initiation archetype and initiation practices as these relate to adolescent ego-development, linking his findings to the notions of adolescent development found in the works of Erikson and the Jungian child analysts, Fordham and Neumann.

Henderson also examined findings from his analytic practice with young adults fixated at adolescent stages of development when they entered analysis, and he agreed with Jung that there is a difference between adolescent development stimulated by psychological treatment and that evoked by traditional initiation ceremonies:

> The transformation of the unconscious that occurs under analysis makes the natural analogue of the religious initiation ceremonies, which do, however, differ in principle from the natural process in that they anticipate the natural course of development and substitute for the spontaneous production of symbols a deliberately selected set of symbols prescribed by tradition. (CW 11: 854,523)

Both collective and individual initiations are psychologically effective, however, in Henderson's opinion, because they activate the initiation motif in the collective unconscious.

All initiations, however, involve the transmission of important cultural attitudes to the initiate. As dynamic, structural elements of the psyche, cultural attitudes are creative centers that are the true origin of values; like other symbols, they function as bridges, in this case from the individual anxieties of the adolescent on the threshold of maturity to the creative and productive cultural activities of society.

> But the attitude itself is a cultural achievement; it is a function that is exceedingly valuable from a biological point of view, for it gives rise to incentives that drive human beings to do creative work for the benefit of the future age and, if necessary, to sacrifice themselves for the welfare of the species. (CW 4: 555,241)

An attitude, in the language of Jungian psychology, is a specific function of relationship between the ego and the expressive centers of motivation in the cultural and collective unconscious.

The cultural attitudes, which Henderson has also studied extensively, mark a real step in adolescent acculturation, and also in the fantasy lives of adolescents, which take on a cultural dimension well beyond the paracosms of Middle Childhood. In the previous stages of symbolic developmental transformation, the ego's "recognition" of the other occurred most often in relation with the parents. In Early Adolescence it is more likely to focus on the heroic creator of a cultural form or on the cultural form itself. Our own approach in this chapter will be to focus on examples of how specific cultural attitudes of the types Henderson has identified – Philosophic/Scientific, Aesthetic, Religious, and Social – emerge in relation to specific cultural forms. There is especially strong evidence for the emergence of strongly differentiated interests in "precocious" adolescents and so we will focus on examples from that group of gifted early adolescents.

In his Fitzpatrick lecture on the history of medicine, *Contributions to the Study of Precocity in Children*, Leonard Guthrie cites a study by Lancaster, who first collected over a thousand biographies and then analyzed two hundred of these in considerable detail. From these, Guthrie compiled the following list of the various types of adolescent awakenings:

> Of these one hundred and twenty showed a distinct craze for reading in adolescence; one hundred and nine became great lovers of nature; sixty-eight wrote poetry; fifty-eight showed a great and sudden development of energy; fifty-five showed great eagerness for school; fifty-three devoted themselves for a season to art and music; fifty-three became very religious; fifty-one ran from their homes in their teens; fifty-one showed dominant instincts of leadership; forty-nine had great longings of many kinds; forty-six developed scientific tastes; forty-one grew anxious about the future; thirty-four developed increased keenness of sensation or at least power of observation; in thirty-two cases health improved at adolescence; thirty-one became passionately altruistic; twenty-three became idealists; twenty-three showed powers of invention; seventeen were devoted to older friends; fifteen would reform the world; seven hated school. (Guthrie 1921: 38)

In this diverse list of adolescent transformations, we can identify the emergence of the primary cultural attitudes and symbolic forms – religion, art, philosophy/science, and society.

Scientific Attitude: Zoology (Jean Piaget)

Henderson describes the scientific attitude as a relatively recent differentiation of the philosophic attitude in post-enlightenment world culture. The psychologist Jean Piaget is a twentieth-century example of how the scientific attitude can shape the orientation of a future career. Although Piaget has not published accounts of the adolescent development of his children, he has presented autobiographical material which marks his own symbolic development at the beginning of the stage of Early Adolescence.

By the time he was eleven years old, Piaget had decided that the curator of the Neuchatel Museum of Natural Sciences embodied the scientific ideal to which he aspired (this was his recognition of a cultural attitude in the other). He wrote his first scientific article, "An Albino Sparrow" (1907), at this same age (demonstrating an awareness of a cultural attitude in himself), and he undertook this ambitious task in order that "he might be granted permission to work at the museum out of regular hours" and so "be taken seriously by the curator, who was to become his master in the field of zoology" (Gruber and Voneche 1977: 6). Subsequently, between the ages of thirteen and eighteen, Piaget published five scientific articles concerning Alpine snails. The *Limnaea* were to become a lifelong research interest (this is an example of an adolescent's creation of a new world view involving a life-task).

Scientific Attitude: Chemistry

The following observations illustrate symbolic development in two other adolescents that culminated in career choices. In the first example, the adolescent's relation with both a peer and his (deceased) father contribute to his transformation.

> When I was thirteen and was a sophomore in high school, I had had a course in general science that was not a bad course and involved a little chemistry. I was walking home one day from high school with a boy I had known very distantly in grammar school, and he said, "Would you like to stop by my house and see some chemical experiments?" He was thirteen years old at the time, and he showed me these experiments which interested me so much [this is recognition of the other] that when I got home that night I found a book on chemistry that had belonged to my father who had died when I was nine. He had been a druggist. I began reading this book, got an alcohol lamp that my mother had around, began boiling things and mixing things together [this is awareness of self]. I had some glassware largely from a man who lived next door who was a curator in a dental college, and I bought some chemicals, scrounged, got them from various places; and from that time on, I was a chemist [again this is the creation of a new view of the world involving a life-task]. (Eiduson 1962: 56)

In the next example, it is a relationship with a teacher that is pivotal in stimulating symbolic transformation.

> I think the dominating factor in getting me oriented toward science was a teacher, a woman teacher I had in junior high. She was a practical kind of woman who took an interest in my welfare at that time. She would, for example, let me help her set up experiments that we had in general science in junior high, and she would let me fool around in the stockroom [recognition of the other]. By that time, I had become interested in chemical sets and reading [awareness of the self], and I read practically everything I could get my hands on [creation of a new world view]. (ibid.: 57)

Crystallization of the Scientific Attitude: Mathematics (Evariste Galois)

Development of the cultural attitudes in Early Adolescence has not escaped the attention of other researchers. Joseph Walters and Howard

Gardner designate the "unusual encounters between a developing person and a particular field of endeavor as 'crystallizing experiences'" (Walters and Gardner 1986: 307). They indicate that "such experiences involve remarkable and memorable contact between a person with unusual talent or potential and the materials of the field in which that talent will be manifest" (ibid.: 307–8).

> ... these crystallizing experiences may appear in advance of formal training. In any case, their dramatic nature focuses the attention of the individual on a specific kind of material, experience, or problem [recognition of a cultural attitude in the other]. Moreover, the individual is motivated to revisit these occasions for the indefinite future [creation of a new world view] and to reshape his self-concept [awareness of a cultural attitude in one's self often associated with a life-task] on the basis of these experiences. (ibid.: 308)

As my interpolations indicate, I believe that these authors' definition of the crystallizing experience corresponds with my view of the sequential differentiation of consciousness in and through which a new mode of the symbolic function emerges during Early Adolescence.

> A crystallizing experience, then, is the overt reaction of an individual to some quality or feature of a domain: the reaction yields an immediate but also a long-term change in that individual's concept of the domain [Ego–Other "Recognition"], his performance in it [Creation of a New World View], and his view of himself [Ego–Self "Recognition"]. (ibid.: 309)

When they compiled biographical materials from a number of musicians and mathematicians, they found that some, though not all, described crystallizing experiences during Early Adolescence.

One of their examples concerns the mathematician Evariste Galois, who, after being tutored by his mother at home, entered public school at the age of eleven.

> Because his unpredictable disposition and stubborn attitude precluded any formal success as a student, he had to make the personal discovery of the world of mathematics on his own. Quite by chance he came across a geometry book written by Legendre: "The book aroused his enthusiasm; it was not a textbook written by some hack, but the work of art composed by a creative mathematician. A single reading sufficed to reveal the whole structure of elementary geometry with a crystal clarity to the fascinated boy ... (ibid.: 306)

This, I believe, is a description of the adolescent Galois experiencing his "recognition" of a Mathematical (philosophic/scientific) cultural attitude in the other (Legendre). His "recognition" of a Mathematical vocation in himself is not reported, but, from this time on, Galois studied mathematics on his own, that is, he was immersed in a new mathematical world view of his own creation. His realization of the developmental potential in this attitude was tragically cut short by his death in a duel at the age of twenty-one. However, his collected papers "served as the basis of a new field of mathematics now called 'Galois Theory'" (ibid.).

Aesthetic Attitude: Painterly (Una Hunt)

Una Hunt has described in her autobiography, *Una Mary* (1914), her development of what Henderson has described as an Aesthetic Attitude. "Una Mary" is an imaginary companion who entered Hunt's life during the Preschool Period and became an inhabitant of the authors symbolic community, "My Country," during Middle Childhood. (The effects of the earlier stages of symbolic development on subsequent stages is demonstrated in a study by Schaefer, which found support for the "hypothesized relationship between childhood imaginary companions and adolescent creativity ..." (Schaefer 1969: 747).) When Hunt was thirteen, a pair of related transformations occurred: she discovered that God was "Beauty" (in our terms, she developed a dominant Aesthetic cultural attitude) and she achieved a synthesis of her ego-personality with that of "Una Mary."

> The wish came true, and after that evening Una Mary vanished as a being of distinctly separate feelings and imaginations. Her world became the deep, encircling background of My World, supporting and sustaining my whole life; a life no longer made up of inner and outer circles that never touched, but one consistent whole with the same depths, reserves, and silences; but they were now depths and silences belonging to the surface and of which the surface strove to speak. Life became like a deep woodland pool, tangling the eye with gold-flecked abysses of blue and green, depth on depth of impenetrable color below the sunlit surface where water-lilies float and children sail their mimic boats. That evening, like Kipling's "Ship that Found Herself," I was suddenly and for the first time in my life
> MYSELF! (Hunt 1914: 267–8)

We note that the emergence of an Aesthetic cultural attitude and the consolidation of Hunt's ego identity are simultaneous events.

Aesthetic Attitude: Musical

Shiniki Suzuki

M. McDonald, drawing upon the autobiography of Shiniki Suzuki, describes his discovery of his vocation as teacher of the violin to young children. McDonald tells us that Suzuki's father was first a Samisen maker but went on to become the largest producer of violins in the world (at one time reaching 400 violins and 4,000 bows a day). Until he was seventeen years old, Suzuki "thought of his father's violin factory as a toy factory." He underwent a transformation when he heard a recording of Elman playing Schubert's "Ave Maria." McDonald quotes Suzuki's description of his experience while listening to Elman.

> To think that the violin, which I had considered a toy, could produce such beauty of tone! ... Elman's "Ave Maria" opened my eyes to music. I had no idea why my soul was so moved. (McDonald 1970: 505)

This describes Suzuki's "recognition" of an Aesthetic cultural attitude through its presence in another, that is, Mischa Elman, who became his hero. The numinous quality of the resulting musical experience is apparent. McDonald states that "this profoundly moving experience led Suzuki to take up the serious study of the violin at the late age of seventeen years [this was awareness of an Aesthetic attitude in himself accompanied by a new world view]." Even then, however, Suzuki's *vocational* path was not yet determined.

When he was in his twenties and studying music in Germany, he found at the end of a performance of the Mozart Clarinet Quartet that he was unable to applaud because of "a temporary paralysis of both arms." He says of the accompanying inner experience:

> It was Mozart who taught me to know perfect love, truth, goodness and beauty. And I now deeply feel as if I were under direct orders from Mozart, and he left me a legacy, and in his place I am to further the happiness of all children. (ibid.: 505–6)

This was the experience that really gave to his life a specific, vocational direction, within the context of the previously constructed Aesthetic cultural attitude.

> Forsaking the possibility of a career as a college teacher or a performer, Suzuki instead took over an abandoned kindergarten in Matsumoto and turned it into a music studio. There he taught the violin to small children, some as young as three years of age. (ibid.: 503)

Suzuki's calling, his life-task, was now established.

Sir George Solti

In his review of Solti's *Memoirs*, P. Driver described the beginning of the conductor's musical ambition.

> Singing at his school in Budapest, 7-year-old Gyorgy was so provoked by the mediocre playing of the boy accompanist that he restarted the piano lessons he had recently abandoned. The experience awakened "my tremendous musical ambition, which has never subsided to this day." (Driver 1997: 24)

It was in Early Adolescence, however, that Solti had the experience which initiated his lifelong devotion to conducting.

> It was conducting, though, that mattered, once he had been "hit by lightning" at an Erich Kleiber performance of Beethoven's Fifth Symphony when he was 14. It mattered more than his father (whom he scolded for tears when he left for Lucerne and Toscanini in 1939 and whom he never saw again) ... "I wanted to get away from my past and everything connected with it." (ibid.)

In psychological terms, we should view this galvanic transformation in Solti as the emergence in Early Adolescence of an Aesthetic cultural attitude, which set him on his life's course.

Aesthetic Attitude: Literary (Chaim Potok)

Chaim Potok is a rabbi and a novelist. His discovery of the Aesthetic cultural attitude, which underlies his literary career, began quite casually. When Potok was about fourteen and a half years old, he had completed his exams at the end of the high school term and had time on his hands. He *found* himself in a public library.

> I decided that I would take a crack at a really tough adult novel. I was intrigued by the title of the book that caught my eye. I took it off the shelf, skimmed its dust jacket, brought it home, and read it. The book was *Brideshead Revisited* by Evelyn Waugh. (Potok 1975: 16)

Unexpectedly, Potok had a primordial, transformative experience.

> I will never forget what it was like reading that book. The space-time slice of that book became more real to me than the space-time slice of the world in which I actually lived. I walked the streets worrying about the mother. I would be doing my homework and would catch myself

being terribly distressed over the disintegrating faith and personality of the son. This world, this strange British Catholic world, had somehow reached into my life through the medium of words on paper. And it had taken on a degree of reality that my own world no longer had for the length of time that it took me to read this book. On finishing, I remember feeling an overwhelming sense of bereavement – these people were gone from me now – and then feeling an overwhelming sense of amazement ... (ibid.: 16–17)

He wondered how and what Waugh had done to him.

How do you take words and put them on paper and using one man's imagination take those words and pieces of paper and create a world that one knows nothing about and make that world more real to the reader than the world in which he is actually living? (ibid.: 17)

This detailed description by Potok, of what we would interpret as his "recognition" of a cultural attitude in the other, is obviously suffused with a numinous quality. He continues his description of the effects of his reading Waugh's novel:

That was the encounter. I report it to you. I do not understand the Why of it. I can report only the What, the When, and the Where. And insofar as I myself am concerned, conjectures over the Why are an exercise in futility. I don't understand the Why. But the commitment to create, using words and paper and my own imagination, was born out of that encounter. And it was an ultimate commitment. (ibid.)

Potok suggests that we have all experienced the emergence of commitments of this kind, which may last only for an hour, a day, a week, or a lifetime: "It is this last kind of commitment that I am describing to you now" (ibid.). I interpret this passage as a description of Potok's "recognition" of an Aesthetic cultural attitude in himself, which became a container for the numinous depths of his experience. Over the objection of his religious teachers, Potok immediately began the creation of a new world view.

Everything that I read from that time on had as its fundamental purpose to teach me to do what Evelyn Waugh had done with words: to be able to create worlds on paper; worlds on paper that would be more real to the reader during the reading than the world in which the reader actually lived. (ibid.)

Potok concludes by saying that there are no secrets to becoming a writer, you read the great writers and you write, and write, and write. In our terms, you "recognize" your vocation in other and self, then actualize it.

Aesthetic Attitude: Poetic

Robinson Jeffers

When Jeffers agreed to write an Introduction to Albert's bibliography of his works, he also agreed to read it. Here was his reaction:

> ... every page of this book brings me a prickly feeling of remembering things that I do not want to remember, like an amnesia victim recalled in spite of himself to a painful past and unsatisfactory present. Those dreadfully juvenile verses reprinted here are the least of it; the pale boy who contributed them to the student-magazines of a college from which he graduated at eighteen was no Chatterton, but he is too far away to annoy me much, and I was quite willing to let his rhymes be included ... There are later things as bad; it seems to me I was still an adolescent at twenty-five. (Jeffers 1933: xv)

In order to compensate for his "prickly" feeling, Jeffers writes of an experience in his adolescence that he remembers with interest.

> My first deeply felt encounter with poetry interests me; for it was rather bizarre, besides being one of the greatest pleasures I ever experienced. I was fourteen or fifteen, at school in Switzerland, and my father on one of his summer visits brought me two little paper-bound books, poems of Thomas Campbell and poems of D. G. Rossetti. Neither name meant anything to my mind; nor did Campbell's poetry; but no lines of print will ever intoxicate as Rossetti's rather florid verses did, from the *Blessed Damozel* to the least last sonnet. I wonder why was that? (ibid.)

A partial answer to Jeffers's question is that he was experiencing the numinous emergence of a Poetic Aesthetic attitude, which later never deserted him.

> My pleasure was pure; I was never a critical reader, and was not yet looking for someone to imitate. And now, if I should ever wonder about the uses of poetry, I have only to remember that year's experience. The book was worn out with reading; when it fell to pieces I was sixteen and found Swinburne. (ibid.: xvi)

Jeffers goes on to describe his subsequent discovery of Shelley, Tennyson, Milton, and Marlowe – all "reasonable raptures," but "never again the passionate springtime that Rossetti (of all authors!) made me live" (ibid.:

xvi). This statement underscores the way the cultural attitude is a vital creative center in the psyche.

Robert Hass

The first American poet laureate from the West, Hass can't remember a time he wasn't interested in language.

> Growing up, he and his older brother would look up unfamiliar words they came across in the *Saturday Evening Post* and compete to use them in the most elaborate possible sentences. (Smith 1996: 10)

Hass is described as someone who has a "knack for communicating the thrill of reading a brilliantly made poem." This must be due in part to the fact that he had such an experience in Early Adolescence.

> He writes about discovering a poem by Wallace Stevens in a book he'd bought with money won in an 8th grade essay contest – the poem was called "Domination in Black" – which he liked so much "that it made me swoon, and made me understand what the word 'swoon' meant. I read it over and over. I read it exactly the way I lined up for a roller-coaster ride with a dime tight in my fist at Playland across the bay in San Francisco. It was the first physical sensation of the truthfulness of a thing that I had ever felt." (ibid.)

It is likely that Hass is describing the emergence of a Poetic Aesthetic attitude, the numinous quality of which is captured in the word "swoon," which goes beyond the *physical* sensation of truthfulness.

Aesthetic Attitude: Dance (Jose Limon)

Limon tells us that he had three sets of parents. The first were his "carnal" father, a "musician, pedagogue, conductor and director of the State Academy of Music" and his "biological" mother, who gave birth to twelve additional children (including two sets of twins), four of whom died. She herself died during her fourteenth pregnancy.

His second set of parents, who never met him and were not aware of their responsibility for his creative being, were Isadora Duncan and Harald Kreutzberg. His third set were foster parents, Doris Humphrey and Charles Weidman, who presided over his emergence into the world of dance. (In addition, Limon claims as illustrious grandparents, Ruth St. Denis and Ted Shawn.) It is his encounter with Kreutzberg which we will recount and interpret here.

In his last years of high school, Limon became acquainted with three young aspiring artists, who became his mentors. Shortly after they moved to New York, Limon followed them. By now, it was taken for granted by Limon and others that he was destined for a career as a painter.

In New York, Limon, twenty years old, discovered that El Greco had done all he had hoped to do.

> New York now became a cemetery, and I a lost soul in torment. I had been earning my living by running elevators, emptying garbage cans, tending furnaces, and posing for artists and art classes. Now that the bottom had fallen out of my life, I spent my days loafing or going to the movies. All ambition was lost. (Limon 1999: 15–16)

During this nadir, Limon was invited by a friend to attend a Sunday matinee dance recital. Here is what happened.

> The house was packed. The lights dimmed, and the curtains rose on a bare stage with black velour curtains. A piano struck up the stirring preamble to the Polonaise in A-flat Major of Chopin. Suddenly, onto the stage, borne on the impetus of the heroic rhapsody, bounded an ineffable creature and his partner. Instantly and irrevocably I was transformed. I knew with shocking suddenness that until then I had not been alive, or, rather, that I had yet to be born. There was joy, terror, and panic in the discovery [note the primal affects]. Just as the unborn infant cannot know the miracle of light, so I had not known that dance existed, and now I did not want to remain on this earth unless I learned to do what this man – Harald Kreutzberg – was doing. (ibid.: 16)

Although Limon was now in Late Adolescence, or even Early Adulthood, there is no doubt that he had "recognized" in Kreutzberg the viability of an Aesthetic cultural attitude.

Fearful that he was too late in making his discovery to prosper as a dancer, he read *My Life* by Isadora Duncan, and found his artistic mother. Having now "recognized" an Aesthetic attitude in himself, he presented himself for training to his foster parents, Humphrey and Weidman, to begin his "realization of a new world view." As he was to write later, "Birth for a dancer is like this. You put on a leotard, and trembling with embarrassment and terrible shyness, you step into the studio" (ibid.).

Limon now entered a "state of pure bliss," each day waiting for the moment of return to the studio, which he did for a period of ten years. Eventually he became a world-famous dancer.

Religious Attitude

In his study of the empirical growth of religious consciousness, *The Psychology of Religion*, E. D. Starbuck (1905) presents the following results concerning religious conversion: (a) that it is a distinctly adolescent phenomenon; (b) that it is a spontaneous awakening of that which has been ripening in the unconscious; and (c) that the whole experience of conversion is a part of the natural process of psychological development.

In her study of the psychology of religious conversion, *The Transformed Self*, C. Ullman (1989) reviewed the evidence that has been collected since Starbuck's work and found that it corroborated his view that conversions are most likely to occur during adolescence. She also came to view religious development as one aspect of normative adolescent development, pointing out that it interacts with cognitive growth and may provide some adolescents with a resolution to the identity question.

J. Fowler formulates a theory of stages in the development of faith consciousness, which designates the pattern of religious feeling characteristic of Adolescence as *synthetic-conventional* faith. He describes the tasks involved in this construction.

> Parallel with this task of integrating a set of images of the self into a sense of identity, the person forming Synthetic-Conventional faith must form a set of beliefs, values, and commitments that provides orientation and courage for living. This shaping of a world view and its values proceeds as adolescents encounter persons and contexts that offer stories, ideals, belief systems, rituals, disciplines, and role models that can capture and fund their imaginations and hunger for adult truth ... (Fowler 1991: 38)

Fowler's description of the emergence of synthetic-conventional faith suggests that what is being formed corresponds to what I, following Henderson, would describe as the development of a Religious cultural attitude. Fowler presents the following example of the construction of synthetic-conventional faith.

Marie, age twenty, recalls a summer camp experience at thirteen years of age.

> On the last night of camp there was a campfire, as there always is in youth camp. The dark night sky was beautiful, the sparks rose from the big campfire against the velvet sky, there was music. Different people told about what God meant to them and had done in their lives. We felt close to each other after an intensive week together. (ibid.: 28)

Embedded in this simple account is Marie's "recognition" of a Religious cultural attitude in her fellow campers. Her awareness of the presence of a Religious cultural attitude in herself follows:

> There came over me a feeling of unexplainable, universal love. I felt like nothing human was alien to me. I thought at the time I could even love Hitler if he were there. (ibid.)

In the next observation, Marie describes her creation of a new world view.

> Out of that experience of closeness to God, I developed a kind of peace and love that I carried with me for the next five years. I seemed to know just what to say to help my friends. They turned to me as a kind of confidant and adviser. It was like God was in me, a part of me. (ibid.)

Social Attitude

J. Adelson's study of the development of political thought during Adolescence illustrates, in Henderson's terminology, the development of a Social cultural attitude. The subjects in his study were drawn from three nations, United States, West Germany, and Great Britain.

Adelson's observations begin, however, at the time which I identify as the completion of Middle Childhood. At this level, the child's view of society is still *personal*.

> The child's adherence to the personal and the tangible makes it difficult for him to adopt a *sociocentric* perspective. Since he cannot easily conceive of "society," or of other abstract collectivities, he does not take into account, when pondering a political action, its function for society as a whole. He thinks instead of its impact upon specific individuals. (Adelson 1971: 1016)

At the completion of Middle Childhood and during the first years of Adolescence a transformation occurs.

> The years of adolescence, twelve to sixteen, are a watershed era in the emergence of political thought. Ordinarily the youngster begins adolescence incapable of complex political discourse – that is, mute on many issues, and when not mute, then simplistic, primitive, subject to fancies, unable to enter fully the realm of political ideas. By the time this period is at an end, a dramatic change is evident; the youngster's grasp of the political world is now recognizably adult. His mind moves with some agility within the terrain of political concepts; he has achieved abstractness, complexity, and even some delicacy in his sense of political textures; he is on the threshold of ideology, struggling to formulate a morally coherent view of how society is and might and should be arranged. (ibid.: 1013)

Age was identified as the major determinant of this transformation, which indicates that it results from a phase of progressive development.

> Surprisingly, it appears that neither sex nor intelligence nor social class counts for much in the growth of political concepts ... What does count, and count heavily, is age. There is a profound shift in the character of political thought, one which seems to begin at the onset of adolescence – twelve to thirteen years – and which is essentially completed by the time the child is fifteen or sixteen ... A twelve-year-old German youngster's ideas of politics are closer to those of a twelve-year-old American than to those of his fifteen-year-old brother. (ibid.: 1014–15)

At the completion of this rapid period of differentiation of consciousness an entirely new view has been established.

> At fourteen, fifteen, and beyond, the youngster's mood begins to be critical and pragmatic ... He senses that law and social policy must take account of the dead hand of the past, entrenched privilege, human stubbornness, the force of habit. He now understands that law and policy must accommodate competing interests and values, that ends must be balanced against means, that the short-term good must be appraised against latent or long-term or indirect outcomes. (ibid.: 1026)

There is, moreover, room for further differentiation within this developmental context.

Adelson found that at the ideological level "the ideological capacity in adolescence is extremely rare, almost never found before the later years of high school, and even then only among the most intelligent, intellectually committed, and politically intense" (ibid.: 1027). We conclude that both a general transformation in the Social cultural attitude occurs during Early Adolescence and that there is further differentiation in those individuals for whom this attitude is the superior cultural attitude.

Interiorization of the Symbolic Process: From Social Realm to Cultural Attitude

My readers will recall that at the beginning of Middle Childhood, the mode of the symbolic process is the social realm and the instrument of assimilation of experience is the symbolic community. The process of constructive interiorization, dissociation of form and content, continues throughout this stage to attain, at its completion and the beginning of Adolescence, the new mode of the symbolic process, the cultural attitude and the new instrument of assimilation, the symbolic form. Structurally, the cultural attitude appears as a dynamic center, which organizes the conscious material according to its own laws of formation.

Our analysis of the interiorization of the symbolic process during Middle Childhood focuses on Piaget's study of the child's consciousness of game rules during this stage. Adaptation of this study for our purposes is possible because games are structures which provide the frameworks for the formation of symbolic communities.

> Games with rules are *social institutions* in that they remain the same as they are transmitted from one generation to the next and are independent of the will of the individuals who participate in them. Some of these games are transmitted with the participation of adults, but others are specifically infantile, like the game of marbles, which the boys of Geneva play until they are eleven or twelve. The second kind, which are both play and exclusively "children's property," are the most favorable for the advancement of social life among children. (Piaget 1969: 119; italics added)

He found three stages in the latency age child's development of a sense of justice.

> One period, lasting up to the age of 7–8, during which justice is subordinated to adult authority; a period contained approximately between 8–11, and which is that of progressive equalitarianism; and finally a period which sets in towards 11–12, and during which purely equalitarian justice is tempered by considerations of equity. (Piaget 1965: 315)

This progression in the child's sense of justice and the child's interiorization of game rules are parallel processes.

In the five- to seven-year-old child, Piaget found that children considered the rules of the game of marbles as objective, obligatory, untouchable, and sacred. They emanated from the "Word of the Elder or Adult," they were eternal, and they could never be changed. Morality at this level is referred to as "heteronomous" and is based on values transmitted from adult to child. At this stage, games and rules are one. The notion of justice at the first level is inseparable from that of reward and punishment and is defined by the correlation between acts and their retribution.

Piaget found that a transitional period followed, for the following reason. Once children learned more about the game of marbles and its rules, they understood that some rules were recent and made up by other children. On the other hand, the *truth* of the rules remained absolute and intrinsic. Developmentally, a first dissociation of form (rules) and content (games) had occurred, complicating moral thinking.

An entirely new conscious understanding of rules would be constructed by the children Piaget studied at about ten to twelve years of age. Rules now were conceived as subject to choice and as laws arrived at by mutual consent, which meant that rules may be altered on the condition of general approval. Players realized, however, that they must respect the agreed upon rules as a sign of peer-group loyalty. Rules, in other words, are no longer viewed as eternal, but as passed on from generation to generation. Morality at this stage is "autonomous," and is based on child–child transmission, which means that rules are now at the disposal of the players themselves. In terms of principles, the idea of justice at this level of moral development implies only the idea of equality. In his analysis of the child's differentiation of *reciprocity*, Piaget identifies two aspects of respect for other's rights, the factual and the ideal:

> Like all spiritual realities which are the result, not of external constraint but of autonomous development, reciprocity has two aspects: reciprocity as a fact, and reciprocity as an ideal, as something that ought to be. The child begins by simply practising reciprocity, in itself not so easy a thing as one might think. Then, once he has grown accustomed to this form of equilibrium in his actions, *his behaviour is altered from within, its form reacting, as it were, upon its content*. What is regarded as just is no longer merely reciprocal action, but primarily behaviour that admits of indefinitely sustained reciprocity ... Just as in logic, we can see a sort of reaction of the form of the proposition upon its content when the principle of contradiction leads to a simplification and purification of the initial definitions, so in ethics, reciprocity implies a purification of the deeper trend of conduct, guiding it by gradual stages to universality itself. (ibid.: 323–4; italics added)

When reciprocity has refined the trend of conduct so that it reaches "to universality itself," the development of a Social cultural attitude has been achieved. At this higher level the game has become a miniature Kantian utopian community governed by rules of equality, justice, and fair play for all, enacting the fantasy of a well-functioning social complex.

What this differentiation of social consciousness reflects is one more interiorization of the symbolic process during Middle Childhood. To review: rules are initially objective because they are experienced as identical with their material context. In the cognitive domain at this same level, operations are designated as *concrete* for the same reason. By the time of the transitional period of moral development, rules have become partially dissociated from their content but remain quasi-objective. At the completion of Middle Childhood, rules have become mobile and under ego control; they are conceived as subjective and susceptible to innovation and modification based on mutual consent.

This mobility of rules indicates, as did the mobility of the secondary schemata in Infancy (Chapter 4), the symbolic schemes in Early Childhood (Chapter 5), and the social schemes in the Preschool Period (Chapter 6), that the child has once again dissociated a symbolic form from its material content, an achievement that indicates a significant interiorization of the symbolic process.

DEVELOPMENT OF THE EGO-COMPLEX

The Dialectical Spiral

In my analyses of each stage of development prior to Adolescence, I have also attempted to demonstrate the continuous nature of the developmental dialectic between Interest–curiosity/exploration and Joy–play/imagination, which is the motor of progressive development. It would be logical to assume that the same happy dialectic informs development during adolescence, including moral development in the cultivation of integrity (Beebe 1992). A detailed continuation of this analysis during Adolescence is not feasible, however, because of lack of extensive empirical data, which may in itself be a revealing finding. Two studies, however, actually provide findings which suggest that this dialectical process continues in a seamless fashion during this stage.

S. R. Gold and B. B. Henderson focus their research on *intellectual style*, which they define as a "category of cognitive dispositions such as creativity, cognitive style, curiosity, and imaginal processes" (Gold and Henderson 1990: 701). They have studied the intellectual style of seventy-four gifted adolescents during one week of two consecutive summer sessions. One of their findings was that individual differences in *daydreaming frequency* were relatively stable over time, although the content of the daydreams was not. Another finding was that the measures of *curiosity* were also relatively stable over the time. The authors refer to the more stable frequency of daydreaming and curiosity measures as *process measures*, "ways of interacting with the environment" (ibid.: 706). The authors drew the following conclusions.

These results suggest developmental patterns in content and process-oriented intellectual styles. When children report how curious they are, or how frequently they daydream, they are indicating something about the way they typically engage their external and internal environments. Individual differences in these processes are fairly stable over time. In contrast, the content or focus of children's daydreaming is much less stable over a period as long as a year. One function of daydreaming is to review current concerns in order to test out alternate behaviors or solutions to problems in imagination ... A similar pattern might have been obtained if a content dimension of curiosity, such as specific areas of interest, had been employed in the self-report battery. (ibid.: 707)

It does not require a great stretch of the imagination to construe this study as describing, in its process findings, the developmental dialectical process between exploration (which reflects curiosity) and play (which would involve daydreaming) during Early Adolescence. Analysis of the cultural and symbolic content of the daydreams would be of interest; my hunch is that they would reveal a healthy growth of cultural imagination.

A study by K. Rathunde and M. Csikszentmihalyi (1993) of engaged and disengaged adolescents provides observations which may be interpreted in a similar way. Grounding their views in the educational philosophy of John Dewey, the authors adopted the "concepts of *serious play* and *undivided interest* ... to describe an optimal mode of task engagement."

> Being playfully involved is not enough, nor is working to reach a goal; it is the *combination of both* that results in productive experience and avoids the divided interests of fooling and drudgery. (Rathunde and Csikszentmihalyi 1993: 387; italics added)

Their hypothesis was that "teenagers who more often reported undivided interest in their early high school years while doing talent-related activities would achieve more in their respective talent areas by graduation than those who reported divided interest" (ibid.: 389). The talents of the engaged group consisted of math, science, music, athletics, or art. The results of the study indicated that "highly engaged students reported twice as much undivided interest in comparison to a group of disengaged students" and "undivided interest while doing talent-related activities was positively correlated with independent assessment of talent area performance three years later" (ibid.: 385).

The concept of "talent area" corresponds in general, I believe, to the notion of a cultural attitude. The optimal mode of task engagement described by the authors, serious play and undivided interest, corresponds to the dialectical process between Interest–curiosity/ exploration and Joy–play/imagination. The "fooling" and "drudgery" of the disengaged students, on the other hand, reflects a disturbance in the functioning of the dialectical process, which suggests that these students are experiencing blocks to the natural process of psychological development.

Culture Hero or Heroine

The symbol that expresses the normal development of ego-consciousness during Adolescence is the *culture* hero or heroine. In contrast to the social daydreams from Middle Childhood, which are populated with *action* heroes and heroines, mighty personages who slay dragons, rescue those in harm's way and capture villains, the collective daydreams of the adolescent provide images of culture heroes and heroines who are prophets for new religions, creators of new artistic styles, promoters of new philosophic truths, and founders of new social orders. Auden (1967) usefully defined the hero as the exceptional individual who possesses above average authority, and says this authority may be one of three kinds – aesthetic, ethical, and religious. His review of various types to be found in literary works includes Ishmael, Ahab, Nemo, Don Quixote, Orestes, and Hamlet.

Such culture heroes serve two functions: first, they provide the adolescent with a bridge to the collective life of the greater world of culture and civilization; second, they supply the adolescent with compelling images of creative adults which makes it possible to move past the symbolic tie with the parents as the repositors of authority.

As early as Chapter 2 of the present book, we described the infant's relation with its parents as composed of two contexts – an unconscious, symbolic relatedness and a conscious, personal relationship. We noted that at the beginning a symbolic relatedness with the parents predominates, and parents and world are experienced as a primary unity. At each succeeding stage of development a new form of symbolic relatedness is established, and the personal relationship to parents and the world is expanded. During Early Adolescence, a decisive shift occurs within this line of development. Both contexts need to be transferred to the greater world. I have found that specific symbolic modalities, the collective daydream and the symbolic form are instrumental in the transfer of the symbolic relatedness to society.

> Father and mother are, whether we know it or not, replaced by something analogous to them – if, that is to say, we succeed in detaching ourselves from them at all. The detachment is possible only if we can step on to the next level. For example, the place of the father is now taken by the doctor, a phenomenon which Freud called the "transference." But in the place of the mother there is substituted the wisdom of a doctrine. (*CW* 17: 158,84–5)

If this detachment does not occur, the individual "will simply transfer the parental tie to the family he himself has raised (if he ever gets that far), thus creating for his own progeny the same suffocating psychic atmosphere from which he suffered in his youth" (ibid.: 158,85).

> No psychic allegiance to any kind of secular organization can ever satisfy the spiritual and emotional demands previously made on the parents. Moreover, it is by no means to the advantage of a secular

organization to possess members who make such demands ... A man cannot properly fulfil even the biological meaning of human existence if this and this only is held up to him as an ideal. Whatever the shortsighted and doctrinaire rationalist may say about the meaning of culture, the fact remains that there is a culture-creating spirit. This spirit is a living spirit and not a mere rationalizing intellect ... A spiritual goal that points beyond the purely natural man and his worldly existence is an absolute necessity for the health of the soul; it is the Archimedean point from which alone it is possible to lift the world off its hinges and to transform the natural state into a cultural one. (ibid.: 159,85–6)

A collective goal originating in a specific cultural attitude can provide the symbolic bridge across which the adolescent may travel from family to society and enter the world of young adulthood. The emergence of collective daydreams, and the discovery through a preoccupation with particular cultural heroes of specific cultural attitudes, immediately precede the adolescent's establishment of a secure ego-identity, able to imagine its way to maturity.

Part II

When Development Stumbles: The Healing Power of Symbols

I am primarily interested in how I can help my patients find their healthy base again.

——C. G. Jung, *Memories, Dreams, Reflections*

8

The Chemistry and Alchemy of the Psychotherapeutic Relationship

Our understanding of disturbances in the personal and symbolic parent-infant double bond during the first year of life is in its own infancy (Chapter 1). Also not very developed is our understanding of the factors which condition the emergence of what we have called the primal experience, which starts the infant on the path to differential consciousness of other, self, and world (Chapter 2). In the present chapter, I will be discussing the treatment of two infant and five adult patients, each of whom can be said to be suffering from a disturbance in at least one of these areas of earliest symbolic development.

NON-RECOGNITION

Before discussing this clinical material, I want to comment on an article by Selma Fraiberg, which has relevance for all the seven cases. In "Pathological defenses in infancy", Fraiberg identified *avoidance* as a defense universally used by infants. She found a pathological pattern of avoidance, however, in a particular subgroup of mother–infant pairs:

> The home observations of these babies and mothers showed avoidance of the mother which I take to be a fluctuating pattern in response to circumstance. It was always associated with discord in the mother–infant relationship and with avoidant patterns in the mother herself. In our population we see avoidance manifest as early as *three months of age* and throughout the age span covered in our study (up to thirty-six months). The patterns of avoidance were total or near total, without fluctuations in the course of extended and intensive home observations. The mother's avoidance of her baby had reached a pathological extreme. (Fraiberg 1982: 618; italics added)

Viewed as a Life Stimulus for the evocation of an Innate Affect, the mother's avoidance appears as Rejection, and we are safe in assuming that the infant is experiencing Shame and Alienation on that basis (Table 1). Fraiberg illustrates this pattern of disturbance with observations of the interactions between a three-month-old infant and his parents.

Gregg is the child of teenage parents, whose mother alternates between states of depression and outbursts of rage. She seemed to avoid Gregg in every situation that was open to the author's observation. Tellingly, Gregg also avoided his mother.

> At three months of age when a baby seeks his mother's eyes, smiles and vocalizes in response to her face and voice, Gregg never looked at his mother, never smiled nor vocalized to her. Even in distress he never turned to her. (ibid.: 619)

The following observation is characteristic not only of Gregg at three months, but also of other babies in the avoidance subgroup.

> The baby is scanning the room, his eyes resting briefly on the stranger, the cameraman, or an object in the room, and in the scanning he passes over his mother's face without a sign of registration or *recognition*. There is not a pause in scanning or a flicker on his face that speaks for registration. In situations where gaze exchange or a gesture is nearly unavoidable because of the line of vision or the proximity of baby and mother, we see the patterns again and again. It is as if perception has selectively edited out the picture of the mother from the pictures in the visual survey. (ibid.: 619–20; italics added)

Similar behavior occurs when the mother speaks: there is no automatic turning in the direction of her voice and no alerting or signs of attention. (This is far from normal for this age. What we expect to see at three months, as a result of the unfolding of the primal experience, is an infant engrossed in the relation with the mother, ready for social exploration and play at every opportunity.)

Gregg's relationship with his father is different from the one he had with his mother: "But when his father was present, there was gaze exchange, smiles, and vocalizations of pleasure" (ibid.: 619). And the clinicians conducting the study were able to establish eye contact with Gregg and elicit smiles from him.

After stating that visual and auditory contact by the infant with the parents are genetically programmed behaviors, Fraiberg offers the following explanation for the pathological pattern of avoidance.

> In the simplest possible terms, it appears that in the biological-social sequence in which sensorimotor systems are activated and organized around the experience with a mother as a nurturant, responsive, need-

gratifying person, the percept of the mother for these infants is a negative stimulus. It is also a defense which may, in itself, belong to the biological repertoire and is activated to ward off registration and, conceivably, a painful affect. (ibid.: 620)

At this first level of explanation, Fraiberg's attachment-theory interpretation and the one I have just presented based on my theory of innate affect dynamics as shapers of symbolic behavior, are in agreement. Fraiberg does consider that these defensive sensorimotor systems may not be activated simply because of deficient nurturance by at least one of the parents, but she discounts this possibility on the strength of the fact that infants who avoid their mothers may proceed not to avoid their fathers or even strangers. I wish to offer another explanation for her findings, by suggesting that pathological avoidance is not simply the result of parental rejection but also reflects the infant's non-recognition of the avoided parent, a serious deficit in the symbolic capacity.

How could such a deficit emerge? It seems reasonable to assume that at least some infants who do not "recognize" or register one or both of their parents at three months have not emerged from the initial phase of non-recognition (see Chapter 2). In such instances, the primal experience, with its social, individual, and world creating differentiations of consciousness has not yet been realized. As the case of Gregg indicates, "recognition" may occur with one parent but not the other, suggesting that the primal experience may be operating in one relationship but not another. Presumably, the avoided parent did not facilitate the child's emergence from the uroboric phase of non-recognition, and that failure of appropriate nurturance freezes their relationship at the level of mutual non-recognition.

TWO STARVING INFANTS

Infants suffering from acute nutritional failure are another class of symbolically challenged babies. The cases presented below, Billy and Nina, are drawn from Fraiberg's (1980) casebook. Our discussion is based in part on Tomkins's notion that drive functioning (in these instances the hunger drive) is conditioned by the affects.

The drive mechanism ordinarily is conceived to lack nothing essential in intensity and motivational urgency. However, part of the seeming urgency of the drive state is, in fact, a consequence of an affective response, which ordinarily amplifies, but may under certain conditions modulate, attenuate, interfere with, or even reduce, the primary drive signal. (Tomkins 1962: 45–6)

Tomkins applies this view to analyze the relation between the hunger drive and *positive affects*, in infant and adult alike.

> Consider next the hunger drive. In the neonate this ordinarily instigates the negative affective response – the cry of distress. This cry undoubtedly makes the hunger appear more urgent and harder to tolerate [negative affect amplification]. The total distress is certainly greater than if there were hunger alone. Indeed, it is possible to comfort such a child by picking him up and walking with him. This will ordinarily stop the crying without stopping the hunger. A child who has been thus soothed and stopped from crying will, nonetheless, eagerly take food when it is offered, indicating that the affect was an independent response which had amplified the hunger [positive affect amplification]. In adult experience it is common enough that hunger plus "impatience," the adult version of the cry of distress, can be much more uncomfortable than hunger alone. If, while waiting for a slow waitress in a crowded restaurant, such impatience is replaced by conversation with instigates positive affect, the hunger pains lose much of their urgency. (ibid.: 49)

These theoretical formulations suggest that when mother and infant are "contained" in mutually activated positive affects, the hunger drive is amplified and nursing will be a shared delight. Tomkins extends his analysis to the relation between the hunger drive and the *existential affects*.

> We have thus far considered concurrent positive affective responses which amplify the hunger drive. There are, in addition, affective responses which can attenuate, mask, interfere with or reduce the hunger drive. Disgust, fear, distress and apathy, depending upon their intensity, will either modulate, mask, attenuate, interfere with or completely inhibit the hunger drive. (ibid.: 50)

It is a well-known fact that a depressed or anxious mood may inhibit the hunger drive for varying periods of time: a person in mourning or a rejected lover may lose weight and visibly "waste away" from lack of appetite and lowered food intake.

The premise I am exploring is that the pattern of infant nutritional failure referred to as *nonorganic failure to thrive* occurs as a result of a disturbance in the constellation of "infant" symbols in the parents, particularly the mother or primary food-giver. In this circumstance, the flow of positive affects, Interest and Joy, from mother to infant is not sufficient for normal amplification of the infant's hunger drive.

Billy

Billy was five months old when he and his seventeen-year-old mother and twenty-one-year-old father were referred to the infant mental health program. Billy was in a "grave nutritional state," his parents were "depleted and without hope," and there "appeared to be no connection between the young parents and their baby." Nearly half-way through the first year of life, the parent–infant double bond had not yet formed: he was not a perfect, Divine Child, and they were not successful Great Parents.

There is no information about the pregnancy except the fact that the parents were married two months before delivery. Billy was a full-term, healthy baby, but, as we are not told of the dreams, fantasies, or emotions of the parents during pregnancy or parturition, we cannot further evaluate the constellation of "infant" symbols in the parents (Chapter 1). We do know that Billy stopped gaining weight when he was *two months old*, the age when the emergence of the symbolic mode of Infancy and a developmental surge are to be expected (Chapter 2).

By the time he was seen, Billy's peril was so great that the initial assessment was limited to three visits over one and a half weeks. His *exploration of things* was advanced: "Billy was motorically very precocious and was able at 5 months to turn over quickly, to creep, to grasp and manipulate objects" (Fraiberg 1980: 199). His play was primarily individual, not social: "He was capable of spending a lot of time in solitary play with toys" (ibid.: 200). Thus, the dialectical process between Interest–Curiosity/Exploration and Joy–Fantasy/Play was energized in the individual pathway, but functioned only sporadically in the social pathway.

> There were few signs of human attachment. Even though he could creep, Billy rarely approached his mother. He rarely made eye contact with her. He rarely smiled unless mother used gross tactile play. When he fussed, his mother put him to bed with a pacifier and honey. (ibid.)

This observation shows that in Billy's case the infant–parent double bond, a necessary precondition for all early infant social exploration and play, only occasionally flickers to life. Rather surprisingly, considering this dismal initial picture, Billy was able to attain nutritional adequacy after the first two and a half months of psychological treatment.

After quickly establishing a positive therapeutic alliance with the mother, and introducing helpful suggestions for feeding Billy, the therapist made what was, in my judgment, the critical intervention.

Seeking a tactful way to guide Kathie to a livelier exchange with her baby, I asked her if she ever told Billy stories. She said, "No." I asked her if I could tell Billy a story while Kathie held him, and she agreed. I began my story, "Once upon a time there were three bears," using what Stern (1973) describes as "normal baby talk expression," elongation of smile, rise and fall of voice, exaggerated nuances. All of these are typical exchange behaviors between baby and mother. All were missing from Kathie's conversation with Billy. Billy and his mother *both* loved the story. Billy began to smile and make eye contact with me and his mother, as together we watched him. Kathie so enjoyed this herself, as both child and mother, that she herself began to tell Billy stories and, of course, Billy quickly began to respond. (ibid: 207)

Billy's response was immediate, for he began to *smile* and make *eye contact* with the therapist and his mother. Mother's response was immediate and sustained, for she was so enlivened by this numinous moment that she began, and then continued, to tell Billy stories, to which he responded with more *smiles*.

Here we are witness to a dramatic improvement in both parent–infant and infant–parent "chemistry," and its effect on Billy's eating was immediate.

Billy began to gain weight steadily. Vomiting virtually disappeared. By 7 months, Billy had gained 2 pounds 8 ounces and reached the 50th percentile in weight; the pediatrician was satisfied that Billy was no longer in nutritional peril. (ibid.: 209)

An additional year of individual psychotherapy for the mother was necessary to assist her in resolving the personal psychopathology that she had brought to Billy's nursery.

Nina

Nina was seven months old and her mother, Karen, was sixteen years old when they were referred to therapy because of the infant's life-threatening nutritional crisis. Karen had been a fifteen-year-old high school student when Nina's conception occurred, as a consequence of a casual sexual encounter: Nina's father was nameless and faceless. In the two years before her pregnancy, Karen had steadily lost weight, so that she weighed a little over eighty pounds when she conceived. As is typical of anorexic adolescents, she had not menstruated for many months prior to conception, so neither she nor her doctor suspected she was pregnant until the fifth month. When her parents were informed, conflict arose in the family.

When her parents learned of her pregnancy they insisted that she give up the baby for adoption. Karen, in a rare instance of self-assertion, insisted that she would keep her baby, and the decision brought further bitterness and fighting in the household where the parents blamed each other for the pregnancy. (ibid.: 111)

We have no information of Karen's dreams, fantasy-images, emotions, or patterns of behavior during pregnancy or parturition. Karen's self-assertion suggests some urge toward individual development, as well as stirrings of a maternal instinct. We cannot be sure, however, that "her baby" was a true "infant" symbol that could be projected onto Nina.

After Nina's birth, Karen returned with her baby to her parent's home, where conflict and rancor continued. When Nina was one month old she began to attend a private nursery during the hours her mother attended high school. In the nursery, baby Nina had an unpredictable series of caregivers and was often assigned to a particularly withdrawn, depressed young woman. Nina stopped gaining weight when she was *three months old* and at seven months her vocalizations were also limited to the range of a *three-month-old*. As in the case of Billy, Nina's development was arrested at the age we have postulated for the emergence of the primal experience and the waking dream, the symbolic mode of Infancy (Chapter 2).

Nina and Karen were interviewed by a therapist for the first time when Nina was seven months old and, instead of presenting as curious and delighted mutual playmates, they appeared as follows.

The schoolgirl mother and her baby presented a striking picture. Karen gaunt, terribly thin, hair disheveled, her face pinched and sad; Nina long and thin, eyes dark and wary, face somber, a pacifier in her mouth during most of the session. (ibid.: 105–6)

There were, on the other hand, "many signs of a positive and reciprocal attachment between Nina and her mother" (ibid.: 107).

During the initial assessment period the therapist noted that in her role as mother Karen "rarely initiated 'conversations' or games with Nina" (ibid: 116). In response to this deficit, the therapist began her treatment with the following intervention:

The therapist initiated games with Nina and introduced Karen into the games. The games themselves were commonplace: the introduction of a toy, a "conversation" with the baby about the toy, praise for the baby who made such fine music on the toy xylophone. All this seemed new to Karen. There were no traditions in Karen's family for *playing* with a baby. (ibid.: 117; italics added)

The therapist observed the following response on Karen's part.

> Karen herself, in her reticent way, began to enjoy the baby games ...
> Karen, who seemed not to have known a playful side of her nature
> before she came to us, took the permission of the therapist to enjoy
> baby games, to allow herself the occasional silliness that is the privilege
> of parents. (ibid.)

Now the emotional momentum of treatment gathered steam: When
Karen realized that her daughter was responding to the therapist by
"talking," the therapist only needed to initiate the dialogue to bring
mother Karen into the exciting and joyful discourses. Then Karen,
without direction from the therapist, began spontaneously to engage
baby Nina in "conversations."

Immediately after these improvements in parent–infant and
infant–parent "chemistry," when first the mother and then Nina
expanded their capacity for social play and exploration, Nina began to
gain weight steadily. With the nutritional crisis resolved, mother
continued in treatment for two and a half years.

Discussion

Fraiberg and her associates have been impressed by the *rapid changes* that
occur in "kitchen psychotherapy" and have suggested that in the case
of the infant it results from the removal of impediments to forward
movement, which unleashes strong developmental currents. They
believed that the rapid changes in the parents, on the other hand, are
best explained as a result of the infant serving as a catalyst for psychological rebirth in the parents.

> The baby, in fact, evokes profound memories and feelings in his
> parents which normally lie deep in personality. This need not lead to
> pathological disturbance. To be in touch with the deepest reservoirs
> of feeling in oneself can lead to a binding together of the elements of
> personality, a form of self-healing. (ibid.: 54)

As we have shown, there is no doubt that infants are a necessary
condition for the constellation in parents of infant symbols and the
impetus to development in the parents which those symbols generate
(Chapter 1). The authors also note that even if old conflicts are also stirred
up, this may not be disadvantageous.

> The powerful conflicts which have led to this crisis have broken
> through into consciousness, or near consciousness, ready, as it were,
> for our help in resolution and healing – perhaps more ready than at

any other time in adult life. If there were strong currents at work to bring developmental progression for the infant, *there are also strong currents at work to bring developmental progression for the parents.* (ibid.; italics added)

Healing of these conflicts may require that the parent's psychotherapy be extended beyond the initial emergency phase. What has repeatedly impressed the therapists, however, is that, even without this resolution of the parent's long-standing conflicts, there is an immediate blossoming of the parent–infant and infant–parent relations, alongside amelioration of the life-threatening nutritional failure. My interpretation of the healing factor in the cases of Nina and Billy differs in certain particulars from that of the authors.

In both of Fraiberg's cases that we have just reviewed, it seems clear to me that the "developmental currents" that eventually jump-started the infants had first to be induced in the mothers. In each instance, the mechanism of action of the "jump-start" is apparent: *playful* interventions by the therapists in the form of spontaneous play, nursery games and "motherese" were what activated the partially constelled "infant" symbol *in the mothers*. Watching the therapist's play with their babies catalyzed the emergence of the positive affects Interest and Joy in the mothers: they were literally "turned on" by the therapist–patient "chemistry." Only then could the symbol of the Divine Child be constelled in the mothers and projected onto their infants so that a healthy flow of positive affects from mother to infant was established. After that, mother–infant social play and exploration could be initiated by the mothers themselves, subsequently to become a self-sustaining dialectical process mother and infant both took for granted.

It is my conviction that in each case the mother's numinous emotions also stimulated further activation of the partially constelled "mother" symbol in the infant. One can read in the descriptions of their interaction how Interest and Joy begin to flow from the infant to the mother, at the same time as the infant becomes socially curious and playful. All this means to me that the infants' connection with the primal self – the ego–self axis – had been strengthened. In the language of the dyad, an infant-parent double bond has now been formed. The establishment of *mutual* double bonds between parent and infant may not seem like divine intervention, but I certainly can recapture an aspect of deepened connection to the self when the authors exclaim, "It's like having God on your side!"

It also seems clear to me that when amplification of the hunger drive by Interest and Joy, originating now in both mother and infant, reaches optimal levels, infant feeding becomes the natural pleasure it is intended to be. With the life-threatening nutritional crisis resolved and the natural developmental process released from inhibition, it is possible to redirect the therapeutic process to the parent's individual conflicts.

THE MAN WHO COULDN'T LAUGH

D. W. Winnicott has published the case of a married man with children, described by Winnicott as "schizoid-depressive," who began analysis because he lacked the capacity for spontaneity. The man felt hopeful about the outcome of the therapy because, not long after starting treatment, he had *laughed once* at the cinema.

Winnicott chose six episodes from this analysis to illustrate his theoretical discussion of withdrawal and regression. I have chosen the first two episodes for a different reason, to demonstrate what I believe is the constellation in this adult patient of the primal experience.

Both events occurred during analytic sessions. The first episode was a spontaneous fantasy.

> The first of these happenings (the fantasy of which he was only just able to capture and report) was that, in a momentary withdrawn state on the couch, *he curled up and rolled over the back of the couch.* This was the first direct evidence in the analysis of a *spontaneous self.* (Winnicott 1954: 256; italics added)

The second episode, equally remarkable to Winnicott, occurred a few weeks later and was another spontaneous fantasy.

> It was at this point that he just managed to tell me that he had again had the idea of being *curled up*, although in actual fact he was lying on his back as usual, with his hands together across his chest. (ibid.)

At this juncture, Winnicott's interpretation to the patient was that in this image the presence of a containing or "holding" *medium* was implied. This enabled the patient to elaborate on the details of both symbolic fantasies.

> Having now received the idea of the medium holding him, he went on to describe in words what he had shown with his hands, which was that he had been *twirling round forwards*, and he contrasted with the *twirling round backwards* over the couch which he had reported a few weeks previously. (ibid.: 257)

The patient referred to this analytic session as "momentous." I would agree: it was, in my judgment, a numinous moment for the patient, because something archetypal had been touched and constellated with healing force.

These two sessions in which a very activated fantasy predominates are perhaps better understood as involving waking dream states, expressions of the earliest moments in the constellation of the primal experience. The first of the moments is the fantasy or vision, in which the "patient," in a fetal position, executes a backward somersault *toward* Winnicott. From the standpoint of symbolic development, I regard this as a rise of consciousness accompanying the differentiation of subject (patient) and object (Winnicott), involving the ego's first "recognition" of the other as "out there." The second fantasy or vision, in which the "patient," again in a fetal position, executes a forward somersault *away* from Winnicott represents the ego's first recognition of the self's own agency as an object in its own right, apart from any human object "out there."

The third constellation that completes the primal experience is the *creation of a new world view*. This is quite evident in Winnicott's account of the developments which occurred immediately after the fantasy episodes that constellated "other" and "self" for this patient. "Following this [session] the patient had a very important dream, and the analysis of this showed that he had been able to discard a shield which was no longer necessary since I had proved myself capable of supplying a suitable medium at the moment of his withdrawal." Unfortunately, Winnicott does not let us hear the dream or what was said in the analysis about its actual imagery. However, he does record that from this point in the treatment, there was a restructuring by the patient of the analytic situation, a "coming to grips with his reality situation both at work and at home in a completely new way," and "an acknowledgment of his own original dependence on his mother."

To return for a moment to the movements of the patient in the second fantasy episode, these are reminiscent of Piaget's subject Laurent's ego–self "recognition" during the third month, which constituted one of his first manifestations of a spontaneous self.

At 0;2(23 or 24) he seemed to repeat this movement with ever-increasing enjoyment and ever-decreasing interest in the external result: he brought his head back to the upright position and then threw it back again time after time, *laughing* loudly. (Piaget 1962: 91; italics added)

The importance Winnicott's patient attached to having finally been able to laugh spontaneously is borne out by this comparison.

The containing "medium" which Winnicott believed he had provided for his patient is more than an interpretation, it is in Jung's sense a true symbol, a living "image," both of the mother–infant symbolic relatedness and the therapist–patient "chemistry." Winnicott's ability to offer this living symbol of their connection to his patient at this critical moment in the treatment has to be predicated upon the fact that Winnicott has already established a double bond with his patient. The personal relationship is quite apparent, but the overriding symbolic relatedness between this great doctor and his interesting patient can also be inferred on the basis of the information available to us. I believe that it is this mutual double bond, an in-touchness with each other's experience in the room and a sense of each other as numinous, that contributes to the transformation of the therapeutic environment into a potential space within which the awesome primal experience of self and other and the new world view that follows can unfold. Neumann's description of the nature of the primal mother–infant relationship draws upon similar symbolism, invoking the notion of a medium:

> The state of complete exteriorization, in which the child has not yet separated himself from the mother or the world, is a state of *participation mystique*, of total extendedness; the "mother liquid" in which everything is still in a "state of solution" and the opposites of ego and self, subject and object, person and world have yet to crystallize. With this phase is associated the "oceanic feeling" which arises even in adults whenever everyday conscious reality is expanded, invaded, or replaced by the unitary reality. (Neumann 1966: 83)

The term "participation mystique" is one Jung borrowed from Lucien Levy-Bruhl, who had used it to describe the "primitive's" animistic immersion in his environment. Today analytic psychologists more often speak of the "emotional continuum" that is created when an analyst and patient are immersed in each other's subjectivity. In contemporary self-psychology, this is referred to as intersubjectivity, where the therapist's self serves as the selfobject of the patient and is thus fully privy to the latter's self-experience. Functionally, the "mother liquid" and the "medium" are symbolic equivalents of the Kohutian notion of selfobject.

Winnicott continues his explanation of the therapeutic value of his interpretation, now considered as an example of the importance of the provision of a "holding" environment.

> I would say that *in the withdrawn state a patient is holding the self* [pathological ego–self relation] and that if immediately the withdrawn state appears *the analyst can hold the patient* [normal ego–other relation], then what would otherwise have been a withdrawal state becomes a regression [regeneration of the ego–self relation]. The advantage of a regression is that it carries with it the opportunity for correction of inadequate adaptation-to-need in the past history of the patient, that is to say, in the patient's infancy management. By contrast the *withdrawn* state is not profitable and when the patient recovers from a withdrawn state he or she has not changed. (Winnicott 1954: 261)

In this clinical work of Winnicott's with an adult patient, it is my view that we are witness to the constellation, or re-constellation, of the primal experience in an adult patient, which Winnicott's sensitive work makes possible. What this means is that the patient is enabled to connect with the natural foundation of his personality. What is interesting for our purposes is that *fantasy episodes* are the first direct evidence of this fact. It is reasonable to speculate that we might also find further evidence for the way fantasy guides the constellation of primal experience if we could study the important dream that appeared after the second fantasy episode. If I am correct in my assumption that it too contains elements that can be linked to the elements of the "waking dream" that we have already seen, and which I would argue is a close recapitulation of the normal symbolic mode of Infancy, we can conclude that disturbances in the natural course of psychological development at the beginning of Infancy are susceptible to correction in adult patients. (We might also assume that they are open to spontaneous healing experiences during fortunate encounters outside the treatment context.)

THE WOMAN WHO NEEDS TO BE ROCKED

After six years of treatment with a female analyst, a forty-year-old woman started a second analysis with Winnicott to see what treatment with a man might produce. During the lengthy analytic process that ensued, the patient exhibited an intermittent need for physical contact with Winnicott. Winnicott did not shrink from the engagement this required of him:

> A variety of intimacies were tried out, chiefly those that belong to infant feeding and management. There were violent episodes. Eventually it came about that she and I were together with her head in my hands. (Winnicott 1969: 258)

Once a "holding" and "handling" environment was established, a potential space created, the patient's unconscious began to express itself.

> *Without deliberate action on the part of either of us* there developed a rocking rhythm. The rhythm was rather a rapid one, about 70 per minute (cf. heartbeat), and I had to do some work to adapt to this rate. Nevertheless, there we were with mutuality expressed in terms of a slight but persistent rocking movement. (ibid.; italics added)

Winnicott says that this experience "often repeated, was crucial to the therapy, and the violence that led up to it was only now seen to be a preparation and a complex test of the analyst's capacity to meet the various communicating techniques *of early infancy*" (ibid.; italics added), that is, of his basic capacity to maintain the holding environment without losing his own integrity. Within this context, however, the shared ritual of rocking moved the therapy forward decisively. Winnicott averred that this "shared rocking experience illustrates what I wish to refer to in the early stages of baby care" (ibid.). In order to provide a context for my own symbolic interpretation of Winnicott's undoubtedly successful, if controversial, treatment, I want to discuss my view of the complex origins of the "rocking rhythm."

The Jungian analyst and theoretician of movement, Joan Chodorow (1984, 1991) has shown that the autonomous acts evoked during analysis or dance therapy may originate in the *personal, cultural,* or *primal* unconscious. These movements are *symbolic* acts which are motivated by and derive their imagery from the *personal-complexes, cultural-complexes,* and the *innate affects* of the primal unconscious, respectively. Chodorow's states that during analysis, spontaneous movement is healing when it becomes a form of active imagination.

> Active imagination in movement involves a relationship between two people: a mover/analysand and a witness/analyst. It is within the relationship that the mover may begin to internalize the reflective function of the witness, i.e., yield to the unconscious stream, of bodily felt sensations and images, while at the same time bringing the experience into conscious awareness. (Chodorow 1991: 113)

Although Chodorow is not referring here primarily to mutual therapist–patient movement, her views have helped me to understand the primal therapeutic process that emerged between Winnicott and his woman patient.

I am suggesting that in their symbolic interactions, Winnicott and his patient were like two homunculi entering their alchemical retort and creating a "chemistry" of their own. This was, as the practice of alchemy was for the Renaissance alchemist and his *soror mystica,* a form of shared active imagination. The archetypal field established by their mutual double bond created for Winnicott and his patient a "potential space" for the emergence of a content from the patient's primal or developmental unconscious. The growth potential of the emergent psychic content was realized in the next period of analysis through the creation of a new world view. Once this potential was actualized, the symbolic actions needed to be repeated to allow the emergence of another symbol of progressive development and the next phase of realization. Consciousness, that is, was literally rocked forward. It is not possible to demonstrate with certainty that this symbolically driven process of development in a woman in mid-life had its roots in elements of the primal experience that had become blocked in the stage of Infancy, but our analysis, expressed in somewhat different language, is in concurrence with Winnicott's judgment that this is the most plausible explanation.

THE YOUNG WOMAN WHO COULDN'T SLEEP

Our next case example, one of C. G. Jung's, provides additional support for the nursery rhyme, play song, and baby game approach to infant development, for its therapeutic symbol was a *lullaby*. There are two accounts of this treatment (Jung 1977b, Jaffe 1989) and I have drawn on both.

The patient was a school teacher, referred to Jung by her doctor, who suffered from almost total insomnia, and was one of those people "who agonize over having done nothing properly and not having met satisfactorily the demands of daily life" (Jaffe 1989: 122). Jung felt she needed relaxing and tried to explain to her that he found relaxation by sailing on the lake, letting himself go with the wind. When he saw that his conscious efforts were ineffective, Jung was saddened, because he wanted to help her and there was only this single consultation. At this moment, he listened to the unconscious for inspiration. This is what he heard, and did.

> Then, as I talked of sailing and the wind, I heard the voice of my mother singing a lullaby to my little sister as she used to do when I was eight or nine, a story of a little girl in a little boat, on the Rhine, with little fishes. And I began, almost without doing it on purpose, to hum what I was telling her about the wind, the waves, the sailing, and relaxation, to the tune of the little lullaby. I hummed those sensations, and I could see that she was "enchanted." (ibid.)

The consultation now came to an end, and Jung regretfully sent the patient away. He forgot the name of the patient and the referring doctor, but it was a story that haunted him.

Two years later, Jung met the doctor at a congress and learned that the insomnia had completely disappeared after the consultation. The girl had told him some story about sailing and wind, but he couldn't get out of her what Jung had actually done. He pressed Jung for an explanation, but Jung was too embarrassed to respond.

> How was I to explain to him that I had simply listened to something within myself? I had been quite at sea. How was I to tell him that I had sung her a lullaby with my mother's voice? Enchantment like that is the oldest form of medicine. (ibid.: 123)

In Jung's own account of the case, he gives the following explanation of the therapeutic process.

But it all happened outside my reason: it was not until later that I thought about it rationally and tried to arrive at the laws behind it. She was cured by the grace of God ... A good dream, for example, that's grace. The dream is in essence the gift. The collective unconscious, it's not for you, or me, it's the invisible world, it's the great spirit. It makes little difference what I call it ... the Power beyond us. (Jung 1977b: 419)

Before we return to a discussion of the "gift" Jung received from the unconscious and gave to his patient, we should really discuss the role of sleep in Infancy. Jung evokes the collective unconscious as the source of healing in this case, presumably because difficulty sleeping is a universal human problem. Sleep, however, is one of the hallmarks of healthy infant development.

To be sure, at any age, going to sleep has the potential of evoking all of the innate existential affects: Sadness at the Loss of loved ones; Fear at the prospect of the Unknown; Anger at the Restriction of Autonomy; and, on occasion, Shame at Rejection. We know, however, that it is a particularly difficult task for infants to modulate these turbulent emotions, especially during the first weeks and months of life. Parents are very careful to manage the falling asleep of their infants. One less recognized source of the infant's adaptation to the necessity of sleep comes from the existential affects themselves, for they motivate infants to create rituals on their own to ease the transition to sleep. Such sleep rituals have been viewed as prototypes of rites of safe passage, which, in contrast to rites marking a transformation of identity, serve to protect and maintain a sense of identity during a liminal period (Albert et al. 1979), that is a period marking passage through a threshold (or "limen") from one state of being to another. The other source of adaptation to sleep during the neonatal period is, of course, parental nurturance, especially when expressed by specifically soothing behaviors, of which the lullaby is the prototype.

It is during the period from birth to the first social smile, Neumann's "uroboric" phase of non-recognition that the infant's initial organization of the sleep–wake cycle occurs. The quality and continuity of caregiving during the first weeks – the parental holding "tree" – have been shown to influence this achievement of initial regulation of this important physiological rhythm (Sander 1988: 70–1). As the lullaby says, "If the bough breaks, the cradle will fall." Of critical importance in this regard is the innate parental capacity for soothing and lulling the infant in the presyllabic vocal-auditory realm (Papousek 1992). This is an inborn parental ability, a true parental instinct, but it requires the constellation in the parent of an "infant" symbol for its realization. In India, it is said that the sound of Krishna's flute was the magical cause of the birth of the world and the pre-Hellenic mother goddesses are shown holding lyres, which have the same significance.

Lullabies, in turn, not only express an essential aspect of this earliest developmental period, but also provide parents with a group of musical symbols to guide them through it. Some lullabies not only induce infant sleep but also help parents metabolize their own crisis affects, as the first stanza of the following lullaby suggests.

Baby, baby, if he [Bonaparte] hears you,
As he gallops past the house,
Limb from limb at once he'll tear you,
Just as pussy tears a mouse.

Lullabies, therefore, are to be viewed as symbolical musical systems, created at the dawn of human existence and then preserved over the centuries to serve as symbolic bridges for the transition from wakefulness to sleep.

Robert Graves has said, "The best of the older [nursery rhymes] are nearer to poetry than the greater part of *The Oxford Book of English Verse*," and Professor Cammaerts has suggested that "The nursery rhyme is essentially poetical because essentially musical They do not fail to satisfy the ear" (Opie and Opie 1973: 1–2). A number of authors have suggested that the affective melodies used by parents while singing (Tomkins 1962: 423, Papousek and Papousek 1981) as well as talking (Fernald 1992) to their infants may be those infant's first musical experiences.

Returning to Jung's case, I believe that Jung first established a compassionate, conscious relationship with his patient, "his heart went out to her." His conscious therapeutic efforts, however, were to no avail. He turned his attention inward and received a gift from the unconscious: "I heard the voice of my mother singing a lullaby to my little sister as she used to do when I was eight or nine, a story of a little girl in a little boat, on the Rhine, with little fishes." This "gift" was a symbol, which expresses positive elements of parent–infant "chemistry," love, devotion, interest, and, in this instance, soothing intonations. Jung then presented this symbol to his patient: "And I began, almost without doing it on purpose, to hum what I was telling her about the wind, the waves, the sailing, and relaxation, to the tune of the little lullaby." Jung had created a *temenos*, a numinous archetypal field, and the effect was immediate, the patient was "enchanted."

What, however, is being enchanted? Neumann (1990) suggests that relaxed transitions from waking to sleeping and sleeping to waking are conditioned by a well-structured and resilient ego–self axis.

Even in states of not-being-an-ego, the ego must be suspended in the sheltering wholeness of the Self and, though of course the ego does not reflect on the matter, this is one of the essential conditions for its existence. For this reason, and not only in children, difficulty in sleeping is often the expression of a deep-seated anxiety springing from a disturbance in the relationship between ego and Self and lack of the unconscious sense of confidence which is one of the essential conditions of health. (Neumann 1990: 39–40)

Presumably, Jung's chanting of his mother's lullaby was restorative to the ego–self axis of this patient, enabling her to trust the self to take over during sleep. The lullaby served as a symbolic bridge to the Self, a transitional ego–self axis around which the patients own ego–self axis could regenerate itself. As Jung has said: "This is the condition by which any man in any time can make a transition: with the symbol he can transmute himself" (Jung 1988: 1249)

The symbolic cure offered by the patient's "enchantment" originates in the *numinosity* of the primal emotions evoked by the lullaby, which is a collective expression of positive parent–infant "chemistry." It is around the archetypal possibility of parental nurturance that the patient was able to reconnect with her healthy base. It was this archetype that Jung was spontaneously moved to provide to his care worn patient. Music expresses (in sound images) the movement of the innate affects of the collective unconscious, the cosmic melody of the universe (de Tolnay 1943). In folklore and legend, the door to the "other world island" reverberates with sleep-bringing music. There is a goddess of the cradle and an angel of insomnia, and the list of objects which produce magic sleep is a long one.

Rudolf Otto (1958) reviewed original numinous sounds, including the holy syllable "om," which he notes is simply an articulated sound, "a growl or a groan." In the Kena Upanishad, the numinous is evoked in the following way.

> This is the way It (*sc.* Brahman) is to be illustrated:
> When Lightnings have been loosened:
>   aaah!
> When that has made the eyes to be closed –
>   aaah!
> So far concerning Deity (*devata*).

Thus, the devata, the Brahman, becomes "that in whose presence we must exclaim 'aaah!'" (Otto 1958: 191–2). This "aaah" may be compared with Laurent's "aa" in the presence of his crib toys.

> With regard to inanimate objects, from the beginning of the third month Laurent revealed great interest in the cloth and celluloid toys hanging from the hood of his bassinet. At 0;2(5) he looks at them as yet unsmilingly but emitting periodically the sound *aa* with an expression of *enchantment* [italics added]. (Piaget 1952: 73)

I am not suggesting an equivalency between devata induced "aaahs" and crib toy induced "aas," but I do want to point to the fact that in each case similar vocal expressions are evoked by numinous symbols of an uncanny otherness.

Finally, we discover that the sleep drive, like the hunger drive, requires support by positive affects for normal functioning. As in the cases of the mothers of the starving infants, there is nothing to suggest that even though her insomnia disappeared that in this one consultation all the young woman's "agonizing" was resolved.

TWO SCHIZOPHRENIC PATIENTS

In one of his *Collected Papers on Schizophrenia and Related Subjects*, Harold Searles (1965) describes his use of Mahler's separation-individuation theory of early development in explaining the therapeutic process with adult patients suffering from schizophrenia. In this context, Searles places special emphasis on the establishment of symbiotic interpersonal fields, both in normal development (mother–infant) and in treatment (therapist–patient). The following two cases are drawn from Chapter 12 of his book, "The Evolution of the Mother Transference with the Schizophrenic Patient."

Case 1

Searles first patient is a twenty-seven-year-old woman, the mother of two children, who had been overtly ill with paranoid schizophrenia for at least five years when he undertook intensive psychotherapy with her. She had suffered from latent schizophrenia since about eight or nine years of age and, at twenty-four, had been hospitalized in a nationally famous institution near her home. Over the course of a year, however, she failed to show even symptomatic improvement, despite psychotherapy, sixty-five insulin coma treatments, and twenty-five to fifty electro-shock treatments. She was transferred to Chestnut Lodge where another therapist on the staff began intensive psychotherapy with her. This was discontinued after fifteen months, because the therapist was discouraged by her adamant opposition to further treatment and a steadily mushrooming of her paranoid delusional system.

When Searles began work with her, he found her verbalizing a luxuriantly delusional experience of her life, past and present, which was saturated with external malevolence.

> She was genuinely unable, evidently, to recall any experience of fondness [positive affect], with anyone at any time in her life and she spent the great bulk of each therapeutic session in paranoid tirades directed towards everyone about her – but, increasingly as time went on, focusing more determinedly upon myself – as being the same

malevolent figures who had surrounded her all her life. (Searles 1965: 351)

The patient incessantly poured out accusations that she was being raped, being subjected to surgical operations for various weird purposes, having money extorted from her, and vowed murderous revenge. She subjected Searles to verbal abuse of "truly battering intensity" and, as the months went by, he became increasingly sure that he was the malevolent mother who was primarily responsible for the whole venomous "master plan." (The patient's negative transference, and the analyst's guilty counter-transference, are both, I believe, conditioned in part by the patient's unconscious projection onto Searles of the archetypal symbol of the Terrible Mother, Kali and her sisters. Nevertheless, there are obvious "hooks" for this projection onto her doctor in the forms of psychiatric treatment the patient has already endured by the time she came to him.)

Then, about a year and a half into her analysis with Searles, a dramatic change in the therapist–patient and patient–therapist "chemistry" occurred.

By the eighteenth month, our relationship had become predominantly one of *intense, mutual fondness of a mother–child sort. I consciously adored her,* perceiving her varyingly as an *adorable childlike person and as an omnipotent mother.* For her part, she evidenced towards me *a comparable adoration, which she always denied and expressed somewhat indirectly.* Whether exhibiting deeply dependent or maternal fondness towards me, she had to pooh-pooh the existence of such feelings in herself. (ibid.: 355–6; italics added)

Case 2

This next patient, thirty-five years old at the time of her transfer to Chestnut Lodge, had been suffering from overt schizophrenia, with paranoid and hebephrenic features, for five years.

She had been hospitalized on four occasions during these years, for periods of a few months to one year; had received a total of 175 insulin coma treatments and an indeterminate number of electro-shock treatments; had been engaged in sporadic psychotherapy throughout these five years; and had been sent to the Lodge for a two-month trial of intensive psychotherapy as a last measure to avoid her being subjected to a prefrontal lobotomy as recommended by a number of psychiatrists. (ibid.: 365)

During the initial period of treatment, there were occasional hints that the patient was reacting to Searles as a mother-figure whose importance to her was not insignificant. But she cold-shouldered him so persistently, while expressing her infatuation with another doctor, that his feelings for her became chronic irritation, dissatisfaction, scorn, and lack of interest. He tolerated, with Olympian detachment, her preference for his colleague.

After one and a half years of treatment, Searles noted a marked change in his attitude towards the patient.

> It was ... when she was now practically mute, disheveled, and continuing to exhibit the extremely bizarre behaviour which was to keep her on a disturbed ward for a total of four years, that *I suddenly became aware, with astonishment and very considerable anxiety, of feelings of adoration towards her and fantasies of being married to her.* (ibid.: 367–8; italics added)

Searles also began to see that he was far more important to the patient than he had realized. After several more years of treatment, Searles and his patient exhibited the following transference and countertransference.

> By now (just one month short of five years) *we had become so consciously, but yet very shyly, fond of one another that we could not look at each other during the session without our faces revealing this fondness.* I recall that I fantasied now, and continued to fantasy for many months thereafter on innumerable occasions during our highly productive hours together, that *I was giving suck to her from my breast.* This was a highly pleasurable experience free from either anxiety or guilt. (ibid.: 369; italics added)

Thus, in the second case we are also witness to a remarkable transformation in patient–therapist and therapist–patient "chemistry," and the constellation of parent–infant and infant–parent double bonds.

Searles uses the word *adoration* to describe his feeling for his patients. In the American Heritage Dictionary, adoration is defined as (1) the act of worship and (2) profound love or regard. In the first case, the "image" which accompanies his numinous adoration is that of a "childlike person." In the second case, it is of an "infant," whom he is "nursing" at his breast. These elements – affect, archetypal image, and pattern of behavior – are the phenomenological components of "infant" symbols (Chapter 1). We are safe, then, in assuming that, in both instances, the symbol of the "Divine Child" has been constellated in Searles and projected upon his patients; this is manifest consciously in his fantasies of being "married" to the second patient. A *double* bond, composed of (1) a conscious personal relationship and (2) an unconscious, symbolic relatedness, is the source of the numinous organic "chemistry" that has been established between Searles and his patients.

Searles points out that with both of his cases, at the same time that his adoration of his patients began, their attitude toward him was transformed. They began to experience an intense fondness and adoration for him. This suggests that a "mother" symbol has been constellated in each of his patients and projected upon him. These two deeply wounded individuals had re-established a connection with the natural ground of their personalities. Searles's perception of his second patient as "an omnipotent mother" accords with this view. In other words, in the countertransference the patient is both a personal and a divine child, and in the transference the therapist is both personal and divine mother. With an archetypal field thus established, on the basis of *mutual* double bonds, deep and healing reconstruction of the patient's psyche along the lines of normal infant development becomes a therapeutic possibility.

9

Rediscovering Pretend

The child's discovery of the symbolic mode "pretend" announces the beginning of the stage of Early Childhood (Chapter 4). Make-believe may be viewed from three perspectives: (a) the interiorization of the symbolic process in social and individual pathways during Infancy; (b) the emergence of pretend itself at the beginning of Early Childhood; and (c) its differentiation during this same stage. I begin the present chapter with an analysis of disturbances in the child's development of pretend as seen from these three standpoints. This is followed by a discussion of the disordered development of pretend in a child and an adult patient, as well as the healing of these disturbances during treatment.

DISTURBANCES IN INTERIORIZATION DURING INFANCY

Selma Fraiberg has presented a longitudinal study of social play between parents and their blind infants, which includes examples both of healthy social play and of social play disrupted by parental enactments. In the following observation, a social play disruption results from an enactment by a father with his two-month-old blind son.

> Father puts Timothy on his lap and begins to play with him. He taps Timothy's fisted hands, knocking them up and down ... Father briskly pats Timothy's bottom as though spanking him and says, "You're bad ... again." He then holds Timothy's arms and moves them in a mock boxing motion. He says, "Bet you like to be beat up, you like to fight. I could break you right in half ..." (Fraiberg 1974: 214)

In addition to the way such parental behavior distorts the natural rhythm of the infant's play, such enactments are bound to have a negative effect on father–infant bonding and color the infant's beginning construction of the feeling-toned father-complex with disintegrative anxiety. Another kind of social play disruption results from a mother's enactment with her eleven-month-old blind son.

Jackie has a game with mother. Seated on her lap, back against her chest, he will lean forward, then backwards, banging against her chest. Mother says he mainly plays this game with her. "He likes to beat me," she says fondly. (ibid.: 213)

We can infer from the budding sadomasochism that significant disturbances have occurred in the differentiation of infant play and its interiorization, which has its roots in faulty mother–infant bonding. Something is off in the affective quality of the resulting mother-complex. The next observation, on the other hand, shows an episode of social play, in the form of a Knee ride, between a mother and her ten-month-old blind daughter that can be described as positively enabling.

Carol is bounded on mother's knee while mother chants the rhyme, "Ride little Horsie/ trot downtown/ watch out Carol/ that you *don't fall down*." The last phrase of the rhyme is slowed down when spoken, and on the word "down," mother extends her legs so that Carol ... falls backward onto her mother's legs. After a few seconds mother pulls Carol back up. (ibid.: 207)

Although Fraiberg has not presented studies which evaluate the emergence of pretend in her subjects, it is my belief that social and individual play disruptions during Infancy will interfere with the interiorization process and result in disturbances in the emergence of pretend at the beginning of Early Childhood. Impingements which impact both a developing individual's exploration and play produce their negative effect on symbolic development through disruption of the developmental dialectic itself.

DISTURBANCES IN EMERGENCE OF PRETEND IN EARLY CHILDHOOD

Stanley Greenspan and Alicia Lieberman have presented a method for assessing whether patterns that emerge in representational elaboration and differentiation during Early Childhood are adaptive or maladaptive. They have been able to link maladaptive patterns with maladaptive environments.

In contrast to the adaptive environment, the maladaptive environment fails to support the development of representational capacities. At its most extreme, such an environment undermines the child's *emerging capacity* to use symbols by discouraging language or representational play or by distracting or misreading the child's symbolic communication. (Greenspan and Lieberman 1994: 11; italics added)

The maladaptive behavior of the mother in the following example can be contrasted with that of the mother who encouraged her child's construction of pretend by beginning symbolic play before the child's first pretend episode (Chapter 4).

> Robbie's 2-year free play with his mother was characterized by the complete absence of representational play. Robbie seemed mesmerized by his mother's activities, and she, in turn, took over the situation and played as gleefully as if she were a child herself. She made cookies with play dough; greeted Robbie through a puppet, and made the puppet squeal and get away when Robbie tried to touch it; started a telephone conversation with Robbie and told him what to say (he dutifully repeated it); made Robbie "write" his name with a crayon; and showed Robbie pictures in a book ... Robbie appears in this session as a pretext for his mother's own play. (ibid.: 28)

We can wonder what this mother's social play with Robbie was like during his infancy and how it effected his earliest interiorization of the symbolic process. In this observation, the potential space between mother and child is filled with the mother's fantasy activity, leaving no room for that of her child. Viewing this narcissistic mother's play behavior from another developmental perspective, it is reminiscent of Jacqueline's first social play with Lucienne at the beginning of the Preschool Period, when she treated her sister like a doll (Chapter 5).

DISTURBANCES IN DIFFERENTIATION OF PRETEND DURING EARLY CHILDHOOD

In her study of the fantasy behaviors of nursery school children, Rosalind Gould writes of a child's inability to distinguish firmly between a pretend and a real danger. She speaks of this state of affairs as *fluctuating certainty*, and she presents Clara as an example of a five-year-old child who is suffering from such a disturbance.

> Clara, whose aggression-ridden fantasy monologues in the Fours will be quoted in detail, was by chance observed by me in a brief interchange with her friend Laura, when she was in the Fives. When I first noticed them in their classroom they were conversing, close together. What held my eye was seeing Laura move quickly back a foot or so, openly don some mask-like covering over her face (which she had been holding in her hand), then advance back towards Clara in a caricature of a menacing monster. Clara drew back, eyes wide in fright, saying in a half whisper, "Take it off, take it off." Laura did so promptly, with apparent surprise at Clara's intense reaction. (Gould 1972: 78–9)

Gould suggests that a child's experience of fluctuating certainty as to what is real indicates some affective interference in utilizing his or her ego-resources to test reality. In this she echoes Erikson's notion of the origin of disruptions in the child's play. She shows that disturbances in the emergence of pretend are accompanied by limitations of *self*-representation, specifically on lessened ability to "become the other" in make-believe. In its most extreme, this leads to an inability to engage in fantasy play at all, which is usually accompanied by a tendency toward acting out. This inability to "become" the other is, I feel, an early indication of a lack of differentiation of symbolic schemes or failure to generalize them during Early Childhood (Chapter 4).

CLINICAL CASE HISTORIES

The first case we discuss is that of Gabrielle, better known by her nickname, *The Piggle* (Winnicott 1977), a girl who lost the capacity for pretend during Early Childhood when her mother became a "witch," and regained it during her consultations with Winnicott. The second case is that of an adult, Kirk Allen, one of the occupants of *The Jet-Propelled Couch* (Lindner 1999), who only realized his capacity for pretend as an adult patient.

Before discussing the case of Gabrielle, I want to present another example of a mother who became a "witch" as part of the *normal* process of her daughter's symbolic development. When Piaget's subject Jacqueline encounters the "horrid lady," that representation results from a momentary transformation of the mother imago from nurturant to malign in response to developmental stresses.

Jacqueline

Jacqueline dreamed of the "horrid lady" three months after the birth of her sister, Lucienne, one stress, when she was also in the midst of toilet training, another stress.

> At 2;8(4) she was wakened by a cock crowing, and said, still half asleep: "*I'm afraid of the lady who's singing. She's singing very loud. She's scolding me.*" At 2;8(11) X. woke with a loud scream: "*It was all dark, and I saw a lady over there* (pointing to her bed). *That's why I screamed.*" Then she explained that it was a horrid lady who stood with her legs apart and played with her fæces. (Piaget 1962: 177)

In contrast to this transitory appearance of the "horrid lady" who was observed only on these two occasions, the "black mama" and/or "blackness" are present in Gabrielle's dreams and fantasies over a period of two years.

Gabrielle

When Gabrielle was two years and four months old, her parents wrote to Winnicott to describe a great change that had occurred following the birth of her sister, Susan, seven months before.

> When Susan was born, Gabrielle seemed thrown out of her mold, and cut off from her sources of nourishment. We found it hurtful to see her so diminished and reduced, and she may well have sensed this. (Winnicott 1977: 20)

The reduced state of Gabrielle's ego was a "complex indicator," in Jung's original terminology (borrowed from Pierre Janet) an *abaissement du niveau mental*. Jung has also referred to the ego whose level of consciousness is affected by a complex as an *affect-ego*.

> By "affect-ego" I mean the modification of the ego-complex resulting from the emergence of a strongly toned complex. In the case of painful affects the modification consists of a restriction, a withdrawal of many parts of the normal ego. Many other wishes, interests, and affects must make way for the new complex, so far as they are opposed to it. (*CW* 3: 86,41)

In its extreme form, an affect-ego becomes what Neumann refers to as a *distress-ego*, quite frequently the signal of the presence of a negative mother-complex.

> ... the predominance of positive factors constellates the image of the positive mother, while the predominance of negative factors constellates the image of the negative mother. The predominance of a negative experience inundates the ego nucleus, dissolves it or gives it a negative charge. The ego of a child thus marked by a negative primal relationship we call a distress-ego, because its experiences of the world, the thou, and the Self bears the imprint of distress or doom. Thus in the child's mythological apperception a positive primal relationship is reflected in the archetypal image of paradise, and a disturbed primal relationship of the distress-ego in that of hell. (Neumann 1990: 74)

In Gabrielle's case, the archetypal images that compromised her ego functioning appeared at night in terrifying dreams and fantasies, which disturbed her sleep and haunted her by day.

> "She has a black mummy and daddy. The black mummy comes in after her at night and says: "Where are my yams?" (To yam = to eat.

She pointed out her breasts, calling them yams, and pulling them to make them larger.) Sometimes she is put into the toilet by the black mummy. The black mummy, who lives in her tummy, and who can be talked to there on the telephone, is often ill, and difficult to make better. (Winnicott 1977: 6–7)

The mother has become a "witch," and even the father imago has darkened.

Gabrielle experiences a *curiosity* disruption: "She becomes easily bored and depressed which was not evident before, and is suddenly very conscious of her relationships and especially of her identity" (ibid.: 6). She also displays a *play* disruption: "She used to play all the time, but since the change occurred she tended to lie in her cot and suck her thumb without playing" (ibid.: 14). With both curiosity and play blocked, their normal developmental dialectic is halted, and Gabrielle suffers a dissolution of her early *ego-identity*.

The mother said that there had been a great change toward ill health in the Piggle recently. She was not naughty and she was nice to the baby. It was difficult to put into words what was the matter. But *she was not herself*. In fact she refused to be herself and said so: "I'm the mummy. I'm the baby." She was not to be addressed as herself. She had developed a high-voiced chatter which was not hers. If she talked seriously, her voice was much deeper. (ibid.: 13)

I have pointed out again and again the need for a vigorous dialectic between curiosity and play in order to maintain a healthy ego-identity. Let us revisit that argument.

Play is intimately entwined with the emotions in the various ways we have discussed; first of all as an expressive aspect of emotion, of the joy of life itself; then in its transformative function of updating identity, developmentally through its never-ending dialectic with curiosity-exploration under the aegis of the affect of Interest, and into maturity through the socialized forms of games which insure an ongoing opportunity for relationship with the expressive world; and finally in its role of potentiating creative imagination through the seizure of consciousness by images and symbols of the expressive world which occurs in play. (L. H. Stewart and C. T. Stewart 1981: 50)

The pervasive nature of Gabrielle's psychological disturbance indicates that she is experiencing a general block to her symbolic development. Without an exuberant capacity for play, she is cut off from her healthy base.

When, one month after the parents' first letter requesting help, Gabrielle has had her first consultation with Winnicott, her mother's report to him indicates that the dialectic process between curiosity and play is beginning to be released from its inhibition: "She is still often listless and sad, but has been *playing more* and has started to take *more interest* in things again, which we find encouraging" (Winnicott 1977: 19; italics added).

After the second consultation a month later, there is evidence of a beginning restoration of Gabrielle's ego-identity.

When the Piggle came back from London she did not mention her visit, but played very zestfully for the rest of the day. Altogether we feel that she has been much freer since her last visit to you; she sometimes plays on her own again, and *talks in what I take to be her own voice.* (ibid.: 31–2; italics added)

Overcoming the inhibition of the developmental dialectic between curiosity and play, the motor to development, evidently has helped Gabrielle strengthen the integrity of her ego–Self axis.

Continuing treatment helps Gabrielle heal her pathological mother-complex. Between the second and third consultations, Gabrielle begins to be aware of a relation between her mother and the "black mummy." As her mother puts it to Winnicott, "I have been told frequently lately that the black mummy comes and makes me black" (ibid.: 33). After the fourth consultation, Gabrielle's awareness of the contagious nature of her mother's "blackness," enables her to begin to "remove" it.

For a few days now she would not let me kiss her, in case I make her black; but she has been much more affectionate with me, and has kissed me spontaneously, which she has never done before. *The other night, she told me that I was a nice mummy, and then proceeded to scrape me. She said she was scraping the black off, and then she tried to blow it off the pillow.* (ibid.: 63–4; italics added)

Gabrielle has begun to understand her mother's "blackness" as the result of a momentary, emotional state. She even says, "You become a black mummy when you are cross." (ibid.: 119). Through these healing behaviors, Gabrielle has transformed her archetypal relation with her mother from negative to positive and subsumed it under a relatively normal personal mother-complex belonging to the depressive position (the mother can be bad *and* good). And during the eleventh consultation, Gabrielle tells Winnicott a tale about witches: "One day there was a witch, a sea witch, a woman witch, not a man witch [play on words]; baby-hugger-horrible" (ibid.: 140).

It is after Gabrielle's twelfth consultation that her mother writes to Winnicott to tell him that she has become aware of her own family-complex that she has brought to (projected upon) Gabrielle in the course of parenting her:

> I would like to tell you – though you may know this – how much writing you has helped me; somehow to give form to my perplexities and fears, with the knowledge that they would be received with great understanding; and the feeling of being in relation with you. I am sure all this helped me to work through our anxieties about Gabrielle and again find our right relationship with her. My anxieties were very intense at the time of Susan's birth – I forget whether I told you that I have a brother, whom I greatly resented, who was born when I was almost exactly the same age as Gabrielle was when Susan was born. (ibid.: 161)

Gabrielle's mother is now actively and consciously integrating the complex which, when it was unconscious, was a necessary condition for Gabrielle's illness. In addition, as Gabrielle is now in possession of the idea of a "witch," a universal cultural image of the Terrible Mother which is at the same time a container for the anxieties stirred up by such a figure, her psychological immune system is, so to speak, fortified for future encounters with "horrid" maternal behavior. Such is the prophylactic value of myth, fairytale, and legend. Neurotic disturbances tend to arise only when the contents that are constellated in the unconscious in the course of life's experiences cannot be contained by any available concepts in the psyche.

> That is why it is so extremely important to tell children fairytales and legends ... because these things are instrumental symbols with whose help unconscious contents can be canalized into consciousness, interpreted, and integrated. Failing this, their energy flows off into conscious contents which, normally, are not much emphasized, and intensifies them to pathological proportions. (*CW* 9ii: 259,169)

(Readers will find discussions of the significance of the symbolic image of the witch during subsequent stages of development in the following articles: *Preschool Period*: Gould 1972; Neumann 1973; Dahl 1989; L.H. Stewart 1992a, Chapter 2; *Middle Childhood*: Hawkey 1948; *Adolescence*: Jung, *CW* 17: 107, 54–5; Levinson 1984; Lane and Chazan 1989; Feldman 1991; *Adulthood*: Hart 1977; Jung, *CW* 7: 280,179; Beiser 1985.)

Kirk Allen

Kirk Allen, a physicist in his thirties, was referred to Robert Lindner for analysis because the research digests he was preparing for his division head were becoming incoherent, covered with unintelligible symbols and pictographs. Kirk appeared normal in every other way, but he was preoccupied about ideas about living part of the time on another planet. He apologized to his boss for the decline in his work and said he would try not to be "gone" so much and "to spend more time on this planet."

This analytic patient was the only child of a US Admiral, who ran his household like the wardroom of a battleship where no playfulness was allowed. His thirty-five-years-younger wife deferred to his authority in the home. Kirk was born in Hawaii, lived the first year in Paris, returned briefly to Hawaii, and then lived until he was fourteen on a mandated South Pacific island where his father was Commissioner. When Kirk was fourteen, his father died and he and his mother returned to the US. She placed him in a prep school, and from this time forward they saw each other only occasionally until her death when Kirk was twenty-nine. After completing undergraduate and graduate studies, Kirk took his job with the US Government.

From birth, his primary caretakers were a series of nurses and governesses. The most significant of these was his Polynesian wet-nurse, who had cared for him from birth until her sudden death when he was six years old. Kirk ate, slept, and played with her. His first language was her native dialect, which he spoke for years before learning English. When a visitor noted that Kirk did not speak a "white language," the nurse was given other duties for several months while he was taught English. Kirk recalled this period of re-education (and separation from his first mothering figure) as a painful time, even though the nurse gradually recovered her place.

As there were no white children on the island, Kirk's playmates were native children. He felt set apart and different from them, both superior and inferior. As his isolation increased, he turned to daydreaming, which eventually occupied most of his time. The conscious content of these fantasies was drawn from his reading; for instance, he identified himself with characters of the Oz books. He ploughed through every book on the island.

After being sexually seduced and then abandoned by a governess when he was eleven years old, Kirk increased his reading and daydreaming.

From the stories he read he constructed another and different universe, peopled with characters from the tales of his favorite authors and infused with vivid movement, dramatic event and colorful detail. In the beginning such fantasies were random, fitful, inconsistent and loosely constructed as most daydreams tend to be. He did not concentrate on any given set of characters, events, or places, but freely developed whatever took his fantasy – which then followed rather closely the book or story he happened to be reading. (Lindner 1999: 177–8)

The vivid pattern of his preadolescent daydreaming underwent a significant transformation when he was twelve years old.

In quick succession he read, and reread: novels by an English author, philosophical reflections by an American stylist, and adventure tales by another American featuring an all-conquering hero who was a prototype for Superman. These last were adventure tales of space travel, and the fictional hero bore the name *Kirk Allen*. At this juncture, the real Kirk entered into a pathological identification with the fictional Kirk.

> As I read about the adventures of Kirk Allen in these books the conviction began to grow on me that the stories were not only true to the very last detail but that they were about *me*. In some weird and inexplicable way *I knew that what I was reading was my biography*. Nothing in these books was unfamiliar to me: I recognized everything – the scenes, the people, the furnishings of rooms, the events, even the words that were spoken – recognized all this with a sense of familiarity that one has when one sees a house in which he has lived or a friend from years gone by. The whole business, if you like, was one long, almost interminable, *déjà vu* experience ... My everyday life began to recede at this point. In fact, it became fiction – and, as it did, the books became my reality. (ibid.: 179)

The corollary was that Kirk's everyday life became fiction:

> To daily affairs, to the task of staying alive, eating, studying, moving about on the island, I gave little attention – for this was my dream. Real life – *my* real life, was in the books. There I lived: there I had my being. (ibid.)

In other words the more Kirk identified with the fictional hero archetype, the more his actual ego-personality was suppressed.

Between his twelfth year and his thirties, when he finally entered analysis, his fantasy underwent progressive differentiation. During this same period he completed his education and commenced work as a government research physicist. By this time, however, Kirk was firmly convinced that the books he continued to read were about him and that somehow the author had obtained knowledge of his future life and had written its story. At first he referred to his fantasy activity as *remembering the future*, which included filling in spaces in the stories with "recollections" of his own. When he became bored reliving his future life, Kirk picked up where his "biographer" had left off and began to "record" the subsequent history of the heroic "Kirk Allen."

Socially, Kirk had lived most of his life isolated from his peers. One night when a female colleague openly expressed interest in him, his identification with the fictional Kirk catapulted itself into a new form.

This was the night that Kirk achieved for the first time what he considered the most unusual experience of his life – "the illusion of actual tenancy of the body and being of the future Kirk Allen on another planet ..." (ibid.: 195)

From that moment on, he spent more and more of his time *being* "Kirk Allen," the interplanetary space traveler.

Kirk shared with his analyst, Robert Lindner, all of the "records" he had constructed to document his life as "Kirk Allen." These included twelve thousand pages of typescript, divided into some two hundred chapters, two thousand more pages of handwritten notes, a glossary of one hundred pages, eighty-two color maps, a two-hundred-page history of the empire Kirk Allen ruled, etc. A sample of the titles included in these "records" is as follows: "The Fauna of Srom Olma I," "The Transportation System of Sereneb," "Science of Srom" ... "The History of the Intergalactic Scientific Institute," "Parapsychology of Srom Norbra X" ... "Sociology on Srom Olma I" ... and "The Religious Beliefs of the Valley Dwellers." Reading these titles from the standpoint of Kirk's symbolic development, the anlage of future cultural attitudes are apparent.

As a psychoanalyst, Lindner was convinced of two things, Kirk's utter madness, and the life-sustaining necessity of his psychosis (compare Jung's comments on the Schreber case in *CW*).

After one year of what appears to be a thorough, reductive analysis this was the situation.

By this time we had been able to work out the entire mechanics of the gigantic fantasy, we had traced its sources to their roots, and we had even elaborated, in meticulous detail, the one-to-one correspondence of experiential fact with imaginative feature. But none of this affected my patient's behavior to the slightest degree. (ibid.: 196)

Lindner reviewed his notes and decided that Kirk's primary developmental trauma occurred when the family severed his symbiotic relation with his first nurse. At that time, Kirk was in Early Childhood. For Lindner, this was an age when the chief mental operation is the testing of reality, and, deprived of an adult he could trust to help him, Kirk never went through this phase. This left the boy with a stunted capacity to distinguish between the real world and that which was the product of his own mental functioning. At best, he suffered from "fluctuating certainty."

Lindner, in a move all child therapists would have approved of, decided there remained but a single unexplored way to handle the case: "In a sudden flash of inspiration it came to me that in order to separate Kirk from his madness it was necessary for me to enter his fantasy and, from that position, to pry him loose from his psychosis" (ibid.: 198).

The results of this new approach were apparent at the end of the first hour in which it was tried: "As Kirk was about to depart he paused in the doorway, from where his eyes swept over me in a long, slow quizzical gaze" (ibid.: 201). Lindner interpreted Kirk's facial expression as indicating that he had forced a slight crack in the apparently unassailable fantasy: "I knew that my participation in it, the evidence I had just given of total acceptance – even of conspiracy to the extent of helping him sustain his defense when it was threatened – had for the first time, made him question it" (ibid.).

At the time Lindner understood his intervention as an application of John Rosen's direct analysis, then just being developed. It involved active engagement with the patient's psychotic complexes on the part of the therapist:

> My direct involvement in the fantasy that had, until then, been his private preserve, constricted his "*lebensraum*," confronted him with his mirror image, and maneuvered him into the critical reality position. As a consequence, slowly but surely, he was being edged out of his psychosis. (ibid.: 203)

Lindner says that in the beginning this approach was a game for him, but it was one that soon "fascinated" him. Although this countertransference condition was one of "enchantment developing toward obsession," Lindner always kept one foot in the everyday world. As a therapist his task was to keep his feet on the ground and fly into the patient's intergalactic world at the same time.

Then, an amazing event occurred, which broke the spell Lindner was under and marked the successful conclusion of Kirk's treatment. The hour in question begins with Lindner absorbed in reviewing some of Kirk's notes, while Kirk stood by looking at Lindner with an expression of concern. They carried the "work" further, Lindner with lively absorption, Kirk in a desultory manner. Then, Kirk makes a "confession."

> Kirk: "All right," he said. "I'll tell you – but you're not going to like it ..." Then, "I've been lying to you."
> Lindner: "Lying to me? What about?"
> Kirk: He leaned across and picked up the notebook. "About this," he said, "and this," indicating the papers on the desk, "and all the stuff I've been giving you these last few weeks. It's all a lie, all of it. I've been making it up ... inventing all that – that – nonsense!" (ibid.: 213)

Lindner queries him and Kirk replies, "It's all foolishness!"

Kirk: He seated himself on the edge of his chair, his whole body rigid and his face tight with tension. "I know what I've been telling you," he said earnestly. "But, believe me, I've been *pretending* for a long time. There've been no trips. I saw through all of that stuff – weeks ago ..."
Lindner: "What do you mean – you saw through?"
Kirk: "Just what I said. I realized I was crazy. I realized I've been deluding myself for years; that there never have been any 'trips,' that it was all – just insanity."
Lindner: "Then why," I asked, "why did you pretend? Why did you keep on telling me ... ?"
Kirk: "Because I felt I had to," he said. "Because I felt *you wanted me to*!" (ibid.: 214; italics added)

Lindner believed that this amusing, almost novelistic denouement, marked both a culmination and a new beginning in the transference.

It has not been a sudden thing, this abandonment by Kirk of his psychosis, but the result of a dawning understanding that he had begun to develop from the moment he became aware I was sharing – or at least appeared to share – his delusion. From that time forward it had lost its potency ... With this reduction in the appeal of the fantasy, moreover, the insights gained but not employed during the long months of our dynamic exploration of the past at last came into their own. Kirk's former ability to enter the fantasy, to achieve that abnormal state of sensitivity to his needs that had catapulted him into his mythical universe, began to diminish. It was not long before the whole amazing defense – for such Kirk now recognized his obsession to be – collapsed or, better, decayed, to be replaced, item for item, by reality. (ibid.: 214–15)

My understanding of the case, however, differs in certain respects from Lindner's.

Certainly I agree that the patient's identification with the fictional hero that started at age twelve was conditioned by an earlier disturbance. Although the developmental history does not provide enough detailed information to identify the nature of the disorder, the available evidence points to a disturbance in the development of the symbolic process when the disruption of the relationship with his nurse occurred. This was during Early Childhood, the stage of Pretend, and the separation also haunted Kirk's Preschool Period, the stage of the Imaginary Companion. Kirk's social isolation diminished the likelihood of interpersonal experiences that might correct pathological fantasy activity. His cognitive development, on the other hand, was intact: in fact, that was his main ego strength.

If Lindner is correct in assuming that Kirk's florid fantasy life was an attempt at self-healing, then we can speculate that the failure of this symbolic solution was due in part to his social isolation. It is this speculation that gains credence from the events which follow upon Lindner's decision to join Kirk in his fantasy world.

Lindner's intervention clearly worked. The question is why? What Lindner did with this adult patient is similar to what the child therapist does everyday with his patients, that is, to join them in sociodramatic role play. In such play, the child selects the role the therapist is to play, or in adult psychological words, projects an unconscious content onto the therapist. If the therapist's enactment is empathically grounded and he or she plays the role correctly, the child is mirrored and experiences integration and healing. Lindner's intervention corresponds even more exactly to the behavior of those mothers who engage their infants and toddlers in symbolic play just as the latter are on the verge of discovering the capacity for "make-believe" in themselves (Chapter 4). In this context, Kirk's "long, slow quizzical gaze" can be seen as a moment of long-delayed "recognition." What dawned on Kirk was that Lindner was *pretending*! This makes it reasonable to assume that at some moment between this "recognition" and Kirk's open confession that he too was only pretending, there was a moment when Kirk discovered, or rediscovered, his own capacity for make-believe. By that time, a process of interiorization and self-recognition had occurred! As the particular fantasy had now achieved its purpose, its marginalization from consciousness as a set of delusional contents could be accompanied by a release of imaginal energy that could be utilized both for consolidation of the symbolic emergence and for future psychological development. "Srom" and "Sereneb" were, moreover, symbolic communities that could after all serve as foundation stones for the real community Kirk would build as he expanded his social relationships and reversed his isolation.

10

Imaginary Companions as Inner Healers

In our previous analysis of the phenomenon of the imaginary companion (Chapter 5), we indicated that many researchers of this phenomenon in normal developmental contexts have concluded that the companion was invented by the child for individual reasons and that it was not a symbolic expression characteristic of a particular stage of development. We have found similar views stated by authors who have encountered the imaginary companion in various clinical contexts (Congdon et al. 1961; Wickes 1966; Bach 1971; Myers 1976; Bliss 1980, 1986; Bass 1983; Young 1988). Our assertion is that the imaginary companion is *the* symbolic mode of the Preschool Period and that, far from being invented by the child at that stage, the companion is produced by the archetypal imagination and discovered by the child.

The implications of this symbolic understanding are profound. The clinical cases that I will analyze in this chapter have been selected both because they provide further evidence that the emergence of the imaginary companion is specific to the Preschool Period and because they demonstrate that the companion is an inner healer. The emergence of the imaginary companion during psychotherapy, in child and adult alike, marks the effort to complete the incompletely realized developmental potential of the preschool stage of development. I will argue that when this constructive process is completed, the imaginary companion can serve as the symbolic base of a structure that functions in the unconscious to compensate the developing ego, as its ego-ideal/shadow.

Margaret

In Chapter 8, "Imaginary Companions," of *The Inner World of Childhood*, Frances Wickes (1966: 164–210) describes her treatment of Margaret. A discussion by Jung of this case is also available (CW 17: 224–7,128–31). We agree with Wickes's view that the imaginary companion is the progressive growing Self, in its ideal and less desirable aspects, and that this symbol serves as a vehicle for the projection of turbulent emotions, which need to be somehow integrated into the developing personality. What Wickes does not offer is a sense of the developmental stage at which the companion appears, and a clear opinion as to whether the companion is invented or discovered. We can differentiate these issues by a clear look at the details of Margaret's case, which Wickes had generously supplied.

Although Margaret began her life with an operation in Infancy that left a train of physical disabilities, her loving parents and "a whole world of people, unseen by other eyes, who came and went, danced, sang, played, or rendered homage as her imagination dictated," created a family atmosphere and an imaginative realm which nourished her early development. When she started school at seven years of age, however, Margaret was confronted by the reality of the greater world and found it too hard: "Now, suddenly, like a cloud that swallowed up the sun, had come school that ate chunks our of the day which had always been exclusively hers and that paid no attention to her realities" (Wickes 1966: 183). Because of her lack of muscular coordination, writing and drawing came very hard. When engaged in fantasy, she would often spoil her school work by scribbling "funnies" over it.

By the time she was eight years old, Margaret was referred for special psychological help because of social and academic problems at school. The first phase of her treatment utilized Margaret's strength of imagination to focus her on the task of developing her reading skills.

> For the sake of stories, carefully selected because of their imaginative appeal, she learned to read and, once started, made rapid progress, though great care had to be taken not to permit overexertion. (ibid.: 184)

It was reasonable to expect that reading stories selected by the therapist would provide Margaret with a stimulus to the development of the symbolic process (Chapter 5). In Margaret's other studies, however, progress was still slow and there were continued resistances.

The second phase of Margaret's therapy was ushered in when she made the following announcement.

> "I have a twin. Her name is Anna. She is just like me except that she always wears beautiful clothes and never wears glasses." (Glasses meant her weak eyes that kept her from poring over the books that she now loved.) "If Anna were here, I should like to work better." (ibid.: 184–5)

This statement marks the emergence of the symbolic mode characteristic of the Preschool Period, the imaginary companion. Margaret has overcome a block to development by establishing a connection with a Self-symbol expressive of her healthy base. The continuation of the therapy session demonstrates not only Margaret's openness to the imaginal world of the Self, but also that of her therapist.

> "I should like to have Anna too," was the [therapist's] answer. "Suppose you invite her." Margaret went out of the room and returned with Anna who was at once provided with a chair and table and instructed by Margaret as to the work to be done. In order to show Anna how to write she began to write. After this Anna was always there. First Margaret would write and then Anna. It was interesting to note that if she became discouraged and wished to show temper or obstinacy she always slipped out of Anna's seat and had her outbursts in her own character of Margaret. (ibid.: 185)

Francis Wickes's support for her patient's symbolic development is apparent when she firmly invites "Anna" into the office! Here, Margaret's capable ego-ideal is personified by "Anna," while she herself is still identified with her underachieving shadow. One day Margaret was frustrated at the difficulty she was experiencing in learning to write: she was uncertain whether or not to blame her mother for this. Again showing her confidence in the developmental potential of the symbol, the therapist directed Margaret to consult her imaginary companion for an answer to this question by saying, "You might ask Anna."

> She left the room, and, after a while she returned saying, "Anna says it is my own fault and I had better go to work," and she immediately did so. (ibid.)

The compensatory function that "Anna" serves is quite striking in this observation, and it reminds us of the moral suasion given to Jacqueline by the "aseau" (Chapter 5). Next we observe how Margaret has interiorized her therapist's suggestion to consult "Anna" on important matters and, in so doing, initiated a new phase in her own development.

> Before this she wouldn't discuss her responsibilities, but now she would go out of the room, and talk it over with Anna, and bring back the result. Sometimes she would return with every sign of rebellion, but she would always tell the truth as to what Anna's dictates were and she would go out again to remonstrate, but Anna insisted, "Margaret, it is you fault. You've got to try." (ibid.: 185–6)

At this injunction, a second companion appeared briefly: this was a blind child whose parents were sorry that they had been bad to her and did everything that she now wanted; she could not be asked to do school work and had to be helped in every way. This seemingly infantile regressive movement appears to have been in the service of the ego, however, for it ushers in an important progressive movement. This transitional phase of partial resistance to treatment culminated when the therapist suggested that Margaret, who was experiencing a storm of anger toward her "horrid" mother, consult "Anna" again: "There was a long pause, then she said, 'Pooh! I guess I know as much as Anna. I'm horrid. I'll go tell Mother'" (ibid.: 187). With Margaret now integrating her ego-ideal and shadow, she no longer needs to consult "Anna."

Jung noted that a block to development was favorable to the growth of a second personality, and in Margaret's case that second personality was a normal developmental one. Jung emphasizes the importance of integrating the emerging potential signified by such an ideal figure:

> Such a condition is most favourable to the growth of a second personality. The fact that her conscious mind fails to progress does not mean in the least that her unconscious personality will also remain at a standstill. This part of herself will advance as time goes on, and the more the conscious part hangs back, the greater will be the dissociation of personality. Then one day the more developed personality will appear on the scene and challenge the regressive ego. This was the case with Margaret: she saw herself confronted by "Anna," her superior twin sister, who for a while represented her moral reason. Later the two merged into one, and this signified a tremendous advance ... (CW 17: 227,131)

Shortly after her imaginary companion's "death," Margaret said that she would die and "they" will weep! Ten days later, with her face pale and her eyes glaring, she said, "I want to see someone die. I want to watch them do it. I *want to*!" (Wickes 1966: 188). This powerful self-assertion was the antecedent to the birth of yet another imaginary companion, who emerged when Margaret was at home.

> This was Daphy who lived in Kiki House. The Kiki House was a little old wooden house which the child passed on her way to the park. It was a house that belonged to the past generations, the only wooden house in that part of the city. It appealed to the child's imagination and immediately she began to people it ... Daphy would not grow up, would not "be good" ... Daphy never appeared at school or during her hours of special work ... It was Daphy who made all the naughty suggestions. It was Daphy who could not dress herself or tie her shoes or keep her temper. When Daphy became quite unbearable and something obviously had to be done, she was put in the Kiki House and not allowed to come out. (ibid.: 189–90)

Margaret's emerging healthy rage has now been personified as "Daphy," a shadow-complex complementary to "Anna," who had to be brought under that ego-ideal's control. (A psychoanalyst would link the figure of Daphy to the likely presence of Oedipal death-wishes directed toward the competitor for father's attention, mother; such wishes would, of course, have to be contained.)

About the time that "Daphy" was born, Margaret joined a play class and found the necessary adjustments none too easy.

> One day when there had been storms she was sent home. She wept bitterly, but insisted that she was weeping for a farm where she had been the summer before and for a very much younger child with whom she had played. She told me this most dramatically and said, "You should have seen me weep." (ibid.: 190–1)

That night Margaret had a dream, which she told her therapist the next day.

> I was in K playing with H (the farm and the little girl). We were in the woods. I filled my wheelbarrow with leaves. Then I ran right over H and killed her dead. Just think, I killed her! squashed and dead! (ibid.: 191)

After a long pause, a wicked gleam appeared in Margaret's eyes and she said: "Some day soon I think I'll run over the twin and squash her dead."

> She was taken back into the play class and began to adjust with the children. The twin ["Daphy"] vanished. She had "killed her dead." (ibid.)

Here the enactment of the death-wish has a more than Oedipal meaning: it signals a healthy resolution of a developmental challenge. In Jungian terms, the *vanishing* of the twin marks the completion of the integration of the ego-ideal/shadow-complex, "Anna-Daphy," which coincides with Margaret's somewhat delayed completion of the Preschool Period. The subsequent achievement of the capacity for social cooperation with peers is characteristic of Middle Childhood, when constellation of the Oedipus complex and its conflicts abates. This is evidence for the stage-specific nature of the imaginary companion.

Betty

Congdon and his co-authors (1961) present the case of Betty, a twenty-three-year-old housewife, and her alternating personality, "Elizabeth," as an example of the transition between an invented imaginary playmate, simple role-playing, and dual personality. In support of this view, they provide clinical observations which show that during the initial phase of her psychotherapy Betty's conscious ego-personality was temporarily replaced by "Elizabeth." I will interpret these same facts as indicating a periodic and necessary identification by Betty with her shadow, or possession of the former by the latter. Although such a view questions the firm separation of identities suggested by the diagnosis of multiple personality, I am in agreement with the authors on other aspects of the case. I agree that "Elizabeth" is a progressive force in Betty's psycho-therapy and development, embodying both ego-ideal and shadow, and that "Elizabeth" was a bridge to repressed phases of Betty's early development.

Betty was first briefly hospitalized for hysterical convulsions and depression, with suicidal potential, and then referred for outpatient psychotherapy.

Her developmental history reveals that she was an only child, reared in the home of her paternal grandparents, with whom her parents lived during their marriage. The patient's father committed suicide when Betty was four years old. The patient's mother was an easy-going, but a passive and ineffective woman. After her husband's death, she worked out of the house and abdicated the direction of the patient's early life to her mother-in-law, the patient's paternal grandmother, who was a formidable tyrant, of stern, unyielding morality based on strict adherence to Victorian standards. In summary, just as she entered the Preschool Period at age four years, Betty experienced major psychological traumata – the death of her father, psychological abandonment by her mother, and tyranny by her grandmother, who, it is safe to assume, was less than playful.

When Betty was seven years old, an imaginary companion, "Elizabeth," emerged.

> Betty spent many hours in play with the fantasied playmate. Elizabeth was always allowed to do things that she herself was forbidden to do, and always has the courage to undertake what the patient herself feared to do. (Congdon et al. 1961: 500)

"Elizabeth", we notice, has the attributes both of ego-ideal and of shadow. The next observation shows that when Betty began to move out of her home into elementary school and the community, "Elizabeth" went with her, and demonstrated the characteristics of a heroine, a young Wonder Woman. When Betty pretended she was "Elizabeth," and these powers became hers to command, she used them effectively to extend her reach in her real community.

> In grammar school, Elizabeth was the subject of fantasy adventures that the patient felt she dared not undertake herself. Throughout the school years the patient came to identify herself more and more with

Elizabeth and to try out in life various little adventures while pretending that she was Elizabeth. For instance, as Elizabeth she would go to the local candy store to buy and eat some candy which was denied her as Betty. (ibid.)

Betty sustained her imaginary companion well into her high school years. Continuing identifications with "Elizabeth" provided her with the she strength needed to face the developmental challenges of teenage life. (This is not so unusual. Although the average age for the disappearance of the imaginary companion is six to seven years, the actual range is from six to eighteen years.)

Social activities such as parties were usually forbidden her and on the few occasions when she was allowed to go she felt quite frightened at the prospect. So she extended the habit of pretending that she was Elizabeth and went to these few parties as Elizabeth. As Elizabeth she could be more free and enjoy herself. This pattern became more and more firmly fixed in her senior year of high school. It seemed her only way to enter into any stressful situation outside her own home. (ibid.)

From the moment of her first appearance and for the next fifteen years, "Elizabeth" was clearly the stronger element in Betty's ego-complex.

When she was twenty-three years old, Betty again identified with (or is possessed by) "Elizabeth," this time to move her psychotherapy forward.

During one interview, about two months after the patient's discharge from the hospital, she was describing her imaginary playmate to the therapist when she suddenly seemed to become that personality. She sat bolt upright in her chair, at the same time assuming a more relaxed and friendly demeanor, and said to the therapist: "I think it's about time I started telling you about me." ... She then proceeded to describe herself (Elizabeth) and her career more fully. (ibid.: 497)

This occurrence points to the fact that "Elizabeth" has continued as Betty's faithful companion from the end of high school to her twenty-third year. The therapist comments indicate that this emergence in therapy brought with it the promise of a more complete integration of "Elizabeth": "From this time on, *until the disappearance of Elizabeth four months later*, it was possible for several observers to study both Betty and Elizabeth under a number of different circumstances" (ibid.; italics added).

I think that the delay of the emergence of the imaginary companion, which is the symbolic mode characteristic of the Preschool Period, until Betty was already seven years old, as well as the delay in its realization until she was twenty-three years old were conditioned by an interruption in normal development, This arrest resulted, in part, from Betty's father's death and her mother's emotional abandonment just as she was entering the Preschool stage. But there was a further challenge to the healthy unfolding of her capacity to symbolize her conflicts and thus grow beyond them. There is little to suggest that the tyrannical and puritanical grandmother who became her primary caretaker was supportive of her symbolic development.

As the next observation suggests, each appearance of "Elizabeth" during psychotherapy was an occasion for Betty's gradual, conscious realization of the unactualized developmental potential of the Preschool Period, which was manifest in the strengths of "Elizabeth."

> After four months of therapy, Elizabeth dropped out altogether and Betty remained dominant. Although still susceptible to tension, depression, and physical symptoms related to these, Betty has remained dominant ever since (now two years) and her condition has gradually improved. She finally became independent enough to leave her grandmother's home and move to another town, where she is gainfully employed. Betty now recalls fully everything she did as Elizabeth and has insight into the value of the secondary personality in protecting her from severe stresses. (ibid.: 501)

The full interiorization of "Elizabeth" marks, as it did in the case of Margaret, Betty's integration of the ego-ideal/shadow-complex as a structural component of her personality. Betty's ego-complex now exhibits the capacities which formerly resided in the character of her imaginary companion.

Peter

Helene Bass (1983) presents an account of the emergence of an imaginary companion, "Harry," during her analysis of a thirty-one-year-old patient, Peter. Peter entered individual and group treatment with the author when he was twenty-eight years old because he wanted help in controlling his impulses to seek out prostitutes and was unhappy in his job as an assembly-line worker. His current aspirations were leading him toward creative writing.

Peter's father had failed in many business ventures, but had pressured Peter to pursue a professional career. When Peter was twenty-one years old his father died and he abruptly ended his pre-med studies. Peter now lived with his fifty-five-year-old, widowed mother, whom he described as a frustrated, complaining woman. His retarded younger sister, whom he had sexually molested during his adolescence, was now living in an institution.

Bass describes as one antecedent to the emergence of "Harry," the patient's preoccupation with a painting in his therapist's office.

> The painting was of a street corner, where a boy and some adults were standing. Peter stared at it for five minutes, commenting that he liked it. "It's a focus on a young man. There is a sense of alienation ... He stands out and the others blend in ... Only by rebelling do you stand out ... (Bass 1983: 520)

Another precursor to "Harry's" emergence was Peter's search for evidence of spiritual parents in the literature he was reading.

> Peter felt the search for the theme of the spiritual father was taking precedence and was easier to find. Although he had sought for the theme of the spiritual mother, he had not come across it in the literature he was reading. (ibid.: 522)

Once again we find *reading* as a stimulus to symbolic development, and to this we can add *art-appreciation*.

Two weeks before "Harry" appeared there was an improvement in Peter's sexual functioning. A week later, he reported the following dream:

> "You didn't tell O. and I that you had canceled the group and someone called us and said you were attending a dance society. I thought, in the dream, 'See – you can't combine the aesthetic and the responsible world.' Then you promised never to do it again." (ibid.)

Peter has encountered his "shadow" in projection upon his therapist. "Harry" himself first appeared in a group therapy session during a moment when Peter felt on the spot and called out for some kind of help. Once Harry emerged, he persisted as a companion for the next three months.

Our analysis of the developmental significance of the imaginary companion has shown that it provides the symbolic foundation for the child's construction of the ego-ideal and shadow (Chapter 5). Peter and his symbolic companion, "Harry," buttress this argument.

Bass states her belief that the "imaginary companion served to promote Peter's *superego* development, ego mastery, and masculine iden- tification" (ibid.: 527, italics added). She thought that at the beginning of treatment "Peter had a primitive superego structure, with a self- punitive attitude" (ibid.: 530). She understands Peter's search for the spiritual parents as a precursor in enabling him to create the idealized self in "Harry."

Bass substantiates the importance of "Harry" as an image of the ego-ideal with the following clinical material. When Peter first called on "Harry" for help, he was being pressured in the group to explain his clinging to his menial job.

> Peter said he had the impression that Harry's office was above mine, that he was a psychiatrist who had "certain types of heavy artillery" that could be lowered into my office if Peter called for it. Peter said Harry had a crane, which could be lowered into my office, scoop Peter up and transport him out of the group. In this way, Peter could avoid troublesome relationships and prying questions. In the individual session following this group Peter said that he needed Harry in order "to survive and escape." (ibid.: 523)

Peter even said that it was "great fun to throw off responsibility onto someone else's shoulders" (ibid.: 524). Peter admitted he "could feel a sense of security in having this 'Harry' image" (ibid.). In contrast to Peter and his father, "Harry" was "someone who had been able to complete his academic studies" (ibid.: 526).

Although the author does not emphasize the negative characteristics of Peter's imaginary companion, we can extract from her report evidence for a shadow side as well. Peter said that the young man in the painting was rebellious: "The rebel also fights himself and there is a symbiosis with society and a rebel – society *needs* criminals....That doesn't function well for me – that rebelliousness ..." (ibid.: 520). Peter's dream, a week before the first appearance of "Harry" also presents a view of the *analyst's* shadow. I have found that a "recognition" of the shadow in the other is a first step in the differentiation of the superego. The patient himself thought the name "Harry" was "an odd mixture of Harris tweed and harass," [ego-ideal and shadow] and mused on the positive and negative sides of his imaginary companion:

> He is a fantasy of someone who can achieve in this society and maintain his own values. Like an artist who achieves – he can rebel and yet reap rewards also. He gets away with murder and almost rape – but not in a pejorative way. There are people who can maintain their integrity in this society. Others get soaked up or defeated. I was just thinking of Harry and his absentmindedness. It's a quality of worldliness and beyond this world – of fantasy and escaping. (ibid.: 525)

For his discoverer, "Harry" now exhibited features both of ego-ideal and of shadow, and thus has become a fully-rounded inner figure capable of compensating Peter's everyday ego.

At this juncture, Peter achieves a new level of development.

> During the next two weeks Peter made a change in his job which
> represented a "thrilling" conquest over a self-defeating pattern. Peter
> said that he was now able to "confront the base line and walk away
> from it, feeling a resurgence. You have to join the sane and the insane
> worlds." (ibid.: 526)

Very shortly after this burst of psychological growth, Peter's imaginary
companion begins to be interiorized:

> In an individual session about two weeks later, Peter referred to
> "Harry" as a "withering fantasy." The group members did ask Peter
> about "Harry" a month later when they urged Peter to explain Harry
> to a new group member. Peter replied with a laugh that "Harry" was
> a past fantasy on whom Peter had "sealed the lid." (Ibid.: 526–7)

About a year after "Harry" had disappeared, he made a cameo
appearance in an individual session in which Peter was changing jobs
and feeling anxious about an advancement.

> "Harry" reappeared briefly about one year later when Peter was
> changing jobs again and feeling anxious about taking a step up. His
> anxiety was manifested by continual yawning during the sessions. He
> made some references to sleeping and to sleeping with me. In
> immediate association, in defense against his incestuous wish, Peter
> brought up Harry. Laughing, Peter said, "Harry will fall asleep – how
> sick! – I just happened to think about Harry." Peter dwelt on how
> Harry might fall asleep during a session. This would make Peter angry
> because Harry wasn't "honest." In the following sessions, Peter
> discarded Harry saying, "I pulled Harry in again as an intermediary,
> so as not to talk or confront you and the sexual feelings." (ibid.: 527)

In this observation, Peter is able to identify his own shadowy, regressive
impulses in projection onto his imaginary companion. "Harry," in other
words, has become a structural component, an ego-ideal/shadow-
complex in the unconscious, capable of functioning as a compensation
to future bouts of one-sidedness on the part of Peter's ego.

It remains for us to comment on the evidence for a possible relation of
Peter's imaginary companion to the Preschool Period. Bass does not
anywhere identify the imaginary companion as stage-specific because,
like most researchers in this area, she does not recognize the ability to
construct such a figure as a developmental step in the symbolic mode.
She believes, moreover, that "Harry" was simply invented by Peter,
rather than considering the ability to construct the figure, as we do, as

the rediscovery by the patient of an archetype belonging to a stage in the development of the symbolic process itself.

Bass does say that Peter's emotional development had remained at a preoedipal level (in our terminology Early Childhood), which is consistent with our view that the emergence of an imaginary companion coincides with the activation of the subsequent stage, the Preschool Period. In Peter's case. I feel this was actually a reactivation. Making his own analysis of the value of "Harry," he says, "I had to have *him* in order to overcome *her*, my mother. It was my achievement. He and I knew that I did it for him" (ibid.: 526).

As we have noted (Chapter 5), the primary task of the child during what Neumann calls the Magic-Warlike stage of ego-development, which in the broader Jungian view of Freud's "Oedipal stage" represents the transition from the matriarchal to the patriarchal perspective, is a hero's victory over his infantile yearnings. These threaten forward motion with the "regressive inertia of the mother complex" (Henderson 1967) and often appear to the symbolic consciousness in the form of the dragon-mother. This challenge is characteristic of the Preschool Period, during which the imaginary companion comes into play as an ally in getting past the Mother. Peter's therapy led him to reexperience the transition from the Preschool Period to Middle Childhood, a development that had been somehow blocked at that time as well, for reasons which were never made clear.

In an individual session following the appearance of "Harry," Peter spoke to his therapist of a fantasy group, which he called his "All-Star Group."

> He included me along with Freud, Woody Allen and Marilyn Monroe. Peter felt that some "warped person. like Charles Manson, should also be included." Peter also wanted Adam and Eve, Picasso, F. Scott Fitzgerald, and Ernest Hemingway. ("He needs therapy a lot.") "The most wicked of all is Eve." ... The group was becoming quite large, so Peter decided to limit the members, choosing Bob Dylan, Freud, Fitzgerald, and Marilyn Monroe. (Bass 1983: 523)

Peter's relation to the group was an ambivalent one:

> I'd be right at home with those people – they are so distinguished ... Being with the dead people is the best solution of all – what this means to me is squashing the arrogance I feel. I don't really have a reason to be arrogant. (ibid.: 524)

In my view, this "group" is further confirmation of the stage-specific nature of the imaginary companion, for I believe that the "All-Star Group" is best understood as a manifestation of the symbolic structure of assimilation of Middle Childhood, the symbolic community. Its appearance shortly after the emergence of the imaginary companion suggests that Peter was completing in therapy an unfinished portion of his psychological development, specifically completion of the Preschool Period and entry into Middle Childhood. It is impossible to say how much of Peter's vocational advances during treatment can be attributed to resolution of later adolescent conflicts, although one can find evidence for the emergence of an Aesthetic cultural attitude, which would support an achievement specific to this later stage. What is clear is that much of his initial work concerned Erikson's stage of Industry versus Inferiority, which comes well before Early Adolescence. We do have one additional clinical observation that supports the primacy Peter's equilibration of latency age conflicts. In the same interview in which he told his therapist of his "thrilling" job change, he added the following:

> There was a brief reference to "Harry" again, but as a baseball coach, a relay man, signaling to the player. Peter said "Harry" was a good coach because he was a man of discretion, capable of making decisions and assuming responsibilities. (ibid.: 526)

This fact suggests that the symbolic community, the archetypal "All-Star Group," is now serving as the basis for the construction of a more realistic or personal group, a "baseball team."

11

Community as Metaphor and Reality

In Chapter 6, we demonstrated that the *social realm* is the symbolic mode characteristic of Middle Childhood, at which time in life the new instrument for the assimilation of experience becomes the *symbolic community*. In this chapter, we will observe how the emergence of symbolic communities during individual and group psychotherapy with children conditions these children's relation to their individual psychopathology as well as their overall psychological development.

INDIVIDUAL PSYCHOTHERAPY

Our discussion of the following psychotherapies (Cases 1, 2, and 3) will focus on the phases of these treatments when symbolic communities emerged. From a developmental standpoint, I took the appearance of the symbol of the "community" as an indication of the child patient's belated entry into normal Middle Childhood. Case 4, below, concerns a child patient suffering from a long-standing block to this development and illustrates the extraordinary healing effects of the constellation of the symbol of an imaginary community on his everyday ego.

Case 1

Marcus was six years old when he began psychotherapy for chronic depression. During the first year of treatment, his play focused primarily upon highly dramatic, make-believe events experienced by a family which lived on the edge of a jungle inhabited by ferocious animals. In this period of treatment, the patient was completing the Preschool Period by consolidating his fragile family identity in the face of irruptions from the unconscious which frequently threatened its survival. When he was seven years old, the next phase of treatment was ushered in by a dream about a city named "Boredom." "Boredom," he told me, had many of the characteristics of his local community, but "not much happened there."

I take "Boredom" to be an example of a symbolic community, and it did mark the patient's completion of the Preschool Period and entry into Middle Childhood. The contents of this imaginary *polis* are, of course, drawn from the patient's conscious representations of his real community, and there is a witty satiric thrust to these representations. "Boredom" nevertheless provided a mythical form for his social interest, which was clouded by his depressive moods, as exemplified by his assertion that "not much happens there." In his continuing treatment, it became apparent that this child's realization of the developmental potential of Middle Childhood had been initiated by the emergence of "Boredom," even though the symbol was overlain by his continuing depression. As we have observed in the mothers of starving infants (Chapter 8), the patient's individual psychopathology had the power to cast a shadow over his development, but it could not altogether prevent the emergence of the symbolic mode characteristic of this stage.

Case 2

Eight-year-old Bill was suffering from depression, with an overlay of anxiety. When I first met him in the waiting room, he asked me, "Do you go to your office?" It took me a few moments to realize that Bill was using the impersonal pronoun "You" to refer to himself; he was asking "Do I go to your office?" This use of the impersonal pronoun to refer to oneself is characteristic of Early Childhood, not Middle Childhood. Evidently, his first visit to a strange therapist had evoked a regression to an earlier level of functioning.

During the first six months of his psychotherapy, Bill created and recreated the following Sand World.

He cleared a central circle of blue by carefully pushing the sand to the sides of the sandtray. Then two men entered the circle, the arena, and began hand-to-hand combat. The form of their battles and their outcomes were endlessly varied, during any one interview and from week to week.

During the seventh month of treatment, the following transformation occurred in his symbolic play.

After a particularly ferocious encounter, the two men left opposite sides of the circle and stood on the sand banks bounding it. The blue area was covered by returning the sand to the center of the tray. In this new center, Bill constructed "Double-Decker," a city which had as its central feature a drive-through restaurant. There was a small park in the city and the two former combatants were maintenance workers there.

The patient's mythical city, haunted by his past history of deprivation, has at its center a "horn of plenty." During the next period of psychotherapy, the two themes, hand-to-hand combat and "Double-

Decker," alternated, within interviews and from week to week. Gradually, however, "Double-Decker," became the predominant theme. The activities in this "city" were progressively differentiated. As the patient in his ego development began to create a social world view, it was clear that this symbolic community served as a foundation for the construction of a reality based, personal community.

The first six months of this treatment should, I believe, be understood as the completion of the developmental project of the Preschool Period: the two "men" who have been in conflict and finally take up their stands on opposite sides of the sand bank bounding the circle, symbolize ego-ideal and shadow; their battles and subsequent face-off suggest a process of equilibration in which stable tension of opposites is achieved, suggesting a psyche with integrity. The emergence of the symbolic community, "Double-Decker," marks the completion of this formative stage of the self and the beginning of Middle Childhood when others become more significant. The transformation of the figures from "combatants" to "workers" expresses the transition from Erikson's crisis of Initiative versus Guilt to the crisis of Industry versus Inferiority. As a Horn of Plenty, the symbolic city, "Double-Decker" suggests an otherness that is compensatory to the patient's severe emotional and physical deprivation. In this individual constellation of the symbol of community, the patient's personal psychopathology conditioned the content of the symbol, but did not block its emergence as a new form for his development.

Case 3

Don – impulsive, aggressive, fearful, and socially maladapted – was six years old when he entered treatment.

During his first three years of group and individual psychotherapy, this child depicted, both in social and solitary symbolic play, continuing struggles with devouring and sadistic figures. This first phase of Don's treatment could be interpreted as his efforts to resolve conflicts in order to complete ego-development relating to the stages of Infancy and Early Childhood.

The theme in his play gradually shifted to recurrent encounters between the "good guys" and the "bad guys," that is between represen-tatives of the Ego Ideal and representatives of the Shadow. This pattern can be understood as marking the realization and completion of the normal developmental tasks of the Preschool Period.

When Don was nine years old, the "Town of the Lone Rider" appeared in his symbolic play and became its central focus. The "Lone Rider" was a mysterious figure, an action hero (see Chapter 6), who embodied the masculine virtues one can associate with the paternal spirit character-istic of Middle Childhood (Neumann 1990, Chapter 6). Don's differentiation of this mythical realm enabled him to create a new world view and to construct a personal community, in which this view prevailed. As a corollary to his construction of the "Town of the Lone Rider," Don's social relations with his peers began to normalize.

In summary: "Boredom," "Double-Decker," and the "Town of the Lone Rider" are all symbolic communities that emerged in clinical contexts. They correspond in many ways to similar constellations observed in normal developmental contexts, such as Jacqueline's "Ventichon," Laurent's "Six-Twenty Balls," and the "paracosms" reported by Cohen and MacKeith (1991) (Chapter 6). The difference is that the communities encountered in clinical work are delayed chronologically in their emergence, and serve the additional function of bridging a lag in development.

Case 4

Mario was nine years old when he entered treatment because of depression, manifested by a general lack of vitality and falling behind at school.

First Interview

In his first interview, Mario was lethargic and sat inertly in a chair for the first twenty minutes. When encouraged by his therapist, he made the following Sand World.

Exposition
The inhabitants of an Indian village, constructed near the front of the tray, were experiencing a drought and were about to die of thirst.

This challenged "village" is a symbolic community, the patient's depressive mood is symbolized as a life-threatening drought. We can interpret this symbolism to mean that the normal flow of libido ("water") from the unconscious to consciousness is blocked.

Plot Development
A scout team left and returned without finding water.

Although this action expresses the inability of the ego-complex to overcome the depressive mood, it also suggests an active engagement with the unconscious which in this instance activated the archetypal layers of the psyche, which eventually came to the patient's aid.

Culmination
A band of cowboys appeared in the back of the tray and rode into the village; they shared their water with the villagers.

The creative introversion has worked. The "band of cowboys" offers a second community to strengthen the initially depressed symbolic community. The cowboys are images of heroic capacity originating not in the patient's ego, but in the patient's collective or developmental unconscious, a mythical realm of pluripotentiality. They represent a spontaneous, compensatory response by the unconscious to the conscious problem. This band of heroes brings life-saving "water," i.e. libido, the psychic energy needed to irrigate the "villagers" ego-consciousness.

Resolution
Before leaving, the cowboys showed the villagers a source of water for their future needs.

This last event indicates a more permanent solution, in the form of a libido channel between the ego and the wellsprings of the unconscious. Neumann calls this vital channel the ego–self axis; the fantasy suggests that it has been reopened and that a block to development has been overcome. When the interview ended, Mario was indeed alert, energized, and engaged.

This vignette is a vivid illustration of the effect of an effectively fantasied symbolic community. This healing symbol was constellated by the patient's active engagement in symbolic play under the watchful eye of his therapist. It was as if the patient had read these words of Jung:

The best way of dealing with the unconscious is the creative way. Create for instance a fantasy. Work it out with all the means at your disposal. Work it out as if you were it or in it, as you would work out a real situation in life which you cannot escape. All the difficulties you overcome in such a fantasy are symbolic expressions of psychological difficulties in yourself, and inasmuch as you overcome them in your imagination you also overcome them in your psyche. (Jung, 1973b, p. 109)

The developmental impetus evoked by this symbolic process is evident in the next visit.

Second Interview

During his second interview, Mario continued to be energized and engaged. He drew the following picture.

Two trees with leaves, one tall, one short, stand side-by-side. An X-ray view of the underground portion of each of the trees reveals that the root system of each tree is planted in a spherical hole filled with water.

As libido-symbols, the trees have various meanings. The large tree is often thought of as signifying the tree of life, making it a "mother" symbol, a symbol of the unconscious developmental matrix. I believe it can also represent the family tree, that is the cultural unconscious as it met Mario through the particular culture of his family, and his place in that culture. The family tree has, according to Lou Stewart, two dimensions.

> As I have said, there are two aspects of the family which are inseparably entwined with all the others, but which nevertheless stand in a distinct relationship to each other. These are the "sibling position" and the "family atmosphere." The child's sibling position is determined by the fated accident of birth. The family atmosphere is in large part determined by the parents' behaviour, attitudes, values, and particularly their unconscious complexes which carry the unanswered questions of the ancestors. These two aspects of the family determine what may be called the child's "sibling" and "ancestral" complexes. In turn they represent the two dimensions of the family tree, the horizontal which relates us to the body social, and the vertical which relates us to the ancestral spirit. (L. H. Stewart 1992a, p. 26)

Viewed in cross-section the family tree is a mandala, a magical containing circle symbolizing the imagined boundaries of the self, whereas in profile it represents a vertical, potentially limitless process of growth, individuation.

The smaller tree may be thought of as signifying in contrast the "son," that is the individual growth potential of developing individual, and is a symbol of the personal self. That the water of life is bathing the root systems of both trees expresses the adequacy of available libido for development. In medieval alchemical texts, the tree frequently represents the transformation (psychological development) of the arcane substance (the abstract totality of the self). As this substance matures into the philosophical gold (the conscious individual) it becomes like "a well-tended tree, a watered plant, which, beginning to ferment because of the plentiful water, and sprouting in the humidity and warmth of the air, puts forth blossoms and fruits ..." (CW 13: 354,274). Taken together, the two trees represent with incredible economy of expression a symbolic community. Their ecological interdependence suggests the patterns of symbolic relatedness between the patient and his mother, the patient and himself, and the patient and his therapist, which were readily observable in the therapy.

At the close of the second interview, Mario again left the office in good spirits. As well he might: he had re-established a vital connection with the foundation of his personality.

GROUP PSYCHOTHERAPY

In her study of the natural gangs and clinical groups formed by latency age children between their eighth and twelfth birthdays, Eve Lewis (1954) identified two types of play, extroverted and introverted. She characterizes the former as helping the individual child differentiate as a person, as involving much planning and discussion, and as being determined to a great extent by the conscious collective will of the children. Lewis characterizes the more individual introverted play as infrequent, "happening to" the children without their initial planning for it, and entirely different from their usual play. The gang or group is seized as a unit and swept into a mythical drama which transcends the strivings of its individual members.

Whereas the content of extroverted play reflects primarily the current personal issues of its individual members, the content of introverted play consists of primordial images that are collectively meaningful to the children. In extroverted play the child is struggling to establish, against the will of his companions, his own best ego attitude and functions. Introverted play seeks to locate the appropriate symbolic impetus for development as a whole to proceed.

Lewis's observations complicate our understanding of the "community" characteristic of Middle Childhood by showing us that there are two dimensions, one of reality (in extroverted play) and one symbolic (in introverted play). My own analysis of the introverted play described by Lewis in two clinic groups follows. It is presented to emphasize the depth as well as breadth of the symbolic "community" in fostering growth.

Group 1

All six of the eight-year-old boys in this group were enuretic, anxious, had various behavior disorders, and were sons of over-protective mothers.

The first nine sessions of lively, extraverted play with plasticine, paint and toys, was accompanied by incessant, noisy chatter.

Eventually, the boys began to light fires. In the first two sessions, the fires were small and easily contained in sand trays. A symbolic group composed of Promethean "fire-bringers" or "fire-kindlers" had been formed.

The next step was that the children brought paper, sticks, and coal from home to light a really large bonfire in the open. The group members talked very little and were intensely serious as they danced round this central fire. Some of them jumped over it or passed hands and feet quickly through it. Lewis interpreted this session as an initiation ceremony, in preparation for the four sessions of introverted play that followed. I would agree: the children have entered a mythical realm and are developing a symbolic community, which is now composed of "Masters of the Fire." This is quite a significant image: "Primitive magic and shamanism both carry the notion of 'mastery over fire,' whether it is a question of involving the power to touch live coals with impunity or of producing the 'inner heat' which permitted resistance to extreme cold" (Eliade 1971: 79–80). Such images of mastery reflect the reality that each child has an improved connection with his developmental unconscious. Such progression often marks the beginning of a phase of healing and development, and we can find evidence for that in the play that followed.

Introverted Play Interview 1

In the first introverted play session, the children used string to convert the playroom into a "web." They flung themselves into this web and cried out: "I'm trapped! Save me!" They were completely absorbed in this for ten minutes. No child spoke and none made any attempt at rescue.

Although the string was never referred to by the children as a *spider* web, it is reasonable to assume that this was intended. The symbolic community constellated in this session was in fact a group of "flies." The drama enacted depicted the individual patients, the "flies," as threatened collectively by the engulfing and devouring powers of the unconscious, or "web." I suspect that the attitude of fear toward the unconscious that is portrayed in this scene is best understood as a consequence of the over-protectiveness of the children's mothers. The primary accomplishment of the group in this session is survival of all its members.

Introverted Play Interview 2

In the second session, the same symbolic community is constellated and its members went through the same performance, again mostly silently, apart from cries of distress. When Lewis told them that time was up, with no discussion of any kind, they suddenly fell on her, tied her to a chair, and ran out shouting "Now you're caught! You'll never get away!"

With this play, the tide has begun to turn, and the fear of the unconscious originating in the mother is being overcome. The progressive libido inherent in the symbolic community is beginning to be realized, providing, for instance, the psychic energy suddenly available to the group to bind the "spider" in her own web. A "symbolic" transference to the therapist as she-to-be-overcome has been established.

Introverted Play Interview 3

At the next session, the children pretended great indignation at finding Lewis free. They announced that she was a "bear," and an elaborate drama of tracking and stalking began. The children were united and prepared to face the enemy. Their committal to the game was absolute;

the only speech was cautionary, and they simulated great terror. Gradually they grew bolder and finally with a wordless, concerted rush killed Lewis, *by hugging her to death*. The transition from the stages of development governed by the mother archetype to those governed by the father archetype requires, according to Neumann, a "deicide."

> In the first phase of a normal primal relationship the mother integrated the necessary denials or rejections by the predominance of her positive existence. Now with the development of the child ego, the mother's "terrible" attitudes are progressively intensified when in reality, that is, objectively, the mother remains a positive, integrating authority. Only in this way can the child develop the necessary opposition to its mother, which ultimately ends in its turning away from her and the matriarchal world. This is the mythological "matricide" which makes possible the transition to the father archetype. (Neumann 1990: 111)

In this play, however, the symbol of the devouring "mother," the unconscious, and the nature of the symbolic community are first transposed to a new level. Once the former becomes a "bear" and the latter a male hunting group, the hunt can be successful and the Terrible Mother vanquished. The positive libido for this successful exercise in progressive development originates in the symbolic community itself.

Introverted Play Interview 4

In the last session of introverted play, seven weeks later, one child took a puppet representing a witch and began to chase the others. They took turns being the "witch" and chasing the others, showing real fear in their half-laughing flights. When caught, they would clutch their hearts and pretend to fall dead; but quickly scrambled up again to hurl triumphant insults at the witch. Ultimately, two boys who had seized soldier and sailor puppets, served as leaders of the group in drowning the witch in a pail of water.

Here, the terrifying symbol of the devouring mother has been transposed to a universal cultural level in the image of the "witch." The actions of the symbolic community in relation to the witch recapitulate those in the three previous sessions: non-fatal entrapment, binding of the enemy with insults, and conquering of the enemy.

Lewis reports that, within a short time after this healing play, the mothers were reporting a diminution or even cessation of the enuresis and other symptoms, saying that the children were generally more responsible, considerate and mature at home.

This suggests that the children assisted each other in completing a phase of development that involved resolving regressive ties to the earlier stages of development – Infancy, Early Childhood, the Preschool Period

– ties that had been reinforced by the over-protectiveness of the mothers. The forceful, purposive play enabled transition to a more appropriate stage of development, using the symbolic modalities available to them in Middle Childhood.

Group 2

All four of the ten-year-old boys in this group were of good intelligence and doing fairly well at school in most subjects, but all were exceedingly backward readers. Each boy had a particularly close tie with his mother, owing to the absence of the father from the home setting.

At the start of the group, the children appeared emotionally immature and there were frequent play disruptions, when individuals would withdraw to suck their thumbs or bite their nails as they daydreamed. The boys also were slow to show any group cohesion.

Then, very suddenly, they became a gang. The precipitating event was that one of the children told the group why he could not learn to read at school: "He complained, with tears in his eyes, that the sun blazed into his class room in such a way that the light, *reflected from the wall* on to his book and blinded him and gave him terrible headaches" (Lewis 1954: 23). Although this account was obviously not entirely factual, the other boys displayed extraordinary sympathy, declaring heatedly to each other that it was "a shame" to expect anyone to read under such circumstances.

This entry of the group into a mythical realm for which the sun was a central symbol, as well as its initial coalescence into a symbolic community is based on mutual identification of its members as victims of the fiery rays of the sun. One is tempted to speculate psychoanalytically. Are they blinded by the paternal, the Terrible Oedipal surrogate for their absent fathers, or is it the first encounter with the fiery rays of their own masculinity that is wounding them? I am reminded of Phaëthon, son of Helios, who failed in his attempt to drive his father's sun-chariot: he was killed by a fiery thunderbolt hurled by Zeus. That is, the masculinity he could not imitate ended up attacking him. Somehow the group of boys understood the plight of their friend at an instinctive level.

Several sessions of animated extroverted play followed, and these led up to four sessions of introverted play.

Introverted Play Interview 1

In this session, fire emerges as an important aspect of their symbolism, for the group spent the whole time trying to make fire by rubbing sticks together.

The symbolic community has developed and, as in Group 1, consists of "fire-bringers" or "fire-kindlers." In ancient myth and legend, fire is considered the "son" of the two pieces of wood used in fire-making, one of which is male, the other female. The group might be thought of as gripped by the what Bachelard (1964) has described as a Prometheus complex, the Oedipus complex of the intellect. It arises in the following way.

> This, then, is the true basis for the respect shown to flame: if the child brings his hand close to the fire his father raps him over the knuckles with a ruler. Fire, then, can strike without having to burn ... Thus fire is initially the object of a *general prohibition*; hence this conclusion: the social interdiction is our first *general knowledge* of fire ... As the child grows up, the prohibitions become intellectual rather than physical; the blow of the ruler is replaced by the angry voice; the angry voice by the recital of the dangers of fire, by legends concerning fire from heaven. Thus the natural phenomenon is rapidly mixed in with complex and confused items of social experience which leave little room for the acquiring of an unprejudiced knowledge. (Bachelard 1964: 11)

As the prohibitions are primarily social in origin, the problem of attaining personal knowledge of fire is the problem of *clever disobedience*.

> The child wishes to do what his father does, but far away from his father's presence, and so like a little Prometheus he steals some matches. He then heads for the fields where, in the hollow of a little valley, he and his companions build a secret fireplace [form a symbolic community] that will keep them warm on the days when they [as a real peer group community] decide to play truant from school. (ibid.)

My interpolations point to the dialectic between the symbolic and real communities that is at work in the Prometheus complex.

Introverted Play Interview 2

In the next session, after lighting a fire with a cigarette lighter, the children began to melt lead and throw the molten metal into water, examining the results most minutely. They saw chiefly human shapes. I believe that this motif signifies that an alchemical transformation has begun.

Lewis too was reminded of Prometheus, whom she recognized as creating humankind. Prometheus had assisted at the birth of Athene, too, and this goddess taught him, among other skills, the art of metallurgy. The alchemists, smiths, and potters were all considered "masters of fire" and skilled in effecting the transformation of matter from one form to another (Eliade 1971). An analogous Aztec myth also depicts the origin of humankind from metals. It is as if the members of the group will themselves be transformed by the symbolic process which has been constellated.

Introverted Play Interview 3

Two weeks later, we observe the results of this transformation when a coincidental event galvanized the interest of the group members.

> From the playroom window, they saw a stretcher being carried into a nearby nursing home. They asked if the patient was going to have an operation, and passed from this to discussing operations and accidents. In the course of this they put a great number of questions about the body. (Lewis 1954: 24)

They then asked if Lewis had ever had an operation, and she said, yes, an appendectomy. They were silent for a moment, then cupped their hands to their eyes, simulating binoculars, and chanted, "I can see you! I can see you!," over and over again. After some minutes Lewis said, "Of course you can see me. There is no earthly reason why you shouldn't!" At this moment, they rushed out of the playroom to the adjacent bathroom, "where they all urinated together, very solemnly, and with the door wide open, though it just concealed them from me" (ibid.) They emerged and left with the utmost naturalness and simplicity.

I believe that release of the innate affect Interest with its characteristic dynamism, curiosity/exploration had occurred, expressed in the chant "I can see you." This was followed by a healthy phallic-narcissistic urination ceremony, which marked the healing and resolution of the development crisis Erik Erikson assigns the Preschool Period, (phallic) Initiative versus (Oedipal) Guilt.

Introverted Play Interview 4

A month later, Lewis found the opportunity to make an indirect connection between these boys being afraid to look and find out and their inability to read. Her interpretation amused the patients, but it led them to admit that in fact they had recently begun to make considerable progress in reading. Then, one patient went silently to a cupboard where he wound a piece of cotton wool round a wooden slat.

> Before I realized his purpose, the other boys had copied him and drenched the wool with methylated spirit which they set alight, afterwards carrying their torches in triumph round the room and through the house. Finally, returning to the playroom, they sat down and placed the torches erect between their thighs, close to the genitals. They were concentrated and grave ... (ibid.)

Lewis was once again reminded of Prometheus: for it was this god who lit a torch from the chariot of the sun, broke off a fragment of glowing charcoal from it, and *thrust it into the hollow of a fennel-stalk* to carry it to humankind.

We can further amplify this image. When the "flame of valour" arose in the Irish hero, Cuchulain, his body became "unrecognizable as if animated by a different spirit" (Onians 1951/1973: 158). The masculine element is the "sphere of fire" and the phallus is a symbol expressing the numinous "hero's flame," i.e. "masculine" libido, or psychic energy in its creative aspect. Among the many ancient associations of fire with masculine procreation is the Italian legend "that Servius Tullius was begotten by a phallus of fire which appeared on the hearth and that Caecilius, the reputed founder of Praeneste, was begotten by a spark from the hearth" (ibid.). It is this libido, flowing from constellated masculine archetypes of the hero, which has ignited the progressive ego-development of the members of the above group.

12

Play and the Emergence of Cultural Attitudes

In Chapter 7, I identified the symbolic mode characteristic of Early Adolescence as the *cultural attitude*, and the new instrument of assimilation of experience during that crucial developmental stage as the *symbolic form*. A cultural attitude – and, as we have seen, there is more than one type of cultural attitude – functions as a symbolic bridge that provides the individual with a connection to the rich symbolic possibilities of the cultural unconscious and thus a path into the cultural life of his or her society. In the present chapter, I will discuss how a cultural attitude emerges during psychotherapy and the therapeutic and developmental benefits it confers.

As a further introduction to the symbolic analysis of clinical cases, I will present an example of the deleterious effects of a block to the emergence of one individual's natural cultural attitude, which in his case was the Aesthetic attitude, and how psychic equilibrium was restored upon removal of the obstruction to this attitude's unfolding.

Joan Miro

The future Spanish artist, Joan Miro, was seventeen years old when he announced to his parents his intention of becoming a painter (Golding 1993: 45). When his father "dismissed the idea and found him a job as a clerk," there were dire consequences.

> The following year, 1922, Miro suffered a breakdown and became severely ill. He convalesced at the small [family] farm at Montroig (Red Mountain), just south of Tarragona ... This was to become Miro's spiritual home. (ibid.)

Miro's breakdown occurred after the emergence of a cultural attitude proper to his own identity, the Aesthetic attitude, was thwarted by his father. In my view, Miro's connection with his healthy base of cultural adaptation had been severed. Golding comments on the nature of Miro's breakdown at this time in his life:

> Although the literature on Miro persists in calling his illness in 1911 "a minor nervous breakdown," it was clearly not minor at all, and at various points in his career Miro's work shows marked signs of mental anguish and an accompanying aggressiveness that manifests itself in the recurrent violence of his iconography. (ibid.: 46)

Once Miro fell ill, the parents realized their error and revoked their decision: "His parents' permission for him to resume his art studies had helped him to break through the crisis in which he had found himself ..." (ibid.). Once Miro's connection with his symbolic base had been re-established, he began to actualize his developing Aesthetic cultural attitude by enrolling in a progressive art school, thereby beginning the creation of a whole new world view. The rest of his development is now art history: he became one of the seminal modern artists.

SCIENTIFIC AND AESTHETIC CULTURAL ATTITUDES

In her article, "Aspects of symbolism in comprehension of the not-self", Marion Milner (1952) draws the conclusion, based on her own experiments in painting (Field 1950) and her analytic work with children, that symbolization is *not* distortion, but rather is essential for maturation. She points out that her judgment agrees with Melanie Klein's view that the capacity to symbolize is the basis of those other skills and talents by which we establish world-relations. In order to substantiate such privileging of the capacity to symbolize, Milner presents excerpts from the analysis of an eleven year old boy in which she focuses on his peculiar mode of symbolic activity, one characterized by intense concentration, minimal verbalization, aesthetic and ritual qualities, and a ready willingness to transcend the common-sense ego, all traits which another therapist might have considered evidence for a schizoid process.

As the participant observer to this process, however, Milner reports that far from becoming detached, her own imagination caught fire. This experience resembles Lewis's characterization (Chapter 11) of the infectious numinosity of introverted play, which originates in the level of affective intensity expressed in the symbols through which the play proceeds. My purpose in revisiting Milner's case here is to show that she has, in my judgment, captured the moment when this particular patient completed the stage of Middle Childhood and allowed the symbolic cultural attitudes characteristic of Early Adolescence to emerge.

Milner's patient was an eleven-year-old boy who was in the top of his class during his first years in school. Then he gradually sank to the bottom of his "form" and began to avoid school by staying home. The patient had lived in London during the blitz, at a time when his father was in service. (Unfortunately, we don't know the patient's exact age during this period of his life.)

Milner reports that for a long time the patient had engaged in a pattern of symbolic play in which he created a village inhabited by people and animals. He would then bomb the community by dropping balls of burning paper on it. The therapist's role was to attempt to save the village and its inhabitants from fiery destruction. Aside from the particular evidence for the trauma visited upon it, such a symbolic community is characteristic of Middle Childhood – simple, concrete, coherent, and maintained by (in this case the therapist's) heroic actions. The traumatic vicissitudes this symbolic form endures are drawn from the patient's personal life experiences, in this case, dramatically, the bombing of London during his earliest years.

My analysis of the following interview, during which the emergence of this symbolic form so characteristic of Early Adolescence takes place before our eyes, treats the session as a kind of dream. To make what transpires clear, I will use Jung's (*CW* 8: 561–4,294–5) schema of the dramatic structure for dreams. Jung says a dream that is really complete has four "acts": (1) the Exposition – statement of place, protagonists, and the initial situation of the dreamer; (2) the Development of the plot; (3) the Culmination, that is, a decisive happening that brings the issue to a peak of tension or change of direction; and (4) the Solution, that is, the final outcome of the situation, whether in terms of action or feeling or both. Using this four-act model, we will now follow Milner's account of the process of the session in which a new symbolic form of playing emerged.

Exposition

[The patient] begins by saying that we are to have *two villages* and a war between them, but that the war is not to begin at once. My village is to be made up of all the people and animals and houses; his of toy trucks, cars, etc., and "lots of junk and oddments to exchange", though I am to have some oddments as well. (Milner 1952: 184; italics added)

The patient has now assigned the original symbolic community that is normal for Middle Childhood to his therapist, Milner. I believe this move indicates that the patient is now approaching the completion of that period of development. The new village of vehicles and oddments that is emerging marks the beginning of Early Adolescence. What is still not sorted out represents the patient's as yet undifferentiated cultural attitude. The "oddments and junk" are, in other words, alchemical *prima materia*, the raw materials, for the process of psychological construction that is to follow.

Plot Development

> He begins by sending along a truck from his village with half a gun in
> it, and takes various things in exchange. He then brings a test-tube
> and exchanges for it a number of objects, including a little bowl, bits
> of metal, a ladder, etc. (ibid.)

Now "oddments and junk" are being differentiated into a recognizable
cultural attitude. That this is a scientific attitude is suggested in the next
observation, when Milner's patient gives the test-tube the highest value.

Culmination

> When I comment on the amount taken in exchange he says: "Yes, the
> test-tube is equal to a lot"; but on the return journey to his own village
> he adds: "I think those people were a bit odd, I don't think I like those
> people much, I think I will give them just a little time-bomb". He bombs
> my village and I am to bomb his village. (ibid.)

Milner's thinks that her comment, although perhaps in adult terms a
mild "complaint," may have provoked the war between the villages. But
it is also noticeable that the patient is taking his relationship with his
analyst to a new level of equality.

Solution

> Then he says: "You have got to bring all your people over to my village,
> the war is over" ... but at once he says they must go back because they
> have to watch the burning of the whole stack of matchboxes ... He
> makes me stand back from the blaze, and shows great pleasure. (ibid.)

In this sequence, there is a brief regression from the dialectic of villages
to only one village, but progression is quickly restored as Middle
Childhood itself is razed and interiorized in ever-living fire. The novel
elements that appear next, also expressing the beginning of Early
Adolescence, confirm that a structural development of the whole
personality is underway. During this observation of the patient's
symbolic play the plot thickens.

Plot Development

> He now decides that his "people" (empty trucks) are to call on mine; his
> are explorers and mine are to think they are *gods*. The trucks arrive, my
> people have to be frightened. He tells me to make them say something;

so I make the policeman ask what they want; but he replies: "You've forgotten, they think it's gods." (ibid.: 185; italics added)

Culmination

He now borrows the "Mrs. Noah" figure from my village and stands her in one of his trucks. (ibid.)

Solution

Then, in a god-like voice, he commands that the villagers go into their houses and prepare food. (ibid.)

Differentiation of the patient's village includes the appearance of gods, along with the female survivor of the deluge, "Mrs. Noah," the Mistress of the Beasts. These male and female archetypes are developmental centers of symbolization awaiting actualization. The patient's village now has the characteristics of those constructed by other early adolescents:

There is a differentiation of form and content, and coherent symbolic or abstract worlds are formed as well as differentiated realistic worlds. Concepts such as "native land," social justice and religious ideas are portrayed. A single coherent overview encompasses complex parts whose interdependence and integration is not quite complete; or an abstract or theoretical overview such as humor or spirituality unites parts that might otherwise seem unrelated; or a single clearly recognizable thematic overview unites complex parts which are interdependent and integrated. (Jones 1982: 57–8)

Consistent with this symbolic progress, the patient completes this interview by singing a religious tune and engaging in novel ritual behaviors.

It is now the end of the session and while I am beginning to tidy up he plays with some melting wax, humming to himself the hymn-tune "Praise my soul, the King of Heaven". He smears some wax on both my thumbs and says he is double-jointed, and asks if I am too. (Milner 1952: 185)

Evidently, a quite potent hyperflexible masculine god has emerged to complement "Mrs. Noah." In the wax ritual, the patient begins to elaborate his symbolic relation to his analyst, now transposed to the stage of Early Adolescence. Double-jointedness is a metaphor that expresses many things, but not least the patient's dawning awareness of the unique quality of his burgeoning individuality.

With this entry in Early Adolescence, the patient's psychic energies become available for development of a resilient ego-complex. For instance, in the session following this one he spent the hour mending his book bag, a job that he would ordinarily get his mother to do for him.

A period of sociodramatic play follows that concerns the healing of a feeling-toned complex from the patient's personal unconscious. He takes the role of a sadistic schoolmaster, while his therapist becomes a bad boy. The former persecutes the latter through a series of long, monotonous tasks, the results of which are treated with scorn. Punishment includes silence on the schoolboy's part, writing of lines, and threatening with the cane. It is apparent that the feeling-tone of the complex in question is one of Contempt (patient)/Shame and that the humiliation associated with being judged, punished, and avoided is projected onto the analyst. We can assume that this complex itself was formed in prior interactions with parents and other adults. In the language of affect theory, Rejection by them had produced Shame/Contempt, and this was not sufficiently modulated. The successful nature of the patient's efforts at self-healing are evident when the bullying tone suddenly vanishes for four days, beginning with the day when he told Milner about something that had happened at school which pleased him very much.

For many weeks, he and his friends at school had been organizing a photography club. On the day in question he had told his therapist that their form master had been supportive; he had given them permission to hold their meetings in school during a time set aside for special activities and had even given them a little room in which to work. One can speculate that the change in attitude on the patient's part, that is a reduction in a sadomasochistic pattern of relating, may have contributed to the form master's supportive actions. What I would like to focus on here, however, is his interest in photography, which may be seen as one aspect of an emerging Aesthetic cultural attitude that organizes his social adaptation.

With this Aesthetic attitude operating, the next phase in the patient's symbolic development consists of a type play activity that Milner tells us set her own imagination on fire.

> ... at times there was a quality in his play which I can only describe as beautiful ... It was in fact play with light and fire. He would close the shutters of the room and insist that it be lit only by candle light, sometimes a dozen candles arranged in patterns, or all grouped together in a solid block. And then he would make what he called furnaces, with a very careful choice of what ingredients should make the fire, including dried leaves from special plants in my garden; and sometimes all the ingredients had to be put in a metal cup on the

electric fire and stirred continuously, all this carried out in the half darkness of candle light. And often there had to be a sacrifice, a lead soldier had to be added to the fire, and this figure was spoken of either as the victim or the sacrifice. (ibid.: 188)

In this observation of aesthetically beautiful ritual play we are witness to the artfully evoked constellation of a numinous and highly individual initiation process, which includes many images of the self's transformative process: mandalas, alchemical furnaces, fires arising from symbolic "ingredients," and initiatory human sacrifices. Alchemy, historically, was a science as well as an "art." In this play which harkens back to alchemical practice, we can observe crystallization of both the Scientific and Aesthetic cultural attitudes. Previously, this patient had considered himself no good at art, but now during a session he said, with pride, that he was talented in both science and art, adding that this was a combination that was not usual among his classmates. On the other hand, although his cultural attitudes were forming, he was still somewhat tentative in claiming them. For instance, he was abashed when he told his therapist how much delight he took in the colors of the various crystals he had studied in his chemistry: "It's childish to like them so much" (ibid.: 189). The "crystals" are natural mandalas, which are emerging from the innate ground plan, the Self. They contain the developmental potential for self-organization and orientation during Early Adolescence.

As this boy's interest in chemistry deepened, an evolution in the symbolic aspect of the transference followed, in which the analyst became a creation of the patient.

He would say [for several weeks in a row], "What is your name?" and I would have to say "What is my name?" Then he would answer with the name of some chemical, and I would say "What is there about that?" And he would answer "It's lovely stuff, I've made it!"; and sometimes he would give me the name of the chemical which is used as water-softener. (ibid.: 190)

In this transference enactment, the patient is continuing to transpose an ongoing symbolic relatedness with the analyst to his own new level of development. Simultaneously, the process whereby he will resolve this transference is initiated: "This boy would sometimes tell me that I was a gas, that he was going to dissolve me down or evaporate me till I became one" (ibid.). Jung has written:

Dissolution into spirit, the body's volatilization or sublimation, corresponds chemically to evaporation ... Psychologically it corresponds to the conscious realization and integration of an unconscious content. (*CW* 14: 318,238)

The content which Milner's patient will in the end withdraw from projection on her is the *anima*, his own creative capacity to access the cultural energies of the Self.

We can observe the creativity of the developing Scientific attitude as it is expressed in the gift the patient plans for his analyst.

> But I think that it was significant that, near the end of his analysis, this boy told me that when he was grown up and earning his own living he would give me a papier-mache chemical clock, which would keep perfect time and would be his own invention. He said it would be of papier-mache because I had an ornament, a little Indian dog, made of this, and also I had remembered how he himself had tried to make papier-mache bowls, during his play with me, but unsuccessfully. (Milner 1952: 193)

In stating what he will be able to give his therapist when he is grown up, the patient is expressing his confidence in the developmental process that has begun to foster his creative cultural activity. He has a realistic hope of realizing his scientific inventiveness in a "future" society in which both he and his analyst are individual members. It is important to recognize this as more than a transference expression of gratitude to his analyst: the patient is also confirming his belief in the continuing creativity of the symbolic process itself, in shaping the direction his life will take.

RELIGIOUS CULTURAL ATTITUDE

Our discussion of the development of a Religious cultural attitude during treatment includes three adolescent cases and one adult case.

Phil

The first patient is Phil, who was ten years old when he began a psychotherapy that lasted two years. Abandoned in early childhood by both parents, he was raised by relatives to become an angry, fearful child, fractious in the classroom, who refused to turn in his completed homework and had frequent fights with his classmates.

During psychotherapy, his relationship with his therapist was generally positive. He worked hard in his interviews. There was a specific symbolic expression that appeared early in his treatment and persisted until termination, even though it waxed and waned over the course of therapy. It was a sandplay theme involving a male figure who suddenly was caught in quicksand. This heroic figure might remain trapped, but sometimes he escaped, either through his own Herculean efforts or with the help of another hero. When the hero did escape, he frequently climbed to the top of a nearby hill.

Late in his treatment Phil asked his guardian if he could join the church he had been attending for several months. Permission was granted, he joined the church, and soon after ended his therapy. At the time of completion, there was an overall improvement in his adaptation at school and in his own sense of well-being. My reconstruction of the symbolic process furthered by the treatment will focus upon this interesting termination.

The patient's termination of treatment when he was twelve years old coincided with the emergence of a cultural attitude. As I have said repeatedly, forming of a cultural attitude is the characteristic symbolic mode of Early Adolescence, so we can see that his symbolic development is right on schedule. In this instance, it took the form of a Religious cultural attitude. The process in and through which the patient constructed this particular attitude can explained in the following way.

Lou Stewart and I have concluded that a Religious cultural attitude has its origin in the expressive aspect of the affect Fear–Terror (see Table 3). We have also discovered that the efficient cause of the innate affect Fear is a symbol composed of the imprinting of a life-stimulus, the Unknown, on the primordial image, the "Abyss." Through his parents' abandonment of him, the patient had certainly experienced the life stimulus for the development of Fear–Terror, because the reason for their abandoning him were unknown. Both they and his relatives were totally mysterious about that. In the patient's symbolic play, however, it was the primordial image of the Abyss which emerged, in the form of the "quicksand." The transcending symbol of the "hill," beside the pit of "quicksand," can be understood as his individual form of the archetypal "Holy Mountain," so regular a motif in religious experience as Lou Stewart (1987a) has described. He and I believe that such an image is created by the compensatory and self-regulatory activity of the unconscious itself, and then discovered by the individual. By climbing up this hill, the patient had achieved entry into Early Adolescence with the symbolic construction of an adapted cultural attitude and felt free enough of anxiety to terminate his psychotherapy.

In "The mystical experience as suicide preventive," Paul Horton (1973) has presented three adolescent cases to illustrate the function of the mystical state as a suicide preventative. Two of these cases, not surprisingly, illustrate the emergence of a Religious cultural attitude.

Case 2

A highly intelligent and sensitive eighteen-year-old youth left home primarily to escape from the intrusive and harassing behavior of his father: "Emotionally, however, he was still very much tied to his family and suffered anxiety and depression of psychotic proportions" (Horton 1973: 295). Reckless driving and numerous auto accidents occurred, at least one of which was probably a suicide attempt. The effect of frightening nightmares in which there was a "sense of complete annihilation" lasted for days. Under these circumstances, he began to pray.

> Far from home, afraid of and for his disturbed father, he began to pray. At first he recited payers his mother had taught him. Finally, he just meditated by "clearing his mind." (ibid.: 295)

From a psychological perspective, his prayer can be seen as an attempt at an introversion, an important move for someone who has been externalizing his conflict so much in enactments. As Jung puts it, "Prayer, for instance, reinforces the potential of the unconscious, thus accounting for the sometimes unexpected effects of prayer" (*CW* 11: 740n2,456). This patient is intuitively attempting, through prayer and meditation, to reestablish contact with the foundation of his personality. The symbolic transformation that follows has a dramatic, numinous beginning.

> One night, exhausted and defeated, having nowhere to turn for solace, he had his first mystical experience: "It was like a fountain bursting forth. I felt a part of everything. And I died. When it stopped, I was changed. I felt limitless courage and strength and I was inspired to do great things. I wanted my life to become a continuous celebration of what I had found within." (Horton 1973: 295)

When the patient reestablishes connection with the springs of his own being, the libidinal energies of the self, the gushing up of psychic energy is a veritable "fountain." But this is followed by a religious "death," which of course was followed by rebirth. The constellation of this creative center in this "born again" patient, in the form of a Religious cultural attitude, was immediately apparent to others.

> A few weeks later he was visited by a friend who had not seen him in several months. His friend was astonished by a profound change in the patient and told him: "If I didn't recognize your features, I wouldn't have known who you were. You are completely different. There is something about you – I can't say what – that wasn't there before." (ibid.)

The progressive realization of this attitude made it possible for the patient "to resist his father's attempt to draw him back into the family circle," enabled him to diminish "his reckless and impulsive behavior" that had led him to "seek out psychotherapy," and to personally experience "recurrent mystical states" which gave him the "courage and strength to go on" (ibid.). This patient was in Late Adolescence, but the process of development that is recorded is actually one that belongs to Early Adolescence. We can only assume that it had been blocked earlier and is at last moving forward now.

Case 3

An eighteen-year-old adolescent was insecure as a child, sucking her thumb, wetting the bed, and using transitional objects into Early Adolescence. She describes her early religious training.

> I was brought up on what was a good dose of "religion." Church and Sunday school every Sunday, youth group once a week, religious instruction classes during grade school, Bible school in the summer time. Bible drills at home – I even taught Sunday school during my high school years, and I went to a Bible-centered college. (ibid.)

After enrolling at this distant college, she "began decompensating out of sheer loneliness" (ibid.). Seeking refuge in drugs "exacerbated her confusion and sense of loneliness."

> A major turning point came in my life January 15, 1969, when I mixed LSD-25 and alcohol. Bingo! I flipped out fast: it was hellish ... I even went so far as to try to kill myself. The only truth I knew was that I was, indeed, in a hopeless situation. Every other thought in my head was utterly distorted and warped. (ibid.)

When a psychiatrist could not help her, other suicide attempts followed. Her emotional state had become unbearable and she had no one with whom to share her suffering.

> Just to give you an idea of how utterly alone I was in the madness of my mind, even since recovering, I still can't find a human being who has or could feel the pain, the fear, the hopelessness, nor aloneness, I felt then. (ibid.)

It was when she had sunk into this abyss of despair without rescue (surely a death experience, symbolically speaking) that she underwent her "conversion." This experience of transformation was also symbolic and had a numinous beginning.

> I remember looking around at the moment I understood I was forgiven past, present, and future saying, "Is that what it is? Oh, is that what it is?" How did I feel? Like a huge knot had been untied inside my head.

For the first time in two months, I slept soundly and peacefully; without fear; I was filled with warmth and love for a living God. (ibid.)

In psychological terms, she is blessed in the embrace of the positive libido flowing from the center of her healthy base, the self, realized through the Religious cultural attitude. From this moment on, the patient's psychological development was progressive.

In the subsequent two and a half years the patient has been a productive member of a campus religious organization and has made no further attempts on her life. Though still quite depressed, she appears to be continuously improving her life situation. (ibid.)

It would appear that the consolidation of a cultural attitude has given this patient the psychological resilience to gradually resolve the continuing depression. Once again we observe that unblocking of symbolic development can occur in spite of the persistence of psychopathology at an exclusively personal level (the depression). The fact that she, like the previous patient, was in Late Adolescence when this important breakthrough occurred again suggests the overcoming of an earlier block to development.

Case 4

In his study of eight adult patients suffering from schizoid personality disorders, Putnam found that each of these patients recalled a recurring dream from childhood of falling into a dark abyss. He tells us that "These dreams were not repressed and the unexorcised image of the abyss found in the dreams was carried silently throughout their lives" (Putnam 1990: 3). Again, the Abyss is the primal image that, when combined with the life-stimulus the Unknown, forms the symbol that evokes the innate affect Fear–Terror, which is the impetus to discover the Religious attitude. We should mention that this attitude is most easily accessed by the psychological type of ego-function Jung called "introverted intuition."

Putnam found that "mountain" imagery was prominent in the dream and fantasy life of his patients, which he considered confirmation of L. H. Stewart's view (1986) that the image of the sacred mountain is compensatory to the abyss of terror. With these facts in mind, let us look at a series of nightmares presented by one of Putnam's patients over a two-week period.

The dreams occurred when the patient had been in analysis for some time and an increase in ego-strength had been achieved. The first dream is as follows.

> I see Christ standing next to a partially open door. He is luminescent white and beckoning me to go through the door. Behind him and the door are stars – like a picture of the Universe. I know that if I go through the door I will die. (Putnam 1990: 63)

The dreamer wakens huddled in his bed and sweating, in the grip of Terror. The second dream occurred the following night.

> I see Christ again. He is again standing with the stars behind him and the door partially open to the stars – just like my previous night. This time I am closer to him and want to put my arms around his legs. But he is beckoning me (without words or motion) to go through the door. I start to move toward the door knowing I will die. I see my hand reach out. (ibid.)

Again the dreamer wakens huddled in his bed and sweating, in the grip of Terror. The third dream occurred ten days later.

> I am again in the same place only very close to the door with Christ to its right. I start to reach out for the handle – I know I am going to go through the door come what will. (ibid.)

The patient wakens, but this time tries to go back to sleep to see what will happen next.

The patient and his analyst interpreted the dream series in the following way:

> We can see here that the fear of death is actually the fear of life. The dreamer associated Christ's luminescence with the Transfiguration. We see that Christ in his transforming aspect is a numinous transpersonal guide ... saying to the dreamer, "you ought to go into the universe," meaning, "you ought to go into *life*." Essentially this man was not in the world or in life, and the dreams indicate how difficult it was for him to get into life as both the dreams and life had a nightmarish quality for him. (ibid.: 64)

I believe these dreams lend themselves to an additional interpretation from a symbolic perspective. They clearly show the patient completing a developmental process which culminates in the construction of a Religious cultural attitude. We do not have enough information to determine whether this development builds on a process begun in Early Adolescence and carries that to completion, or is the true beginning of a mid-life individuation process with strongly religious overtones. Perhaps in certain patients it is destined to be both. As Erikson pointed out in *Young Man Luther* (1958), for the *homo religiosus*, the concern for integrity that is more typical of late life begins early, as part of the early adolescent identity crisis. Even if that turns out not to be the case in this patient, it remains reasonable to claim that what did occur was profound and enduring.

Part III

Summing Up

Incomplete realization explains much that is puzzling both in the individual and in the contemporary scene.
——C. G. Jung, *Collected Works* 16

13

Explaining an Amazing Transformation: The Symbolic Analysis of a Classic Case

Energy is eternal delight.
——W. Blake, *The Marriage of Heaven and Hell*

There are several ways in which the classic case of five-year-old Dibs (Axline 1964) lends itself to an integration of the views expressed in this book. There is the unique "chemistry" between Dibs and his therapist, Miss A, which is accompanied by the initial development and subsequent resolution of the patient-therapist "double bond." The symbolic impetus to development and healing initiated by the patient's fantasies is apparent, and the motivational significance of the innate affects and their dynamisms is a recurrent theme. Finally, as the patient completes the Preschool Period, the new mode of the symbolic process characteristic of Middle Childhood emerges. We are witness to construction by the patient of important elements of the ego-complex, i.e. specific ego-functions and a particular cultural attitude. Axline's non-directive approach to psycho-therapy makes it possible to observe the innately symbolic aspects of the therapeutic process without the need to factor in the effect of considerable verbal interpretations and cues. On the other hand, we are allowed to observe the skill, grace, and unwavering appreciation of individuality which the empathic and insightful Miss A brings to bear upon her work, and it is obvious that this has profound effects upon her patient.

THE INITIAL SITUATION (Axline 1964: 13–19)

The reader first meets five-year-old Dibs in the nursery school which he has been attending for two years. During this time he has never smiled, laughed, or seemed happy. He has never made eye-contact and his response to invitations for social interaction or play has been to roll into a ball or strike out. Nor has he ever engaged in individual play. He has crawled around the room, rocked, chewed his hands, and sucked his thumb. His parents have concluded that he suffers from mental retardation or organic brain damage, but the teachers believe he may have hidden strengths.

For instance, it has been observed that he stayed nearby and listened attentively when a teacher read or demonstrated interesting objects to the class. He has accepted books, and some teachers have thought he can read. He has also spontaneously and carefully explored the objects in the nursery school room. We can conclude that despite the severe, chronic disruption of Dibs ability to play, the dialectic precursor to normal play, the curiosity dynamism, is functioning well.

INTERVIEW 1 (ibid.: 20–31)

The first interview contained several surprises. Miss A (the name Dibs gave to his therapist, Virginia Axline) was surprised when Dibs took her hand and walked to the playroom with her. In reviewing her description of this session, I was surprised to see that Dibs undertook and completed an episode of healing symbolic play. Dibs was also surprised, especially by his assertiveness at the end of the visit. On the way from the playroom to the waiting room, Dibs spoke to Miss A and at her suggestion walked part of the way on his own. He then engaged in the following interaction, according to Miss A's account:

> He walked down the hall, opened the door of his room, then *looked back*. I waved. The look on his face was interesting. He looked *surprised* – almost *pleased*. He walked into his room and closed the door *firmly* behind him.

Now, we know from L. H. Stewart's work that differentiation of the innate affect Surprise–Startle and its dynamisms, Reflection and Orientation, contributes to the development of ego-consciousness and its twin, the self-reflective psychological attitude (Table 9).

Table 9: Surprise–Startle

	Innate Image		
	Darkness		
	Life Situation		
	The Unexpected		
	Innate Affect		
	Surprise–Startle		
Expressive Dynamism	Reflection	*Apperception*	Orientation
Symbolic Cultural Attitude	Self-Reflective Psychological Attitude	*Ego Function*	Ego Consciousness

During a discussion of the importance of the patient's creative playing during treatment, in which he also refers to Virginia Axline's approach, Winnicott has commented upon the importance of the child's experience of Surprise during psychotherapy.

> I appreciate Axline's work in a special way because it joins up with the point that I make in reporting what I call "therapeutic consultations", that the significant moment is that at which *the child surprises himself or herself.* It is not the moment of my clever interpretation that is significant ... (Winnicott 1971: 50–1)

Another psychoanalyst, Henry Smith, first took interest in the significance of Surprise during deep work when his first analytic patient lay down on the couch. *Unexpectedly,* Smith experienced the fact that he could not see his patient's face. In his subsequent study of Surprise during the analytic process, he presents a series of clinical vignettes which convey such moments of emerging Surprise, often not only in himself but also as an impetus to his patient's ego-consciousness and attendant self-reflectiveness. Smith recalls that the initial moment of Surprise in his office "led to an extended self-inquiry ... outside the hour, which was conceived at that moment in the hour and had a life of its own long after" (Smith 1995: 70) and he suggests that a similar process must take place in the patient who has experienced Surprise. This transference/countertransference function of Surprise is well illustrated in Interview 1, when Miss A's Surprise led to expansion of her own awareness even as Dibs's shared Surprise at his strength in play led to expansion of his self-reflectiveness.

INTERVIEW 2 (Axline 1964: 40–7)

In the second visit, Dibs expanded his verbal dialogue with Miss A and even began one with himself. As he explored the objects in the playroom, he said, "Is this a car? This is a car.", etc.

He continued his symbolic play by developing new fantasy themes. He built an Eriksonian tower of blocks (Erikson 1951) and, when it fell, called to Miss A for help. In providing a holding, containing, and sheltered space, Miss A response shows the art of psychotherapy at its finest.

> Miss A: "You really like to have me help you, don't you?" [This is about as close to an interpretation as Miss A comes.]
> Dibs: "That's right." He shot a fleeting glance in my direction.
> Miss A: "Well, what do you want me to do? You tell me, Dibs."
> Dibs: He stood beside the table, looking down at the blocks, his hands still clasped tightly against his chest.

Both were silent. Then the climax occurs.

> He reached out suddenly, took a small block in each hand and crashed them together. "A wreck," he said.

A collision of opposites has occurred, passive has become active, and with the admission of the possibility of a destructive outcome to the conflict, the therapeutic dyad has become a dynamic duo. Jung is our best formulator of why this path of development is so healing:

> ... life can flow forward only along the path of the gradient. But there is no energy unless there is a tension of opposites; hence it is necessary to discover the opposite to the attitude of the conscious mind ... Seen from the one-sided point of view of the conscious attitude, the shadow is an inferior component of the personality and is consequently repressed through intensive resistance. But the repressed content must be made conscious so as to produce a tension of opposites, without which no forward movement is possible. The conscious mind is on top, the shadow is underneath, and just as high always longs for low and hot for cold, so all consciousness, perhaps without being aware of it, seeks its unconscious opposite, lacking which it is doomed to stagnation, congestion, and ossification. Life is born only of the spark of opposites. (CW 7: 78,53–54)

The "wreck," to return to Dibs's word-image for what Jung calls the clash of opposites, is a libido-symbol, and its verbal representation (in a phrase like "wreck") is itself a psychological achievement. As Jung explains:

> Libido can never be apprehended except in a definite form; that is to say, it is identical with fantasy-images. And we can only release it from the grip of the unconscious by bringing up the corresponding fantasy-images. (ibid.: 345,215)

The psychic energy immanent in the symbolized wreck is immediately realized in Dibs as confident self-assertion and strengthening of the will.

When Dibs left Miss A and rejoined his mother in the Waiting Room he appeared to act out another wreck.

> His mother stood there waiting for him, looking very much like Dibs – uncomfortable, ill at ease, not at all sure of herself or the situation. When Dibs saw her, he threw himself face down on the floor and kicked and screamed his protest ... There was a fuss in the waiting room while his mother tried to get him to leave. She was embarrassed and aggravated by his behavior.

Miss A left them to work it out. (This same reunion pattern had occurred each day in the nursery school when Dibs was picked up by his mother or the chauffeur.)

INTERVIEW 3 (Axline 1964: 48–59)

During his two years in the nursery school and during Interviews 1 and 2, Dibs has been referring to himself by his first name or "You." Now, at the beginning of Interview 3, Miss A attempts to focus his attention on the pronoun "I."

> Dibs: "You will take off your hat and coat."
> Miss A: "You want me to take off *my* hat and coat?"
> Dibs: "That's right."
> Miss A: "But *I* don't have a hat or coat on."
> Dibs: "You will take off your hat and coat."

Later in the interview, Dibs has difficulty fastening the front panel of the doll's house, but persists and is successful. The following dialogue occurs:

> Dibs: "There it is. Locked tight."
> Miss A: "I see. You got it on and locked it."
> Dibs: Dibs looked at me. He gave me a brief, fleeting *smile*. "*I* did," he said, falteringly.
> Miss A: "You really did. And by yourself too."
> Dibs: He *grinned*. He seemed very *pleased* with himself. (italics added)

Dibs's use of the person personal pronoun "I," is preceded by a *smile*. The smile indicates his "recognition" of Miss A's acknowledgment of his "I-ness." His grin must be understood as a symbolic *laugh*, indicating his own "recognition" of his "I-ness," that is, a new level of ego-consciousness and a new sense of self. Developmentally, the progression in self-referential pronoun use, the child's recognition of his own ego as cognizing subject, designated as "I," marks the transition from the stage of Early Childhood to that of the Preschool Period (Huxley 1970, Fraiberg and Adelson 1973, Charney 1980).

When there are five minutes left in this hour, Dibs paints a picture with a house, a tree, sky, grass, flowers, and the sun. The door to the house has a lock, its lower windows are barred, and the basement is dark, but there is a lighted upper window with a pot of red flowers in it. This painting is to be a gift for Miss A, for it is her house: the lighted room is a playroom.

When Miss A indicates that time is up, Dibs begins a series of delaying actions, interspersed with verbal protests at leaving and going home: "Dibs not go home. Not never!" Miss A acknowledges that he doesn't *feel* like going home, but indicates firmly it is time for him to go. As she helps him on with his boots, she notices he is sucking on the baby bottle just like a small baby. After a last, brief flurry of delaying actions and, with his resources exhausted, Dibs sighs and walks out the door. He stops abruptly and turns the sign on the door from "Do Not Disturb" to "Play Therapy Room." He patted the door and said, "Our playroom." He then walks down the hall to the reception room. " He leaves with his *surprised* mother without a fuss." (The emphasis is mine.) A momentous surprising change has occurred that demonstrates how symbols that provide a fresh, unexpected impetus to development often do so by exploiting the affect of Surprise.

Dibs's unanticipated painting, his gift to Miss A, is a numinous symbol of wholeness that expresses a constellation of Dibs's whole personality. Suddenly in this deeply troubled child, there is both differentiation and integration of consciousness; boundaries appear between the "outer" world of nature and the "inner" world of the house and its contents. The contents of these two "worlds," moreover, are paired, suggesting a healthy recognition of opposites: the sun outside, the yellow playroom light inside; the flowers outside, the red flower inside; the earth outside, the dark basement inside; the tree outside, uniting heaven and earth, the wooden house inside, containing above and below.

The illuminated happy playroom and the dark basement of fearful unhappiness are also opposites, but the important fact is that these opposites are contained in the house where therapy occurs: the numinous playroom is itself a symbol uniting the opposites of conscious and unconscious. The luminous yellow light and the glowing red flower express the dialectic between Interest and Joy, which in Jungian terms can be termed Logos and Eros, that is enlightened discrimination and warm relatedness. These opposites of focused insight and diffuse illumination have been assigned to the masculine and feminine, but it is better not to be dogmatic about them, and rather simply to see them as the healthy polarity in any psyche.

Progressive psychological development is a process of both internal, subjective integration and objective relationship. Relationship is expressed in Dibs's offering the painting to Miss A as a *gift*. At this moment, what passes between Dibs and Miss A becomes *both* personal *and* symbolic. "Miss A" herself has become a living symbol for Dibs; she represents a supraordinate maternal figure to whom Dibs is willing to entrust himself. At the same time, Miss A is a real person to him, a fellow human being toward whom he can is extend his hope, trust, friendship, and love for the first time. Viewed as two aspects of the same process, the personal relationship with the therapist and the symbolic relatedness to her mark the constellation, in the transference, of a child–therapist "double bond."

The immediate effect of this double bonding is to provide Dibs with the strength of self he needs to attempt to overcome the long-standing dissociation of consciousness and the unconscious that has produced his symptoms and driven him to therapy. It is to avoid losing himself again to the dissociation that he attempts to prolong the interview.

Once the healing transference has been constellated, both the image of the Terrible Mother and the healthy dependency needs denied by her are introduced into the relation with Miss A, in the form of his clinging attempt to delay his departure from the playroom. Miss A's response to Dibs's delaying tactics – her simultaneous sympathy for his feelings and support for his will to adapt – are necessary factors in the overcoming of his regression The integration of the dissociated, more vulnerable element of Dibs's personality is completed when Dibs sucks on the nursing bottle like a small baby. Miss A is able to allow him to be a baby *as well as* a more mature child, thus ensuring that the baby self is not once again dissociated in therapy in a forced attempt to "act his age" now that the healing interview is over. I believe that Virginia Axline's ability to do this is based on a sensitive integration, on her part, of the patient's symbolic communication during the hour. In Interview 1, Dibs had added the figure of a "baby" to his actual family constellation. Now we can see that this "baby" of Interview 1 symbolized a healthy dependency, presumably balked by over-expectant parents and driven into dissociation. Properly integrated, this symbolic "baby" carries the impetus for future development: it is a symbol of the magical pluripotential of the divine child.

That Dibs is conscious of the crucial role that therapy can play in his development is evident in the statement, "Our room." His integration of the dissociated infantile element of his personality is actually a step toward maturity, a fact made evident in his leaving with his surprised mother without a fuss.

INTERVIEWS 4–7 (Axline 1964: 60–107)

In these sessions, there is much movement, which confirms the fact that in Interview 3 Dibs reestablished contact with the healthy base of his personality in the developmental unconscious. In Interview 4, Dibs make intentional extended eye-contact for the first time and Miss A records *another laugh*. Dibs increases his control over his ability to name and define things and makes room for the conscious emergence of a tricksterish shadow figure.

In Interview 5, a little duck completes his search, begun in the previous visit, for a safe pond where "nothing is alone."

In Interview 6, the integration of the "baby" culminates in the following way:

He stretched out full-length ... He rolled over, He wiggled down ... and scooped the sand on top of him. His movements were free, expansive, relaxed. "Hand me the nursing bottle." (I handed it to him.) "I'll pretend this is my crib. I'll curl up in a nice, cozy ball and play I'm a baby again." He did, sucking contentedly on the nursing bottle.

In each of these four visits, Dibs has also spent part of the therapy time in symbolic destruction of the Terrible Father, the archetypal barrier to accepting the law of the father at a personal level in his ego and superego development. In Interview 6, he repeatedly strikes a toy soldier, spits on it, and says: "I spit in your face, I spit in your eye. I gouge your head down deep in the sand." In the seventh session, he put this unacceptable "father" in his "grave" and sings a funeral dirge.

He picked up the drum and beat it slowly. "I beat the drum for Papa ..." Dibs beat the drum slowly and deliberately. "Sleep. Sleep Sleep. Sleep. Sleep. Sleep. Sleep. SLEEPSLEEPSLEEPSLEEPSLEEPSLEEPSLEEP!" As he called out each letter, he gradually increased the tempo. He ended with a flourish of beats on the drum.

In each interview, he deepens his relationship with Miss A and asserts his own individuality in the therapeutic context, showing mastery of his therapy and an early consolidation of his anima as a healthy step in masculine development.

INTERVIEW 8 (ibid.: 109–16)

The symbolic mode characteristic of Middle Childhood is, as we have seen in earlier chapters, a social one, manifest in the social "realm" described in Chapter 6 and the fantasy of a symbolic community, e.g. Jacqueline's "Ventichon." In his eighth session with Miss A, Dibs not only constructs a symbolic community but also, and for the first time, expresses contents that are clearly referable not to earlier stages but to Middle Childhood. These symbolic achievements actually mark his entry into this new stage of development.

Dibs's first acts during this visit to see Miss A are to distinguish between the number of Miss A's office, 12, and that of the playroom, 17. That is, *personal* images of Miss A, Miss A's office, and *symbolic* images of Miss A, "Miss A's playroom," now appear side-by-side.

Then Dibs makes a village, a town, a "whole world!", with a church, houses, and trees.

I created this little town. I have made here a little world of houses. I have planted trees around it. I have imagined the sky and the rain and the gentle winds. I have dreamed up the seasons. And now I'll call forth the spring. The trees are growing into leaves. It is nice and comfortable in this quiet little town. There are people walking down the street. The trees grow silently along the way. The trees are different. The trees have different kinds of bark on their trunks.

After placing more trees around the village, he comments again:

> This tree has green edges. It stands here, pointing up, up, up to the sky. It whispers secrets as the winds pass by. "Tell me where you have been?" asks the tree of the wind. "Tell me what you have seen? For I have roots that tie me to the earth and I must stand forever here." And the wind whispers back "I never stay. I blow away. Away today. Away, I say. Away. Away." And the tree cries out "I want to go with you. I don't want to stand here, alone and sad. I want to go with you. You seem so glad."

The natural, numinous imagery of the tree's growth occasions appreciative reverie, befitting this constellation of a symbol of progressive development. After completion of the "town," Dibs makes immediate reference to a school activity, the singing of "Tom, Tom the Piper's Son" by the class. Just as Jacqueline's dream (in Chapter 6) included contact with her teacher, so Dibs begins now to talk of Miss Jane, one of his teachers. Further confirmation that the symbolic process characteristic of Middle Childhood is underway is indicated by his continuing expansion of the community of adults he is willing to discuss with Miss A: his family's laundress, Millie, and their gardener, Jake, are mentioned. The echo of the therapeutic dyad is unmistakable, but it would be a mistake to reduce these figures to transference derivatives; rather these figures expand out of the therapy, as the symbolic process released by the treatment creates the symbolic community. Dibs and Miss A have a particularly long conversation about Jake, who in real life allied himself with Dibs in his struggle with his tyrannical, insensitive father.

Dibs, who had been locked in his playroom a good part of his life, explains that he often found solace in being able to watch the seasonable changes in a tree outside his window and to touch one of its branches. Even when his father was intransigent, in the face of pleas from Dibs and Jake, and ordered Jake to trim the tree, Jake understood Dibs's need and acted sensitively:

> But Jake saved me the tip end of the branch I used to touch. Jake told me I could keep that part of the tree *inside* my room – that not every tree had a chance to have its favorite branch live in a house. He told me it was an old, old elm tree. He said it was probably two hundred years old and in all that time probably no one had ever loved it as much as I did. So I kept the tip-end branch. I still have it.

In other words, Jake, as a symbolic initiatory father, has given his beloved "son" a *churinga*.

> The rites with which the sacred objects are surrounded often reveal very clearly their nature as transformers of energy. Thus the primitive rubs his *churinga* rhythmically and takes the magic power of the fetish into himself, at the same time giving it a fresh "charge." ... The transformation of the libido through the symbol is a process that has been going on ever since the beginnings of humanity and continues still. Symbols were never devised consciously, but were always produced out of the unconscious by way of revelation or intuition. (CW 8: 92, 48–9)

Jake also told Dibs the story of St. Francis of Assisi and of the last leaf left on the tree.

> He said the little leaf was sad because it thought it had been forgotten and it would never be free to go anyplace. But the wind came back after that one lonely little leaf and blew it on one of the most wonderful trips anyone had ever had. He said the little leaf was blown all around the world and had seen all the wonderful things there are in the world. And when it had gone all around the world, it came back to our yard, Jake said, because it missed me. And Jake found it back under our tree one winter day. It was all tired and thin and worn from its long trip. But Jake said it wanted to come back to me because it hadn't met anybody else in all the world it liked as much as it liked me. So Jake gave it to me ... I keep that leaf. It is very tired and old. But I keep that leaf. I mounted it and framed it. And I imagine some of the things it must have seen, flying all around the world with the wind. And I read in my books about the countries it saw.

The richness and vitality of even this fragment of the tree symbol is certainly evident here. Jung has noted the tree's endless empirical variations: "the commonest associations to its meaning are growth, life, unfolding of form in a physical and spiritual sense, development, growth from below upwards and from above downwards, the maternal aspect (protection, shade, shelter, nourishing fruits, source of life, solidity, permanence, firm-rootedness, but also being 'rooted to the spot'), old age, personality, and finally death and rebirth" (CW 13: 350, 272). To these, of course, must be added the ever-developing self: "If a mandala may be described as a symbol of the self seen in cross section, then the tree would represent a profile view of it: the self depicted as a process of growth" (ibid.: 304, 253). The common denominator of all these diverse significations is generative energy, or what Jung calls libido: the tree for him is a libido-symbol *par excellence*. Whenever Dibs touched the tip-end branch, he would be infused with libido streaming to him from the projected self.

When the tip-end branch was hewn from the tree by Jake and placed in his care, it became a source of self-transforming, life-giving libido.

Through his careful observations of the natural life cycle of the tree, Dibs was thus getting in contact with the eternal, self-renewing quality of the collective unconscious as it operates within as well as outside himself and raising his own experience to the level of a common humanity. At the age of five, he had joined a symbolic community of psychological peers.

For Dibs, who had reason to feel imprisoned and isolated in his locked room, the voyage of the last leaf is a symbolic promise of a future graced by freedom and a genuine relation to the world. The "last leaf" was in this sense an "imaginary companion," a sign that he will be able to continue to access the symbolic mode that had carried him through the stage he was just beginning to complete, the Preschool Period.

Finally, of course, the tree is an archetype with a human face: it stands for Dibs's personal St. Francis, his loving friend Jake, who is the ally and companion who has stood fast against the tyranny and insensitivity of his more impersonal, superego-driven, and frequently hostile father.

Dibs decides to spend the last eight minutes playing with the doll family in the doll house, creating a drama in which the family-complex is hierarchically integrated into a much larger symbolic social community, which appropriately includes individuals outside the nuclear family, and involves male and female opposites working together toward harmony.

TERMINATION (Interviews 9–18)

Given the intensity of the relationship Dibs established with Miss A, his ability to terminate the psychotherapy with lasting integration of its achievements after only eighteen interviews requires particular attention. I believe the explanation lies in Dibs's outstanding ability to use a symbolizing process to transform not only his relations with Miss A but also his relation to the members of his family. This successful use of symbolization is particularly evident in the final termination interview.

"Miss A" and Miss A

At the start of Interview 8, in which he made his first symbolic community, Dibs referred to Miss A's "office" for the first time: he clearly distinguished it from the "playroom." In Interview 10, Dibs spent part of his time in the playroom and part in Miss A's office. This alternation was repeated in Interviews 11, 13, 14, 17, and 18 (the final interview). I believe this pattern significantly contributes to the resolution of the transference to "Miss A." Before I return to a detailed analysis of the process of these sessions, I'd like to reiterate the theoretical perspective which informs my analysis of Dibs's symbolic development.

Throughout this book I have pointed to the dual nature of the parent–child relation. During the stages of a child's development from Infancy through Adolescence, it is fairly obvious that parents have both an unconscious symbolic relatedness and a conscious, personal relationship with their child. Throughout these same stages, however, the child is experiencing the unconscious symbolic relatedness with the parents, and it is that unconscious relationship with them upon which a conscious, personal psychological relationship is constructed. This is particularly so in the case of the child because, unlike the parents, the child has no previous history of conscious relationships to bring to the table.

Therefore, in the child, unconscious images have to guide. The supra-ordinate mother-symbols and father-symbols provided by archetypes *are* the structural and dynamic basis of the infants capacity to symbolize the parents. The earliest mothering and fathering experiences imprint these archetypes to form the parental imagoes, the mother and father images that provide the foundation for the construction of the personal parental-complexes. In the parents, too, despite their history of at least conscious understanding of relationships, supraordinate child-symbols are the structural and dynamic basis of much of the capacity parents seem to have to symbolize their developing child's psyche. The image of the divine or magical child projected upon the magical newborn child, with its extraordinary potential for development, provides the foundation for the construction of the personal child-complex. Once the child-complex is in place in the minds of the parents, the child's need and ability to develop becomes a source of ongoing fascination, pleasure, curiosity, and concern for them.

Both parent and child, however, must renounce these initial symbolic achievements to a considerable degree when the child goes through normal separation-individuation to achieve by the second year of life, the autonomy and "unit status" of an individual. An individual, after all, is someone with a psychic life independent of the parental relationship and the parent's fantasies about who the child is. In order for the child to achieve a satisfactory liberation from the parents, and the parents from the child, transformations need to occur at both personal and archetypal levels of relationship, but most importantly at the archetypal level of symbolic-relatedness. As Jung has written: "Separation from the mother is sufficient only if the archetype is included, and the same is true of separation from the father" (*CW* 8: 374). During the natural process of psychological development, in a "good enough" family, and with adequate sociocultural environmental influences, these transformations occur naturally. In more disturbed families, they require outside mediation, as from a psychotherapist or counselor.

When a child (or adolescent) participates in a successful psychother-apy, as Dibs did, the transference to the therapist will be composed of the same two relational elements that governed the relations with the parents, a symbolic relatedness and a personal relationship. Thus, successful termination of treatment, liberation from the therapist, will have to follow the same path as would normal differentiation from the parents.

Returning to how Dibs resolves the transference with Miss A, my premise is that Miss A's "office" must be understood symbolically as the primary context for his *personal* relationship with his therapist, and that the "playroom" is to be understood symbolically as the primary context for his more archetypal relationship to his symbolic friend "Miss A." Support for this differentiation begins with the fact that the first reference Dibs makes to Miss A's office does not occur until Interview 8, when he is almost halfway through his treatment. This is the interview in which the normal symbolic developmental transformation of Middle Childhood toward creation of a symbolic community is expressed in the image of the little town. This "town" I think marks a significant differentiation from the contexts both of his parents and Miss A and looks forward to Dibs one day taking his place in the wider whole of society itself. The recurrence of the theme of "the two Miss A's," in Interviews 10, 11, 13, 14, 17, and 18, can be understood as reflecting the two levels of personal and symbolic relatedness with Miss A. It comes up so often because Dibs is attempting to interiorize *both* levels of his connection to his therapist. The final phase of this work, in fact, leads to his successful construction of an interiorized relationship with her, a "Miss A-complex," in which the interplay between the personal and symbolic is apparent. Let us see how this occurred in the sessions themselves.

INTERVIEWS 9–17 (Axline 1964: 117–62, 177–200)

In this series of interviews, Dibs engages in further healing of the pathological elements of several family constellations: the combined-parental-complex, the father-complex, the mother-complex, and the sister-complex. In Interview 12, a giant boy locks his screaming and crying "mother and father" in a burning house, only to rescue them at the last moment. In Interview 14, he records a "make-believe" story of his hatred for a mean, but now contrite, "father" and then goes on to tell of a gift he made for his real father. In Interview 15, he puts a deadly poison in his "sister's" food and punishes his cruel "mother" unmercifully; then he expresses his caring for his actual sister and tells of a flower book he made for his actual mother. In Interview 16, he makes a world with the World Test Kit and declares himself a "builder of cities." Again his "parents" are locked screaming and crying in a burning house, and again they are rescued. The energies reclaimed through this work are then combined with already available energies in his ego to ensure Dibs's entry, as a "builder of cities," into a symbolic world that is normal for Middle Childhood. With his symbolic development secured, Dibs's relationships with the members of his family, as well as with his classmates, become ever more loving and playful.

In Interview 17, Miss A re-enters his fantasy life for the first time since Dibs painted her "house" in session 3. Now, they have become neighbors in the symbolic community Dibs has created for himself:

> "The jail is right next to Miss A's house now and she says she does not like jails and she takes it far away and buries it in the sand and there isn't a jail any more for any one." Dibs buried the jail in the sandbox. "Then there are these two houses. Your house and my house and they begin to slowly move farther and farther apart." He slowly moved the two houses apart. "My house and Miss A's house are getting farther and farther apart – about a mile apart."

INTERVIEW 18 (ibid.: 201–9)

Dibs's last interview with Miss A, which occurred after a three-month summer break, is truly remarkable. In this interview, Dibs engages in a series of symbolic acts, which are to be seen as rituals serving to complete the resolution of the symbolic relatedness with "Miss A." He says goodbye to the "dear wonderful lady of the playroom." (We might conjecture that in the unconscious archetypal context of the patient–therapist symbolic relatedness, Miss A has been assimilated to the image that inspired the Greeks to envision the nymph Paidia (Play), an attendant upon the god Dionysus.) Dibs also engages in a series of interpersonal actions, which serve to deepen, commemorate, and further differentiate his personal relationship with Miss A. He sums up their relationship: "*As you said you wanted it. As I said I wanted it. As we said we wanted it.*"

In Interview 10, Dibs identified yellow as the color of anger. He now empties the vessel of rage on the floor. Then he wipes it up. He signals that he is finished with the baby bottle, which comforted him when he needed it, by smashing it on the iron radiator. He then bequeaths the playroom to other children: "It will make the children happy."

At his request, they visit the church, which has always been visible from the playroom. The organ music makes him "cold" and gives him "goose pimples." He has never seen anything as beautiful as the sun shining through the stained glass windows.

He completes the visit by telling Miss A that he has asked his father to teach him baseball, as he wants to play with the children at school. (He admits he's better at cops and robbers.) In the waiting room, he tells his mother this was his last visit Miss A and that he's not coming back anymore. As he explains, "This today was for goodbye."

DEVELOPMENT OF A SOCIAL CULTURAL ATTITUDE (ibid.: 210–14)

Dibs's was in his sixth year when his eighteen visits with Miss A, spanning a period of nine months, came to an end. Miss A's first follow-up of the treatment occurred when, shortly after his family moved into her neighborhood, she had a chance meeting with Dibs, now nine years old. He was glad to see her, showed her his well-tended garden, and seemed like a normal latency age boy.

The second and last follow-up occurred when Dibs was fifteen years old. It consisted of a letter written by him and brought to Miss A's attention by a friend who taught in his school. The letter, addressed to the headmaster and faculty, appeared in the school newspaper.

This is an open letter of protest against the recent dismissal of one of my classmates and one of my friends. I am indeed indignant at your callousness and lack of understanding and feeling. It is whispered about that my friend was "suspended with dishonor" because he was caught cheating. My friend said he was not cheating and I believe him. He was verifying ... an important date in history – since accuracy of date is essential to establish its very existence, then it should, indeed, be verified ... Do you call it a fault when a person seeks to verify accuracy? Would you prefer that he cloud his honest doubt in ignorance? What are the purposes of examinations anyhow? Are they to increase our educational attainment? Or are they instruments to bring *suffering and humiliation and deep hurt* to a person who is trying hard to succeed?

As educators, you *must* unlock the door of ignorance and prejudice and meanness. Unless my friend is given your apologies for this hurt he has received to his *pride and self-respect* and is reinstated, then I shall not return to this school in the fall.

With sincerity and intent to act, I am, Sincerely, Dibs. (italics added)

Miss A asked the person who sent this letter what Dibs was like. She was told:

He is a brilliant boy, Full of ideas, Concerned about everybody and everything. Very sensitive. A real leader ... They will probably follow his suggestion ... Do you want to keep it for your collection of brave new words for justice and equality for all?

Miss A replied by echoing Dibs's own sign-off: "'With sincerity and intent to act.' I believe that."

Those who have read this book with attention will note that Dibs's letter embodies the social values of the Good – Equality and Justice – and expresses the ideals of a utopian community, implying that his symbolic development has matured into what we expect from Early Adolescence in a gifted child. As such, it reflects the living presence, in the now fifteen-year-old Dibs, of a creative center in the personality, a Social cultural attitude. Of course, it is also the letter of a challenging, creatively oppositional person, unafraid to rebel: it is Dibs to the core.

It is interesting to note that when Dibs was two years old, the parents had taken him for a psychiatric evaluation because of their concern that he was schizophrenic or autistic. The psychiatrist told them, that in view of their backgrounds, he would be very frank with them. He said that Dibs was not mentally defective or psychotic or brain-damaged, but the most *rejected and emotionally deprived* child he had ever seen. It would seem that by age fifteen Dibs had differentiated his early fate enough to articulate a response to similar rejections suffered by others.

Let us recall that rejection is not just catastrophe. It is the life stimulus to the innate affect Shame/Contempt, and that a Social cultural attitude can develop from this innate affect, even in "negative" circumstances. The social attitude can also come into play through creative shaming among children on the playground or the later rebukes of the Establishment delivered to many effective social activists in adulthood. In other words, the impetus of the symbol can enable a pathological complex of early childhood to be transformed, by the time of adolescence, into a cultural attitude that supports a healthy adaptation.

Epilogue

The wolf also shall dwell with the lamb and the leopard shall lie down
with the kid; and the calf and the young lion and the fatling together;
and a little child shall lead them.

Isaiah 11: 6

The familiar Old Testament verse carrying, as a divine dispensation, the
promise of peace and a Golden Age of harmony, depicts from a psychological standpoint a progressive reconciliation of highly energized,
primordially instinctual opposites that would seem incompatible – the
aggressions and vulnerabilities of early childhood that threaten to
interrupt development. An explanation for the miracle of their coming
together as an energy that can move life forward may lie in the final
phrase "and a little child shall lead them." This striking image can be
read, in tandem with the prophet's tender way of evoking the "lamb,"
the "kid," the "calf," and the "young lion," as an evocation of the divine
child, who functions as the earliest symbol of the newborn's capacity to
make the difficult passage out of affective conflict to the growth-
enhancing state of psychological unity easy.

The tension of opposites and the primordial energy of the child in
resolving them appear as essential concepts also in the writings of
Heraclitus of Ephesus (536–470 BC), who proclaimed, "I see nothing
other than becoming." Nietzsche, with an uncanny empathy for the psychological implications of such a cosmology, believed that the intuition
of the impermanence of everything actual had to have been a "paralyzing
thought" for the pre-Socratic philosopher. Nietzsche felt that it must have
taken tremendous strength on Heraclitus's part to transform his
apprehension of life's flux into a world view characterized by "sublimity
and the feeling of astonishment."

Heraclitus achieved this by means of an observation regarding the
actual process of all coming-to-be and passing away. He conceived it
under the form of polarity, as being the diverging of a force into two

qualitatively different opposed activities that seek to re-unite. Everlastingly, a given quality contends against itself and separates into opposites; everlastingly these opposites seek to re-unite. (Nietzsche 1962: 54)

Nietzsche found it particularly extraordinary that his great philosophical ancestor, after designating the principle governing all becoming in the cosmos as *aion* (time), conceived this exigency not as later generations would, as Saturn, Father Time, the Grim Reaper, but as a *child playing*: "Time," Heraclitus tells us, "is a child moving counters in a game; the royal power is a child's." Nietzsche saw the liberating quality in this image, which drew inspiration from the primordial element fire that Heraclitus had already selected as the fundamental process of creation, for it is at the same time a purging of previous, impure forms of being.

Before his fire-gaze not a drop of injustice remains in the world poured all around him; even that cardinal impulse that allows pure fire to inhabit such impure forms is mastered by him with a sublime metaphor. In this world only play, play as artists and children engage in it, exhibits coming-to-be and passing away, structuring and destroying, without any moral additive, in forever equal innocence. And as children and artists play so plays the ever-living fire. It constructs and destroys, all in innocence. Such is the game that the aeon plays with itself. Transforming itself into water and earth, it builds towers of sand like a child at the seashore, piles them up and tramples them down. From time to time it starts the game anew. An instant of satiety – and again it is seized by its need, as the artist is seized by his need to create. Not hybris but the ever self-renewing impulse to play calls new worlds into being. The child throws its toys away from time to time – and starts again, in innocent caprice. But when it does build, it combines and joins and forms its structures regularly, conforming to inner laws. (ibid.: 61–2)

It is these laws I have tried to explicate in this book.

Bibliography

Abrams, D. M., and Sutton-Smith, B. (1977) The development of the trickster in children's narrative. *Journal of American Folklore* 90: 29–47.

Abt, R., Bosch, I., and MacKrell, V. (2000) *Dream Child: Creation and New Life in Dreams of Pregnant Women*. Einsiedeln, Switzerland: Daimon Verlag.

Adelson, J. (1971) The political imagination of the young adolescent. *Daedalus, Fall 1971: Twelve to Sixteen: Early Adolescence* 100, No. 4: 1013–50. Proceedings of the American Academy of Arts and Sciences.

Ainsworth, M. D. S., Bell, S. M., and Stayton, D. J. (1974) Infant–mother attachment and social development: Socialisation as a product of reciprocal responsiveness to signals. In *The Integration of a Child into a Social World*, ed. M. P. M. Richards, 99–135. London: Cambridge University Press.

Albert, S., Amgott, T., Krakow, M., and Marcus, H. (1979) Children's bedtime rituals as a prototype rite of safe passage. *Journal of Psychological Anthropology* 2: 85–105.

Ames, L. B., and Learned, J. (1946) Imaginary companions and related phenomena. *Journal of Genetic Psychology* 69: 147–67.

Appleyard, J. A. (1990) *Becoming a Reader*. New York: Cambridge University Press.

Auden, W. H. (1967) *The Enchafed Flood*. New York: Vintage Books.

Axline, V. (1947) *Play Therapy*. San Francisco: Houghton Mifflin Company.

Axline, V. (1964) *Dibs: In Search of Self*. New York: Ballantine Books.

Bach, S. (1971) Notes on some imaginary companions. *Psychoanaltyic Study of the Child* 26: 159–71.

Bachelard, G. (1964) *The Psychoanalysis of Fire*. Boston: Beacon Press.

Bachelard, G. (1971) *The Poetics of Reverie*. Trans. © 1969 Grossman Publishers, Inc. Boston: Beacon Paperback.

Bainum, C. K., Lounsbury, K. R., and Pollio, H. R. (1984) The development of laughing and smiling in nursery school children. *Child Development*, 55: 1946–57.

Baring-Gould, W. S., and Baring-Gould, C. (1962) *The Annotated Mother Goose*. New York: Clarkson N. Potter, Inc.

Barth, J. M., and Parke, R. D. (1993) Parent–child relationship influences on children's transition to school. *Merrill-Palmer Quarterly* 39: 173–95.

Bass, H. (1983) The development of an adult's imaginary companion. *Psychoanalytic Review* 70: 519–33.

Beebe, J. (1992) *Integrity in Depth*. Foreword David H. Rosen. 1st edition College Station: Texas A&M University Press. Carolyn and Ernest Fay series in Analytical Psychology; no. 2.

Beiser, M. (1985) The grieving witch; A framework for applying principles of cultural psychiatry to clinical practice. *Canadian Journal of Psychiatry* 30: 130–41.

Bender, L., and Vogel, F. (1941) Imaginary companions of children. *American Journal of Orthopsychiatry* 11: 56–65.

Blake, W. (1977) *Songs of Innocence and Experience*. New York: Oxford University Press.

Blehar, M. C., Lieberman, A. F., and Ainsworth, M. D. S. (1977) Early face-to-face interaction and its relation to later infant–mother attachment. *Child Development* 48: 182–94.

Bliss, E. L. (1980) Multiple personalities. *Archives of General Psychiatry* 37, 1388–97.

Bliss, E. L. (1986) *Multiple Personality, Allied Disorders, and Hypnosis*. New York: Oxford University Press.

Blurton Jones, N. (1967) An ethological study of some aspects of social behaviour of children in nursery school. In *Primate Ethology*, ed. D. Morris. London: Weidenfeld and Nicolson.

Blurton Jones, N. (1972a) Non-verbal communication in children. In *Non-Verbal Communication*, ed. R. A. Hinde. Cambridge: Cambridge University Press.

Blurton Jones, N. (1972b) Categories of child–child interaction. In *Ethological Studies of Child Behaviour*, ed. N. Blurton Jones. London: Cambridge University Press.

Botvin, G. J., and Sutton-Smith, B. (1977) The development of structural complexity in children's fantasy narratives. *Developmental Psychology* 13: 377–88.

Bowyer, R. (1970) *The Lowenfeld World Technique*. London: Pergamon Press.

Brazelton, T. B. (1973) Effects of maternal expectations on early infant behavior. *Early Child Development and Care* 2: 259–73.

Brazelton, T. B., and Als, H. (1979) Four early stages in the development of mother–infant interaction. *Psychoanalytic Study of the Child* 34: 349–69. New York: International Universities Press, Inc.

Brown, R. (1973) *A First Language*. Cambridge, Mass.: Harvard University Press.

Callimachus (1901) *Hymn to Delos*. In *The Works of Hesiod, Callimachus, and Theogonis*. Prose trans. J. Banks; metrical trans. Elton, Tytler, and Frere. London: G. Bell.

Campbell, J. (1956) *The Hero With a Thousand Faces*. New York: Meridian Books.

Cassirer, E. (1944) *An Essay on Man*. New Haven: Yale University Press.

Cassirer, E. (1955) *The Philosophy of Symbolic Forms*, Vol. 1: *Language*. New Haven: Yale University Press.

Cassirer, E. (1957) *The Philosophy of Symbolic Forms*, Vol. 3: *The Phenomenology of Knowledge*. New Haven: Yale University Press.

Charney, R. (1980). Speech roles and the development of personal pronouns. *Journal of Child Language* 7: 509–28.

Chatterjee, G. (1999) Nursery rhymes and socialization. In *Culture, Socialization and Human Development: Theory, Research and Applications in India*, ed. T. S. Saraswathi. Thousand Oaks: Sage Publications.

Chodorow, J. (1984) To move and be moved. *Quadrant* 17: 39–48.

Chodorow, J. (1991) *Dance Therapy & Depth Psychology: The Moving Imagination.* London: Routledge.

Cohen, D., and MacKeith, S. A. (1991) *The Development of Imagination.* New York: Routledge.

Congdon, M. H., Hain, J., and Stevenson, I. (1961) A case of multiple personality illustrating the transition from role-playing. *Journal of Nervous and Mental Diseases* 132: 497–504.

Dahl, E. K. (1989) Daughters and mothers: Oedipal aspects of the witch-mother. *The Psychoanalytic Study of the Child* 44: 267–80.

Davis, M. E., and Wallbridge, D. (1981) *Boundary and Space.* New York: Brunner/Mazel.

de Tolnay, C. (1943) The music of the universe. *Journal of the Walters Art Gallery,* VI; 83–104.

Deutsch, H. (1945) *The Psychology of Women,* Vol. 2: *Motherhood.* New York: Grune & Stratton.

Dixon, R. B. (1916) Oceanic mythology. *The Mythology of All Races,* Vol. IX, ed. L. H. Gray. Boston: Marshall Jones Company.

Dougherty, N. (1998) Vampires, eroticism, and the lure of the unconscious. In *The Soul of Popular Culture.* ed. M. L. Kittelson. Chicago: Open Court.

Driver, P. (1997) Maestro. *The New York Times Book Review,* November 2, 1997.

Dyson, A. H. (1996) Cultural constellations and childhood identities: On Greek gods, cartoon heroes, and the social lives of schoolchildren. *Harvard Educational Review* 66: 471–95.

Eiduson, B. T. (1962) The beginings of scientists. In *Scientists, their Psychological World,* ed. B. T. Eiduson and L. Beckman. New York: Basic Books.

Ekman, P., and Friesen, W. V. (1971) Constants across cultures in the face and emotion. *Journal of Personality and Social Psychology* 17: 124–9.

Eliade, M. (1958) *Rites and Symbols of Intiation.* New York: Harper & Row.

Eliade, M. (1971) *The Forge and the Crucible: The Origins and Structures of Alchemy.* New York: Harper & Row.

Eliade, M. (ed.) (1987) *Encyclopedia of Religion.* New York: Macmillan Publishing Company.

Elkind, D. (1967) Editor's Introduction to *Six Psychological Studies* by J. Piaget. New York: Random House, Inc.

Emde, R. N. (1989) The infant's relationship experience: developmental and affective aspects. In *Relationship Disturbances in Early Childhood,* ed. A. J. Sameroff and R. N. Emde, 33–51. New York: Basic Books.

Emde, R. N., Gaensbauer, T. J., and Harmon, R. J. (1976) Emotional expression in infancy: A biobehavioral study. *Psychological Issues* 10, Monograph 37.

Emde, R. N., Swedberg, J., and Suzuki, B. (1975) Human wakefulness and biological rhythms after birth. *Archives of General Psychiatry* 32: 780–3.

Erikson, E. H. (1950/1963) *Childhood and Society.* (2nd edition) New York: W. W. Norton & Company, Inc.

Erikson, E. H. (1951) Sex differences in the play configurations of preadolescents. *American Journal of Orthopsychiatry* 21: 667–92.

Erikson, E. H. (1958) *Young Man Luther.* New York: W. W. Norton & Company, Inc.

Erikson, E. H. (1959) Identity and the life cycle. *Psychological Issues* 1 (1).

Erikson, E. H. (1964) *Insight and Responsibility.* New York: W. W. Norton & Company.

Escalona, S. K. (1968) *The Roots of Individuality*. Chicago: Aldine Publishing Company.

Feldman, B. (1991) Adolescents with bulimia. In *Personal and Archetypal Dynamics in the Analytical Relationship*, ed. Mary A. Matoon. Proceedings of the Eleventh International Congress for Analytical Psychology, 1989. Einsielden, Switzerland: Daimon Verlag.

Fernald, A. (1992) Meaningful melodies in mother's speech to infants. In *Nonverbal Communication: Comparative and Developmental Approaches*, ed. H. Papousek, U. Jergens, and M. Papousek. New York: Cambridge University Press.

Field, J. (1950) *On Not Being Able To Paint*. London: W. Heinemann.

Field, T. M., and Fox, N. A. (1985) *Social Perception in Infants*. Norwood, New Jersey: Ablex Publishing Corporation.

Fordham, M. (1979) The self as an imaginative construct. *Journal of Analytical Psychology*, 24: 18–30.

Fordham, M. (1994) *Children As Individuals*. London: Free Association Books.

Fowler, J. (1991) Stages in faith consciousness. In *Religious Development in Childhood and Adolescence*, ed. F. K. Oser and W. G. Scarlett. *New Directions for Child Development*, 52: 27–45. San Francisco: Jossey-Bass Inc.

Fraiberg, S. (1974) The clinical dimension of baby games. *Journal of the American Academy of Child Psychiatry* 13: 202–20.

Fraiberg, S. (1980) *Clinical Studies in Infant Mental Health*. New York: Basic Books, Inc.

Fraiberg, S. (1982) Pathological defenses in infancy. *Psychoanalytic Quarterly* 11: 612–35.

Fraiberg, S., and Adelson, E. (1973) Self-representation in language and play: observations of blind children. *Psychoanalytic Quarterly* 42: 539–63.

Furth, H. G. (1969) *Piaget and Knowledge*. Englewood Cliffs, New Jersey: Prentice-Hall, Inc.

Gaster, T. (1952) *The Oldest Stories in the World*. Boston: Beacon Press.

Gloger-Tippelt, G. (1983) A process model of the pregnancy course. *Human Development* 26: 134–48.

Gold, S. R., and B. B. Henderson (1990) Daydreaming and curiosity: stability and change in gifted children and adolescents. *Adolescence* 25: 701–8.

Goldberg, S. (1984) Parent-infant bonding: another look. *Annual Progress in Child Psychiatry and Child Development*, ed. S. Chess and A. Thomas, 17–57. New York: Brunner/Mazel.

Golding, J. (1993) Sophisticated peasant. *The New York Review of Books*, December 16: 45–51.

Gould, R. (1972) *Child Studies Through Fantasy*. New York: Quadrangle Books, Inc.

Greenberg, M., and Morris, N. (1974) Engrossment: the newborn's impact upon the father. *American Journal of Orthopsychiatry* 44: 520–31.

Greenspan, S. I., and Lieberman, A. F. (1994) Representational elaboration and differentiation: a clinical-quantitative approach to the assessment of 2- to 4-year-olds. In *Children at Play: Clinical and Developmental Approaches to Meaning and Representation*, ed. A. Slade, D. Palmer Wolf, et al. New York: Oxford University Press.

Gruber, H. E., and Voneche, J. J. (eds) (1977) *The Essential Piaget*. New York: Basic Books, Inc.

Guthrie, L. G. (1921) *Contributions to the Study of Precocity in Children*. London: Eric G. Millar.

Haight, W., and Miller, P. J. (1993) *Pretending At Home*. Albany, NY: State University of New York Press.

Halliday, M. A. K. (1975) *Learning How to Mean – Explorations in the Development of Language*. London: Edward Arnold.

Harkins, D. A., Koch, P. E., and Michel, G. F. (1994) Listening to maternal story telling affects narrative skill of 5-year-old children. *Journal of Genetic Psychology* 155: 247–57.

Harrison, J. E. (1922) *Prolegomena to the study of Greek Religion*. 3rd edition Cambridge: Cambridge University Press.

Harrison, J. E. (1962) *Epilegomena to the study of Greek Religion and Themis*. New York: University Books.

Hart, D. L. (1977) Dreams of escape from bewitchment. *Spring* 1: 42–5.

Hastings, J. (ed.) (1926/1969) *Hastings Encyclopedia of Religion and Ethics*, Vol. 9. New York: Charles Scribner's Sons.

Haviland, J. M., and Lelwica, M. (1987) The induced affect response: 10-week-old infants' responses to three emotional expressions. *Developmental Psychology* 23: 97–104.

Hawkey, M. L. (1948) The witch and the bogey. *British Journal of Medical Psychology* 21: 12–29.

Henderson, J. L. (1964) Ancient myths and modern man. In *Modern Man and His Symbols*, ed. C. G. Jung and M. L. von Franz. Garden City, New York: Doubleday & Company, Inc.

Henderson, J. L. (1967) *Thresholds of Initiation*. Middletown, Conn.: Wesleyan University Press.

Henderson, J. L. (1984) *Cultural Attitudes in Psychological Perspective*. Toronto: Inner City Books.

Henderson, J. L. (1990) *Shadow and Self: Selected Papers in Analytical Psychology*. Wilmette, Ill.: Chiron Publications.

Hillman, J. (1962/1992) *Emotion*. Evanston, Illinois: Northwestern University Press.

Hillman, J. (1972) *The Myth of Analysis*. New York: Harper & Row, Publishers.

Hogenson, G. B. (1994) *Jung's Struggle with Freud*. Wilmette, Ill.: Chiron Publications.

Holmberg, U. (1927) Finno-Ugric mythology, Siberian mythology. *The Mythology of All Races*, Vol. IV, ed. J. A. MacCulloch. Boston: Marshall Jones Company.

Horton, P. C. (1973) The mystical experience as a suicide preventive. *American Journal of Pyschiatry* 130: 294–6.

Hunt, U. (1914) *Una Mary*. New York: Charles Scribner's Sons.

Hurlock, E. B., and Burstein, M. (1932) The imaginary playmate; a questionnaire study. *Journal of Genetic Psychology* 41: 380–92.

Huxley, R. (1970) The development of the correct use of subject personal pronouns in two children. In *Advances in Psycholinguistics*, ed. G. B. Flores d'Arcais and W. J. M. Levelt. New York: American Elsevier.

The Hymn to Hermes I (1970) In *The Homeric Hymns*, trans. C. Boer. Woodstock, Conn.: Spring Publications, Inc., 1995.

Jaffe, A. (1989) *From the Life and Work of C. G. Jung*, trans. R. F. C. Hull and M. Stein. Am Kosterplatz, Einsiedeln, Switzerland: Daimon Verlag.

Jeffers, R. (1933) Remembered Verses. Introduction to S. S. Albert's *A Bibliography of the Works of Robinson Jeffers*. New York: Random House.

Jones, L. (1982) The development of structure in the world of expression: a cognitive-developmental analysis of children's "sand worlds". *Dissertation Abstracts International* (University Microfilms No. 8303178).

Jung, C. G. (1954) *The Development of Personality. Collected Works*, Vol. 17. New Jersey: Princeton University Press.

Jung, C. G. (1961) *Freud and Psychoanalysis. Collected Works*, Vol. 4. New Jersey: Princeton University Press.

Jung, C. G. (1964) *Civilization in Transition. Collected Works*, Vol. 10. New Jersey: Princeton University Press.

Jung, C. G. (1966a) *The Spirit in Man, Art, and Literature. Collected Works*, Vol. 15. New Jersey: Princeton University Press.

Jung, C. G. (1966b) *Two Essays on Analytical Psychology. Collected Works*, Vol. 7. New Jersey: Princeton University Press, 2nd edition.

Jung, C. G. (1967) *Alchemical Studies. Collected Works*, Vol. 13. New Jersey: Princeton University Press.

Jung, C. G. (1968a) *Aion. Collected Works*, Vol. 9ii. New Jersey: Princeton University Press, 2nd edition.

Jung, C. G. (1968b) *Symbols of Transformation. Collected Works*, Vol. 5. New Jersey: Princeton University Press, 2nd edition.

Jung, C. G. (1969) *Psychology and Religion: West and East. Collected Works*, Vol. 11. New Jersey: Princeton University Press, 2nd edition.

Jung, C. G. (1970) *Mysterium Coniunctionis. Collected Works*, Vol. 14. New Jersey: Princeton University Press, 2nd edition.

Jung, C. G. (1972) *The Psychogenesis of Mental Disease. Collected Works*, Vol. 3. New Jersey: Princeton University Press.

Jung, C. G. (1973a) *Experimental Researches. Collected Works*, Vol. 2. New Jersey: Princeton University Press.

Jung, C. G. (1973b) *Letters*, Vol. 1: *1906–1950*, ed. G. Adler and A. Jaffe, trans. R. F. C. Hull. New Jersey: Princeton University Press.

Jung, C. G. (1974a) *Psychological Types. Collected Works*, Vol. 6. New Jersey: Princeton University Press.

Jung, C. G. (1974b) *Psychology and Alchemy. Collected Works*, Vol. 12. New Jersey: Princeton University Press.

Jung, C. G. (1975a) *The Practice of Psychotherapy. Collected Works*, Vol. 16. New Jersey: Princeton University Press.

Jung, C. G. (1975b) *Psychiatric Studies. Collected Works*, Vol. 1. New Jersey: Princeton University Press.

Jung, C. G. (1975c) *The Structure and Dynamics of the Psyche. Collected Works*, Vol. 8. New Jersey: Princeton University Press.

Jung, C. G. (1976a) *Letters*, Vol. 2: *1951–1961*, ed. G. Adler and A. Jaffe, trans. R. F. C. Hull. New Jersey: Princeton University Press.

Jung, C. G. (1976b) *The Symbolic Life. Collected Works*, Vol. 18. New Jersey: Princeton University Press.

Jung, C. G. (1977a) *The Archetypes and the Collective Unconscious. Collected Works*, Vol. 9i. New Jersey: Princeton University Press.

Jung, C. G. (1977b) *C. G. Jung Speaking*, ed. W. McGuire and R. F. C. Hull. New Jersey: Princeton University Press.

Jung, C. G. (1984) *Dream Analysis*. New Jersey: Princeton University Press.

Jung, C. G. (1988) *Nietzsche's Zarathustra*, 2 vols, ed. J. J. Jarrett. New Jersey: Princeton University Press.

Jung, C. G., and Kerenyi, C. (1963) *Essays on a Science of Mythology.* New York: Harper & Row.

Kaitz, M., Meirov, H., Landman, I., and Eidelman, A. I. (1993) Infant recognition by tactile cues. *Infant Behavior & Development* 16: 333–41.

Kennell, J. H., and Klaus, M. H. (1984) Mother–infant bonding – weighing the evidence. *Developmental Review* 4: 275–82.

Kitzinger, S. (1972) *The Experience of Childbirth.* Baltimore: Penguin Books Inc.

Kitzinger, S. (1979) *Birth at Home.* New York: Oxford University Press.

Klaus, M. H., and Kennell, J. H. (1982) *Parent–Infant Bonding.* St. Louis, Missouri: The C. V. Mosby Company.

Konner, M. (1998) Behavioral changes around two months of age in a population of African hunter-gatherers. Abstracts of Papers Presented at the Eleventh International Conference on Infant Studies, special ed. R. Bakeman and L. B. Adamson. *Infant Behavior and Development,* 21S: 185.

Lagercrantz, H., and Slotkin, T. (1986) The "stress" of being born. *Scientific American* 254: 100–7.

Lane, R. C., and Chazan, S. E. (1989) Symbols of terror: The witch/vampire, the spider, and the shark. *Psychoanalytic Psychology* 6: 325–41.

Langdon, S. H. (1964) Semitic mythology. *The Mythology of All Races,* Vol. V, ed. J. A. MacCulloch. New York: Cooper Square Publishers.

Leifer, M. (1980) *Psychological Effects of Motherhood.* New York: Praeger Publishers.

Levinson, L. (1984) Witches – bad and good: maternal psychopathology as a developmental interference. *Psychoanalytic Study of the Child* 39: 371–92.

Lewis, E. (1954) The function of group play during Middle Childhood in developing the ego complex. *British Journal of Medical Psychology* 27: 15–29.

Lieberman, A. (1999) Negative maternal attributions: effects on toddlers' sense of self. *Psychoanalytic Inquiry* 19: 737–56.

Limon, J. (1999) *An Unfinished Memoir.* Hanover: Wesleyan University Press; University Press of New England.

Lindner, R. L. (1999) *The Fifty-Minute Hour.* New York: The Other Press.

Lockard, J. S., Fahrenbruch, C. E., Smith, J. L., and Morgan, C. J. (1977) Smiling and laughter: phyletic origins? *Bulletin of the Psychonomic Society* 10: 183–6.

Lum, P. (1951) *Fabulous Beasts.* New York: Pantheon Books, Inc.

Macculloch, J. A. (1964) Celtic mythology. *Mythology of All Races,* Vol. III, ed. L. H. Gray. New York: Cooper Square Publishers.

McDonald, M. (1970) Transitional tunes and musical development. *Psychoanalytic Study of the Child* 25: 503–20.

Macfarlane, A. (1977) *The Psychology of Childbirth.* Cambridge, Mass.: Harvard University Press.

McKernon, P. E. (1979) The development of first songs in young children. In *New Directions for Child Development, No. 3, Early Symbolization,* ed. D. Wolf. San Francisco: Jossey-Bass Inc.

Main, M. (1983) Exploration, play, and cognitive functioning related to infant–mother attachment. *Infant Behavior and Development* 6: 167–74.

Malatesta, C. Z., Grigoryev, P., Lamb, C., Albin, M., and Culver, C. (1986) Emotion socialization and expressive development in preterm and full-term infants. *Child Development* 57: 316–30.

Malatesta, C. Z., and Haviland, J. M. (1982) Learning display rules: the socialization of emotion expression in infancy. *Child Development* 53: 991–1003.

Malatesta, C. Z., and Wilson, A. (1988) Emotion cognition interaction in personality development: a discrete emotions, functionalist analysis. *British Journal of Social Psychology* 27: 91–112.

Manosevitz, M., Fling, S., and Prentice, N. M. (1977) Imaginary companions in young children: Relationships with intelligence, creativity and waiting ability. *Journal of Child Pschology and Psychiatry* 18: 73–8.

Manosevitz, M., Prentice, N. M., and Wilson, F. (1973) Individual and family correlates of imaginary companions in preschool children. *Developmental Psychology* 8: 72–9.

May, K. A. (1982) Three phases of father involvement in pregnancy. *Nursing Research* 31: 337–42.

Milner, M. (1952) Aspects of symbolism in comprehension of the not-self. *International Journal of Psycho-analysis* 33: 181–95.

Murdoch, I. (1973) *The Black Prince*. New York: The Viking Press.

Myers, B. J. (1984) Mother–infant bonding: the status of this critical-period hypothesis. *Developmental Review* 4: 240–74.

Myers, W. A. (1976) Imaginary companions. fantasy twins, mirror dreams, and depersonalization. *Psychoanalytic Quarterly* 45: 503–24.

Nagera, H. (1969) The imaginary companion. *Psychoanalytic Study of the Child* 24: 165–96.

Nietzsche, F. (1962) *Philosophy in the Age of the Greeks*, translated, with an Introduction by M. Cowan. Chicago: Henry Regnery Company.

Neumann, E. (1954) *The Origins and History of Consciousness*. New Jersey: Princeton University Press.

Neumann, E. (1966) Narcissism, normal self-formation, and the primary relation to the mother. *Spring 1966*: 81–106.

Neumann, E. (1973) *Depth Psychology and a New Ethic*, trans. E. Rolfe. New York: Harper & Row.

Neumann, E. (1990) *The Child*. Boston: Shambhala Publications, Inc.

Nwokah, E. E., Hsu, H., Dobrowolska, O., and Fogel, A. (1994) The development of laughter in mother–infant communication; timing parameters and temporal sequences. *Infant Behavior and Development* 17: 23–35.

Onians, R. B. (1951/1973) *The Origins of European Thought About the Body, the Mind, the Soul, the World, Time, and Fate*. Cambridge at the University Press. New York: Reprint edition by Arno Press, Inc., 1973.

Opie, I., and Opie, P. (1959) *The Lore & Language of Schoolchildren*. London: Oxford University Press.

Opie, I., and Opie, P. (1959) *Children's Games in Street and Playground*. London: Oxford University Press.

Opie, I., and Opie, P. (1973) *The Oxford Dictionary of Nursery Rhymes*. London: Oxford University Press.

Otto, R. (1958) *The Idea of the Holy*. New York: Oxford University Press.

Papousek, H., and Papousek, M. (1983) Interactional faillures: their origins and significance in infant psychiatry. In *Frontiers of Infant Psychiatry*, Vol. 1, ed. J. D. Call, E. Galenson, and R. L. Tyson. New York: Basic Books, Inc.

Papousek, H., Papousek, M., and Koester, L. S. (1986) Sharing emotionality and sharing knowledge: a microanalytic approach to parent–infant communication. In *Measuring Emotions in Infants and Children*, Vol. 2, ed. C. E. Izard and P. B. Read. New York: Cambridge University Press.

Papousek, M. (1992) Early ontogeny of vocal communication in parent–infant interactions. In *Nonverbal Vocal Communication: Comparative and Developmental*

Approaches, ed. H. Papousek, U. Jergens, M. Papousek. New York: Cambridge University Press.

Papousek, M., and Papousek, H. (1981) Musical elements in the infant's vocalization: their significance for communication, cognition, and creativity. In *Advances in Infancy Research*, Vol. 1, ed. L. P. Lipsitt and C. K. Rovee-Collier, 163–224. Norwood, N.J.: Ablex Publ. Corp.

Parke, R. D. (1981) *Fathers*. Cambridge, Mass.: Harvard University Press.

Piaget, J. (1927) The first year of life. In *The Essential Piaget*, ed. H. E. Gruber and J. J. Vonèche. New York: Basic Books, Inc., 1977.

Piaget, J. (1952) *The Origins of Intelligence in Children*. New York: International Universities Press; London: Routledge and Kegan Paul.

Piaget, J. (1954) *The Construction of Reality in the Child*. New York: Basic Books, Inc.

Piaget, J. (1960) *The Child's Conception of the World*. Totowa, N. J.: Littlefield, Adams & Co.

Piaget, J. (1962) *Play, Dreams and Imitation in Childhood*. New York: W. W. Norton.

Piaget, J. (1965) *The Moral Judgment of the Child*. New York: The Free Press; London: Routledge and Kegan Paul.

Piaget, J. (1967) *Six Psychological Studies*. New York: Random House, Inc.

Piaget, J. (1969) *The Psychology of the Child*. New York: Basic Books, Inc.

Piaget, J. (1970) *The Place of the Sciences of Man in the System of Sciences*. New York: Harper & Row.

Potok, C. (1975) Rebellion and authority: the adolescent discovering the individual in modern literature. *Adolescent Psychiatry* 4: 15–20.

Provine, R. R., and Yong, Y. L. (1991) Laughter: a stereotyped human vocalization. *Ethology* 89: 115–24.

Putnam, T. C. (1990) The Abyss Complex: a Jungian perspective on a repetitive nightmare and the phenomenon of the abyss image. Dissertation, Union Institute, Ann Arbor, Mich.: UMI dissertation services.

Rathunde, K., and Csikszentmilhalyli, M. (1993) Undivided interest and growth of talent: a longitudinal study of adolescents. *Journal of Youth and Adolescence* 22: 385–405.

Sander, L. W. (1977) Regulation of exchange in the infant caretaker system: a viewpoint on the ontogeny of "Structures." In *Communicative Structures and Psychic Structures*, ed. N. Freedman and S. Grand. New York: Plenum Press.

Sander, L. W. (1983) To begin with – reflections on ontogeny. In *Reflection on Self Psychology*, ed. J. Lichtenberg and S. Kaplan. Hillsdale, N.J.: Analytic Press.

Sander, L. W. (1988) Reflections on self psychology and infancy: the event-structure of regulation in the neonate-caregiver system as a biological background for early organization of psychic structure. In *Progress in Self Psychology*, Vol. 3: *Frontiers in Self Psychology*, ed. A. Goldberg. Hillsdale, N. J.: Analytic Press, Inc.

Schaefer, C. E. (1969) Imaginary companions and creative adolescents. *Developmental Psychology* 6: 747–9.

Schuster, C. (1956/1958) Genealogical patterns in the old and new worlds. *Revista do Museu Paulista* 10: 7–123.

Schroer, T. (1984) Archetypal dreams during the first pregnancy. *Psychological Perspectives* 15: 71–80.

Scott, R. D. (1930) *The Thumb of Knowledge in Legends of Finn, Sigurd, and Taliesin*. New York: Publications of the Institute of French Studies, Inc.

Searles, H. F. (1965) *Collected Papers on Schizophrenia and Related Subjects*. New York: International Universities Press.

Sered, S. and Abramovitch, H. (1992) Pregnant dreaming: search for a typology of a proposed dream genre. *Social Science and Medicine*, 34, 1405–11.

Shereshefsky, P. M., and Yarrow, L. J. (1973) *Psychological aspects of a First Pregnancy and Early Postnatal Adaptation*. New York: Raven Press.

Sherwen, L. (1981) Fantasies during the third trimester of pregnancy. *The American Journal of Maternal-Child Nursing (MCN)* 6: 398–401.

Smith, H. (1995) Analytic listening and the experience of surprise. *International Journal of Psycho-Analysis* 76: 67–78.

Smith, J. (1996) Poetry Man. *Examiner Magazine, Sunday Examiner and Chronicle*, March 31, 1996.

Sorell, W. (1968) *The Story of the Human Hand*. Indianapolis: Bobbs-Merrill.

Sperling, O. E. (1954) An imaginary companion, representing a prestage of the superego. *Psychoanalytic Study of the Child* 9: 252–8.

Spivak, L., Spivak, D., and Wistrand, K. (1993) New psychic phenomena related to normal childbirth. *European Journal of Psychiatry* 7: 239–43.

Starbuck, E. D. (1905) *The Psychology of Religion: An Empirical Study of the Growth of Religious Consciousness*. New York: Charles Scribner's Sons.

Stenberg, C. R., Campos, J. J., and Emde, R. N. (1983) The facial expression of anger in seven-month-old infants. *Child Development* 54: 178–84.

Stern, D. N. (1977) *The First Relationship*. Cambridge, Mass.: Harvard University Press.

Stern, D. N. (1985) *The Interpersonal World of the Infant*. New York: Basic Books, Inc.

Stevens, A. (1990) *On Jung*. London: Routledge.

Stewart, C. T. (1981) The developmental psychology of sandplay. In *Sandplay Studies: Origins, Theory and Practice*. ed. G. Hill, 39–92. San Francisco: C. G. Jung Institute of San Francisco.

Stewart, C. T., and Stewart, L. H. (1981) Play, games and stages of development. Paper presented at the 7th annual conference of The Association for the Anthropological Study of Play (TAASP), Fort Worth, April 1981.

Stewart, L. H. (1976) Kinship libido: toward an archetype of the family. *Proceedings of the Annual Conference of Jungian Analysts of the United States*, pp. 168–82, San Francisco: C. G. Jung Institute of San Francisco.

Stewart, L. H. (1977) Sand Play therapy: Jungian technique. B. Wolman (ed.) *International Encyclopedia of Psychiatry, Psychology, Psychoanalysis and Neurology*, 9–11. New York: Aesculapius Publishers.

Stewart, L. H. (1981a) Play and sandplay. In *Sandplay Studies Origins, Theory and Practice*, ed. G. Hill, 21–37. San Francisco: C. G. Jung Institute of San Francisco.

Stewart, L. H. (1981b) The play–dream continuum and the categories of the imagination. Presented at the 7th annual conference of The Association for the Anthropological Study of. Play (TAASP), Fort Worth, April 1981.

Stewart, L. H. (1984) *Affects and Archetypes I and II*. Paper presented at active imagination seminar in Geneva, Switzerland.

Stewart, L. H. (1985) Affect and arcehtype: A Contribution to a comprehensive theory of the structure of the psyche. In *Proceedings of the 1985 California Spring Conference*, 89–120. San Francisco: C. G. Jung Institute.

Stewart, L. H. (1986) Affect and archetype: A contribution to a comprehensive theory of the structure of the psyche. In *The Body in Analysis*, ed. N. Schwartz-Salant and M. Stein, 183–203. Wilmette, Ill.: Chiron Publications.

Stewart, L. H. (1987a) A brief report: Affect and archetype. *Journal of Analytical Psychology* 32: 35–46.

Stewart, L. H. (1987b) Affect and archetype in analysis. In *Archetypal processes in psychotherapy*, ed. N. Schwart-Salant and M. Stein, 131–62. Wilmette, Ill.: Chiron Publications.

Stewart, L. H. (1987c) Kinship libido: Shadow in marriage and family. In *The archetype of shadow in a split world*, ed. M. A. Matoon, 387–99. Einsiedeln, Switzerland: Daimon Verlag.

Stewart, L. H. (1988) Jealousy and envy: complex family emotions. In *The Family: Personal, cultural and archetypal dimensions*, ed. L. H. Stewart and J. Chodorow. Boston: Sigo Press.

Stewart, L. H. (1990) Foreword to *The Child*, by E. Neumann. Boston: Shambhala Publications, Inc.

Stewart, L. H. (1991) The philosophic attitude. *Symposium on Cultural Attitudes in Honor of Jospeh L. Henderson*, 6–14. Friends of ARAS.

Stewart, L. H. (1992a) *Changemakers: A Jungian Perspective on Sibling Position and the Family Atmosphere*. Routledge: New York.

Stewart, L. H. (1992b) The Archetypal Affects. Paper presented at the Friends of C. G. Jung of Greater Kansas City, May 1–2.

Stewart, L. H. (1996) One Man's Journey. Unpublished manuscript.

Stewart, L. H., and Stewart, C. T. (1981) Play, games and affects: a contribution toward a comprehensive theory of play. In *Play as Context*, ed. A. T. Cheska. *Proceedings of The Association for the Study of Play* (TAASP), 42–52. Westpoint, N.Y.: Leisure Press.

Sutton-Smith, B. (1972) *The folkgames of children*. Austin: University of Texas Press.

Sutton-Smith, B. (1975) The importance of the storytaker: an investigation of the imaginative life. *Urban Review* 8 : 82–95.

Taylor, M. (1999) *Imaginary Companions and the Children Who Create Them*. New York: Oxford University Press.

Taylor, M., Carthwright, B. S. and Carlson, S. M. (1993) A developmental investigation of children's imaginary companions. *Developmental Psychology* 29: 276–85.

Tomkins, S. S. (1962) *Affect Imagery Consciousness. Volume I: The Positive Affects*. New York: Springer Publishing Company, Inc.

Tomkins, S. S. (1963) *Affect Imagery Consciousness. Volume II: The Negative Affects*. New York: Springer Publishing Company, Inc.

Tonkova-Yampol'skaya, R. V. (1973) Development of speech intonation in infants during the first two years of life. In *Studies of Child Language Development*, ed. C. A. Ferguson and D. I. Slobin. New York: Holt, Rinehart and Winston, Inc.

Tronick, E. Z. (1989) Emotions and emotional communication in infants. *American Psychologist* 44: 112–19.

Tronick, E. Z., Beeghly, M., Weinberg, M. K., and Olson, K. L. (1997) Postpartum exuberance: not all women in a highly positive emotional state in the postpartum period are denying depression and distress. *Infant Mental Health Journal* 18: 406–23.

Ullman, C. (1989) *The Transformed Self: The Psychology of Religious Conversion*. New York: Plenum Press.

Van de Castle, R. L. (1994) *Our Dreaming Mind*. New York: Ballantine Books.

Van Gennep, A. (1960) *The Rites of Passage*, trans. M. B. Vizedom and G. L. Caffee. Chicago: University of Chicago Press.

Van Hooff, J. A. R. A. M. (1972) A comparative approach to the phylogeny of laughter and smiling. In *Non-Verbal Communication*, ed. R. A. Hinde. Cambridge: Cambridge University Press.

Virgil (1980) *The Eclogues of Vergil*. Verse trans. Barriss Mills. New Rochelle, N.Y.: Elizabeth Press.

Walker, V., and Lunz, M. E. (1976) Symbols, fairy tales, and school-age children. *Elementary School Journal* 77: 94–100.

Walters, J., and Gardner, H. (1986) The crystallizing experience: discovering an intellectual gift. In *Conceptions of Giftedness*, ed. R. Steinberg and J. Davidson. Cambridge: Cambridge University Press.

Warner, M. (1999) *No Go The Bogeyman: Scaring, Lulling, and Making Mock*. New York: Farrar, Straus, and Giroux.

Werner, H. (1957) The concept of development from a comparative and an organismic point of view. In *The Concept of Development*, ed. D. B. Harris. Minneapolis: University of Minnesota Press.

Wickes, F. G. (1966) *The Inner World of Childhood*. New York: Appleton-Century, revised edition.

Winnicott, D. W. (1954) Withdrawal and regression. *Collected Papers: Through Paediatrics to Psycho-Analysis*, 255–61. New York: Basic Books, 1958.

Winnicott, D. W. (1956) Primary maternal preoccupation. *Collected Papers: Through Paediatrics to Psycho-Analysis*, 300–305. New York: Basic Books, 1958.

Winnicott, D. W. (1958) The capacity to be alone. *The Maturational Processes and the Facilitating Environment*, 29–36. London: Hogarth Press, 1965.

Winnicott, D. W. (1962) Ego integration in child development. *The Maturational Processes and the Facilitating Environment*, 56–63. London: Hogarth Press, 1965.

Winnicott, D. W. (1964) *The Child, the Family, and the Outside World*. Baltimore: Penguin Books.

Winnicott, D. W. (1965) *The Maturational Processes and the Facilitating Environment*. London: Hogarth Press.

Winnicott, D. W. (1971) *Playing & Reality*. New York: Routledge.

Winnicott, D. W. (1972) The basis for self in body. *International Journal of Child Psychotherapy* 1: 7–16.

Winnicott, D. W. (1977) *The Piggle*. New York: International Universities Press, Inc.

Winnicott, D. W. (1989) Fear of breakdown. In *Psycho-Analytic Explorations*, ed. C. Winnicott, R. Shephard, and M. Davis. Cambridge, Mass.: Harvard University Press.

Wolff, P. H. (1961). Observations on the early development of smiling. In *Determinants of Infant Behaviour II*, ed. B. M. Foss. London: Methuen.

Young, W. C. (1988) Observations on fantasy in the formation of multiple personality disorder. *Dissociation* 1: 13–20.

Zimmer, H. (1938) The Indian world mother. In *The Mystic Vision: Papers From the Eranos Yearbooks*, Vol. 6, trans. R. Mannheim. New Jersey: Princeton University Press, 1968.

Index

Compiled by Sue Carlton